Derek Parfit: His Life and Thought

Derek Parfit: His Life and Thought

Edited by

JEFF McMAHAN

OXFORD
UNIVERSITY PRESS

Great Clarendon Street, Oxford, OX2 6DP,
United Kingdom

Oxford University Press is a department of the University of Oxford.
It furthers the University's objective of excellence in research, scholarship,
and education by publishing worldwide. Oxford is a registered trade mark of
Oxford University Press in the UK and in certain other countries.

Published in the United States of America by Oxford University Press
198 Madison Avenue, New York, NY 10016, United States of America.

British Library Cataloguing in Publication Data

Data available

Library of Congress Control Number: 2024952964

ISBN 9780192894243

DOI: 10.1093/9780191915307.001.0001

Printed and bound by
CPI Group (UK) Ltd., Croydon, CR0 4YY

The manufacturer's authorised representative in the EU for product safety is Oxford University Press España S.A. of El Parque Empresarial San Fernando de Henares, Avenida de Castilla, 2 – 28830 Madrid (www.oup.es/en or product.safety@oup.com). OUP España S.A. also acts as importer into Spain of products made by the manufacturer.

MIX
Paper | Supporting responsible forestry
FSC® C013604

Contents

Preface

This book is the third of three volumes that together constitute a posthumous Festschrift for Derek Parfit. The first two volumes, *Principles and Persons* and *Ethics and Existence*, which I co-edited with three younger philosophers who were Parfit's friends and students, consist of philosophical essays on issues on which Parfit had worked and thought important. Although this final volume of essays contains a certain amount of intellectual biography, its essays are primarily biographical rather than philosophical. It is thus complementary to David Edmonds's recent, magnificent biography, *Parfit: A Philosopher and His Mission to Save Morality*.[1] Even though a number of Edmonds's most important sources of information about Parfit's life are also contributors to this book, we have been able to ensure that there is comparatively little overlap between the two books; for the authors of the essays that follow have sought for the most part to avoid repeating stories and musings about Parfit that they shared with Edmonds.

Parfit was both legendarily brilliant and legendarily eccentric. The child of missionaries, he aspired, until the age of 8, to become a monk, but at that age became instead an atheist and remained one for the rest of his life. In many respects, though, he fitted the profile of a saint. He was highly ascetic, though he had no conscious commitment to asceticism as an ideal. He was a recluse but nevertheless maintained deep friendships. He was devoid of egotism and was invariably kindly and—again legendarily—generous, both in his devotion to his students and others in philosophy and in his support for charities and political organizations opposed to injustice or supportive of beneficence. He was acutely sensitive to injustice, to cruelty, and to suffering, in both people and animals. Even as an undergraduate at Oxford, he wrote vigorous and passionate editorials for the student paper arguing for the redistribution of wealth to eliminate global poverty, the ending of the unjust war in Vietnam, the abolition of apartheid, and the pursuit of arms control and eventual nuclear disarmament.

1 Princeton University Press (2023).

The contributors to this book are among those who were closest to him in various ways. They include his widow, his surviving sister, and a number of his best friends, who were also his colleagues at the various universities at which he taught and, in many instances, his former students as well. Alternately poignant and humorous, the observations and anecdotes in the following chapters together provide a vivid portrayal of the life, character, values, and ideas of one of the greatest moral philosophers of the last quarter of a millennium. All of us who have written for this volume miss him and his presence in our lives—indeed, in some cases, in our very selves—most profoundly.

Jeff McMahan

Notes on the Contributors

Ruth Chang is the Chair and Professor of Jurisprudence at the University of Oxford. She was a graduate student and friend of Derek Parfit.

Jonathan Dancy is Professor Emeritus at the University of Texas at Austin. He previously taught at Keele University and the University of Reading in the UK. He is the editor of *Reading Parfit* (Blackwell, 1997) and the author of *Moral Reasons* (Blackwell, 1993), *Practical Reality* (Oxford University Press, 2000), and *Ethics Without Principles* (Oxford University Press, 2004).

Jonathan Glover is the author of, among other books, *Causing Death and Saving Lives* (Pelican, 1977), *Humanity: A Moral History of the Twentieth Century* (Cape, 1999); *Choosing Children: Genes, Disability, and Design* (Clarendon Press, 2006); *Alien Landscapes? Interpreting Disordered Minds* (Belknap Press, 2014); and *Israelis and Palestinians: From the Cycle of Violence to the Conversation of Mankind* (Polity, 2024).

F. M. Kamm is the Henry Rutgers University Professor of Philosophy and Distinguished Professor of Philosophy in the Department of Philosophy, Rutgers University. She focuses on normative ethical theory and practical ethics in numerous articles and ten books, including *Creation and Abortion, Morality, Mortality* Vols. 1 and 2, *Intricate Ethics, Bioethical Prescriptions, The Trolley Problem Mysteries, Almost Over: Aging, Dying, Dead,* and *Rights and Their Limits: In Theory, Cases, and Pandemics* (all from Oxford University Press). Kamm is a member of the American Academy of Arts and Sciences.

Thomas Kelly is Professor of Philosophy at Princeton University, where he has taught since 2004. At Harvard University, he wrote a doctoral dissertation on the relationship between theoretical and practical rationality that was supervised by Derek Parfit and Robert Nozick. He works primarily in epistemology, and his book *Bias: A Philosophical Study* was published by Oxford University Press in 2022.

Jeff McMahan is Sekyra and White's Professor of Moral Philosophy at the University of Oxford and a Fellow of Corpus Christi College. He is the author of *The Ethics of Killing: Problems at the Margins of Life* (Oxford University Press, 2002) and *Killing in War* (Oxford University Press, 2009). He is currently writing a book on *The Ethics of Creating, Preserving, and Ending Lives.*

Theodora Ooms, Derek Parfit's older sister, lives in Washington DC. Born in Chengdu, China, she attended Somerville College, Oxford, and obtained a degree in Philosophy, Politics, and Economics (PPE). Trained as a clinical social worker and family therapist, she focused on helping low-income children and their families with a variety of challenges in New Haven and Philadelphia. From 1981 to 1999 she was the executive director of the Family Impact Seminar, a nonpartisan policy research institute based in Washington DC. She organized monthly policy seminars for congressional and executive branch staff on a wide range of family health, economic, education, and social service issues. She has edited or authored three books (Temple University Press) and a series of background briefing reports for Washington policy staff.

Ingmar Persson is Emeritus Professor of Practical Philosophy, University of Gothenburg, and Distinguished Research Fellow, Oxford Uehiro Centre for Practical Ethics, Oxford University. His main publications are six books with Oxford University Press.

Janet Radcliffe Richards is Derek's widow. She is Professor Emerita of Practical Philosophy at Oxford, and is a Distinguished Research Fellow at the Oxford Uehiro Centre for Practical Ethics. She formerly held appointments at the Open University and UCL, and is the author of *The Sceptical Feminist* (Routledge, 1980), *Human Nature after Darwin* (Routledge, 2000), and *The Ethics of Transplants: Why Careless Thought Costs Lives* (Oxford University Press, 2012).

Larry S. Temkin is Distinguished Professor of Philosophy, Emeritus, at Rutgers University. An expert in ethics, and social and political philosophy, Temkin has lectured extensively around the world and received numerous distinguished fellowships and teaching awards. He is the author of *Inequality* (1993), *Rethinking the Good: Moral Ideals and the Nature of Practical Reasoning* (2012), and *Being Good in a World of Need* (2022), all published by Oxford University Press.

Fig. 1 Sister Theodora, sister Joanna, father Norman, mother Jessie, and Derek.

Fig. 2 Derek, Joanna, and Theodora.

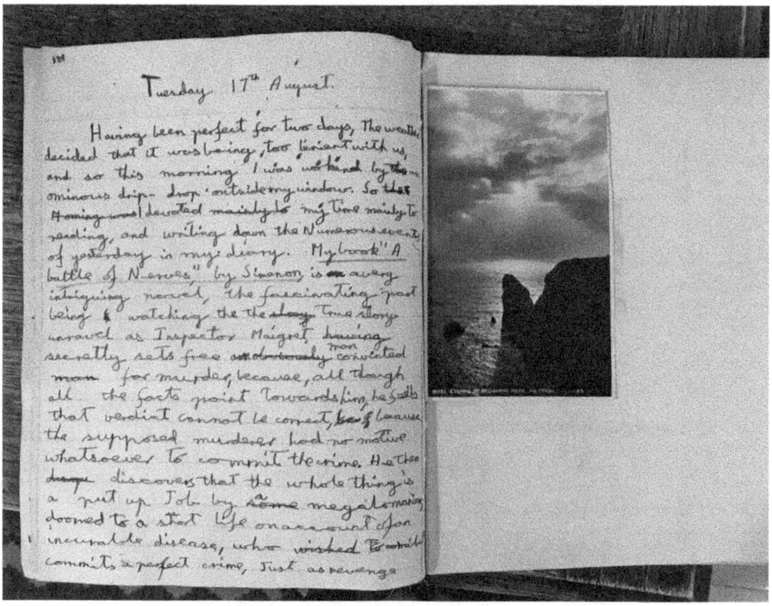

Fig. 3 A page from Derek's diary when he was 10.

Fig. 4 A talent unfulfilled.

Fig. 5 Eton schoolboy.

Fig. 6 Portrait.

Fig. 7 The young philosopher.

Fig. 8 Later 1970s.

Fig. 9 A playful moment.

Fig. 10 Conference at Rutgers on the manuscript of what was then titled *Climbing the Mountain* (later *On What Matters*), April 2003. Left to right: Larry Temkin, Stephen Darwall, Thomas Nagel, T. M. Scanlon, Derek, and John Broome.

Photo: Saba Bazargan-Forward.

Fig. 11 Portrait.

Fig. 12 Birthday gathering, 2014. Left to right: Larry Temkin, Jeff McMahan, Meg Temkin, Derek.

1

Derek Parfit, 1942–2017

Biographical Memoir for the British Academy

Jonathan Dancy

Biography

Derek Parfit was born in Chengdu, Szechwan, West China. His parents, Jessie and Norman Parfit, both doctors, were medical missionaries; all four of his grandparents were missionaries too. His parents lost their faith when Parfit was very young, but it was because of the war that in 1945 the family moved back to the UK, first to London and then to Oxford, where Parfit attended the Dragon School as a day boy; from there he won the top scholarship to Eton. At Eton he specialized in history, which was effectively the only alternative offered to Classics, which he detested. But it was at Eton that he first came across philosophy, and this became the subject he most enjoyed; there was a philosophy club, to which practising philosophers were invited and at which Parfit read papers about free will and desert, God, and the problem of evil. He also edited the *Eton College Chronicle* and in fact left Eton a little early, during the summer of 1961, in order to take up a temporary post at *The New Yorker*, which he was offered out of the blue by the then editor, William Shawn; during that period he wrote a poem which was published in *The New Yorker* a year later.

From Eton Parfit won a scholarship in history to Balliol College, Oxford, where he read history (1961–4). He also engaged in various journalistic activities, just as he had at Eton. But in his second term there he was already considering switching to PPE, which was the only way in which a non-classicist could study philosophy; what prevented him from doing so was that the PPE syllabus required one to study logic, which he hated and which made him feel very uncomfortable.

This piece was originally published in *Biographical Memoirs of Fellows of the British Academy*, XIX, pp. 37–57.

Jonathan Dancy, *Derek Parfit, 1942–2017* In: *Derek Parfit: His Life and Thought*. Edited by: Jeff McMahan, Oxford University Press. © Oxford University Press 2025. DOI: 10.1093/9780191915307.003.0001

His intention on graduating was apparently to continue as an academic of some sort, since he took the examination for an All Souls prize fellowship in 1964, with history as his subject; he did not succeed, but the then Warden of All Souls, John Sparrow, wrote to him saying that he had been as close as a whisker to being elected and that he should consider trying again. He put that idea on the back burner, because he already had a Commonwealth (Harkness) Fellowship for the years 1964–6, which required him to travel in the US and enabled him to take classes at Columbia University and Harvard University. (David Wiggins reports that Parfit somehow impressed the Harkness selection committee by talking about American conceptions of the future.) Parfit said later that his main motivation for taking up the offer of a Harkness Fellowship was that it gave him two years in which he could study whatever he wanted at American universities, and this would give him the time to decide whether to continue as an academic and whether to try to change his subject from history to philosophy. His experiences in the US led to his official conversion. The influence of Stuart Hampshire (who himself had switched from history to philosophy, but during his undergraduate years) seems also to have been involved in this process.

A typescript of a paper of Parfit's on moral justification dated March 1967 has recently been unearthed, with a handwritten note, "14 months after I changed my subject to philosophy". This gives us a date of January 1966 as the moment of decision, with nearly half of the Harkness still to run.

So on his return to the UK in January 1967 Parfit started as a graduate student at Balliol, reading for the BPhil in philosophy. He says in *Reasons and Persons* that he owes a great deal to his first teachers—Sir Peter Strawson, Sir Alfred Ayer, David Pears, and Richard Hare—who gave him tutorials during this period. But he sat the All Souls examination again at the beginning of the autumn term 1967, taking the philosophy papers this time, and was successful. (On election he announced his subject as "philosophy, in particular philosophy of mind and moral philosophy".) Thus began his long association with the college which he never left and which he loved so dearly.

On his election, he was urged by the Warden, John Sparrow, to withdraw from the BPhil, and so he switched to do a DPhil on "the philosophical concept of personal identity". Alan Montefiore was his supervisor 1970–3—an interesting choice, but in fact Parfit never got as far as submitting. This hardly mattered: he published his first article, "Personal Identity", in January 1971 to considerable acclaim and from then on enjoyed an international reputation which made degrees an irrelevance. He did win the T. H. Green Prize in 1977 with an essay entitled "Against Prudence". But like other leading younger philosophers at Oxford (such as John McDowell and Gareth Evans), he never got a graduate degree in philosophy. At least the others had an undergraduate degree—in McDowell's case, two of them.

One consequence of his peculiar path into philosophy was that Parfit was much less broadly based in the subject than most academic philosophers nowadays. He learned up what he needed to learn up to pursue the topics that interested him. He did not need to concern himself with epistemology, logic, philosophy of language, or philosophy of science, and he did not worry about such matters. There is a letter to the Warden of All Souls in 1971 in which he says that he wants to learn some philosophical logic. But I doubt that he went very far in that direction, for, as he confessed to me, or perhaps boasted, he had a sort of blindness where symbols are concerned; this was what had led to his decision not to switch to PPE at Balliol. So the general habit at that time of dressing up every argument in symbolic logic would have rendered much of what was written in certain fields impenetrable to him anyway.

Parfit's essay for the T. H. Green Prize was an interesting forerunner of what was to emerge later as *Reasons and Persons.* It discussed cases where, if each of us does what is best for him, that will be worse for everyone. It asked whether a rational person should be equally concerned with all the temporal parts of their future; and it discussed the implications for rationality of different views about the nature of personal identity.

All Souls suited Parfit perfectly, but a prize fellowship only lasted for seven years maximum, and after that, if one wanted to stay on, one had to apply for a research fellowship and then again for a senior research fellowship. To be kept on, one needed to be able to show significant achievement, and at each of these steps Parfit faced a challenge because he found it so hard to finish anything. In his application for a research fellowship (in October 1973, towards the end of his prize fellowship) he promised three books. Material about personal identity was to form the heart of the first one: does personal identity have the importance we usually suppose, and is the concern for one's own future somehow specially rational? The second book was to be about rationality, with the aim of bringing the different kinds of reason for action within a unified account. The third book was to ask about societies what the other two books asked about individuals. But these promised books did not materialize. Already in 1975 Parfit had reported that he had got stuck, was considering writing a book entitled "Future Generations", and thought he could only make progress by concentrating on rationality (which would include such notions as what is in one's own best interest and the incommensurability of values).

The non-appearance of the three promised books led to difficulties. In 1980, as his tenure of a research fellowship neared its end, Parfit applied for a senior research fellowship to start in 1981, but there was considerable reluctance within All Souls to give him this position when he had not produced a book of any sort, let alone the three promised books. Eventually he was given a limited extension of his research fellowship until 1984, with encouragement but also a warning that if no book (of suitable weight) appeared by then, he would be out. The pressure this put on him was enormous, but the result was *Reasons and Persons*.

A month after the book's appearance in 1984, to enormous acclaim, Parfit reapplied for and was granted a senior research fellowship at All Souls, enabling him to continue to work there for the rest of his life.

In his application Parfit stated that his interests lay in "the central and most debated subjects, such as the choice between conflicting views about what is in a person's own best interests, the many objections to consequentialism, different theories about liberty and justice, and the claimed incommensurability of different values". He also suggested that work in epistemology and metaphysics—on the nature of time, free will, and the kind of objectivity we can achieve—could make the same sort of difference to our substantial beliefs about ourselves as could his own work on personal identity. He was nothing if not optimistic about the effect that good philosophy can have. But what actually happened was rather different.

In *Reasons and Persons* there is no sign of metaphysics (other than what might be called the metaphysics of persons) or of metaethics, and the only ethical theory that makes a significant appearance is consequentialism. But by the end of the century Parfit's interests had moved to a focus on two main themes. The first theme is the question whether three great philosophical understandings of ethics—consequentialism, contractualism, and Kantianism—could not in the end be shown to be different expressions of the same position. (This fits his stated aim of considering "the many objections to consequentialism".) The second theme is an uncompromising realism about the moral and more generally the normative, as evidenced by the title he chose for his great three-volume work: *On What Matters*.

So the next phase of Parfit's philosophical trajectory was one in which he gradually converted himself into a metaethicist. He had always been haunted by the thought that Hare's prescriptivism (and other forms of non-cognitivism) had the consequence that nothing really matters. There are things that we care about, but there is no possibility of mistakenly caring about things that don't matter, or not caring about things that do matter.

Parfit wanted to fight this sort of metaethical nihilism with all the strength he could muster. *On What Matters* was the result; its first two volumes were published in 2011, with a third (posthumous) volume in 2017.

For the historian of ideas, and especially of Parfit's ideas, the path that led the author of *Reasons and Persons* to *On What Matters* is an interesting one. In the first book, as I said above, there is really no metaethics at all; it is all normative ethics, and the only ethical perspective considered is consequentialism, which grounds the right on the good. In the second book—which is a peculiar compilation with substantial contributions from other authors—it is pretty much all metaethics and the theory of reasons. The three names that now stand out are Kant, Sidgwick, and Scanlon. Sidgwick had made a significant appearance in *Reasons and Persons*, but there are only two references to Scanlon in that book and Kant mainly appears in an extended example (in Part 3 on personal identity), which concerns the question whether Kant could have been born to parents other than his actual parents.

Part of the impetus which drove this change of focus was an attempt to respond to the various contributions to a collection I was putting together in the 1990s, consisting of responses to *Reasons and Persons*. With Parfit's enthusiastic help, I assembled an excellent list of contributors/critics and, as their papers came in, Parfit set himself to work out his replies. And the replies grew and grew until it became clear that there was far more material here than could be accommodated in a single volume that included both the critical contributions and Parfit's responses. It got to the stage where three volumes were in sight, one on Parts 1 and 2, one on Part 3, and one on Part 4 of *Reasons and Persons*. Blackwell, who were publishing this volume, or rather these volumes, were very tolerant over several years as this process unfolded. But during that period Parfit began to recognize that he was also beginning to develop a framework within which all this might fit, and which would be far better presented as an independent contribution than as a set of responses to anything. So he pulled out and the contributors' papers were published, very late and without his replies, in 1997, under the title *Reading Parfit*. Meanwhile, he began to assemble the material that became *On What Matters*.

It was my privilege during that period to be involved in Parfit's construction of his metaethical position, and to find a friend. For several years we met pretty regularly to discuss philosophy—his and mine. He devoted as much care and attention to my efforts as to his; his enthusiasm was sometimes more than I could match, but the excitement of climbing the stairs to his room in the Great Quad at All Souls remains with me.

Topics on which we had endless discussions during that period included Bernard Williams's paper on internal and external reasons, to which Parfit returned over and over again, and the arguments for metaethical naturalism; also the theory of motivation, his views on which emerged as "Reasons and Motivation" (Proceedings of the Aristotelian Society, 1997). In the latter there occurs one of the most striking examples of what later became a dominant motivation for Parfit—to show somehow that the proponents of positions that had been taken to be in opposition were "really" in agreement. The example in this case was the contrast between psychologistic and non-psychologistic, or realist, conceptions of what it is to act for a reason. A psychologistic account will claim that "motivating reason" is a term for whatever psychological states cause the agent to act as she does, normally taking such states to consist of combinations of beliefs and desires; a realist conception will try to maintain that the reasons for which we act are such things as that this is too expensive, which is not a psychological state of anyone. Parfit maintained, very implausibly in my view, that these accounts are both right. There are two kinds of motivating reason: psychological states and matters of (supposed) fact. For normative purposes, it is more natural to think of reasons as matters of fact; for explanatory purposes, it is more natural to look for something capable of causing action, for which psychological states of the agent look like excellent candidates.

In addition to these private meetings, there were regular meetings of a small group consisting of John Broome, Roger Crisp, Brad Hooker, Philip Stratton-Lake, Parfit, and myself (a sort of Oxford–Reading nexus). Later this group expanded with the arrival of Julian Savulescu, and it was then not long before it became so large as to be quite a different sort of occasion.

A personal note: after several years of regular train rides from Reading to Oxford and back, I began to find that I could not keep up. Other duties (of which Parfit had none) made it increasingly difficult to give his material the necessary attention if I was to contribute meaningfully to our discussions. And it didn't seem fair to take up so much of his time when I was getting far more than I gave; so I began to withdraw—which I now greatly regret. Another disincentive, of a different sort, was the fact that Parfit revisited the same material over and over again in a continuous search for perfection, and the law of diminishing returns began to set in for me in a way that it never did for him. He was still reworking this material fifteen years later.

Peter Momtchiloff has shown me letters written during this period, in which Parfit, seeking a contract from OUP, reveals his current thinking about books he might write. In 1996 he offers five books. The last of these, to be titled *Truth, Evil, and the Sublime*, is, he says, too remote to talk about. The first, to be titled *Practical Realism*, would defend a realist and irreducibly normative conception of practical reasons. The second would rework his conception of personal identity in response to the relevant papers in my *Reading Parfit*. The third, to be titled *On What Matters*, would discuss various questions about the goodness of outcomes and the rightness of acts, focusing on problems about distributive justice and future generations. The fourth, to be titled *Reasons, Persons, and Reality*, would be a reworking of various themes in *Reasons and Persons*. (Parfit never abandoned this dream of eventually publishing an improved version of *Reasons and Persons* which would enable the latter to go out of print.)

In 2003 (the year after he gave the Tanner Lectures at UC Berkeley), Parfit's thinking about publication had changed, though no book had yet appeared. His main aim now was to finish two books. The second and the larger of these, to be called *Rediscovering Reasons*, would have one part on reasons, one on normative ethics (consequentialism, Kantianism, and contractualism), and one on metaethics. The first and smaller book would be a shorter version of the second part of *Rediscovering Reasons*, to be published together with comments by Scanlon, Wood, Herman, O'Neill, and Wolf. These comments (apart from those of O'Neill) all eventually appeared in Volume 2 of *On What Matters*.

Parfit's life revolved around two completely engrossing interests. The first was philosophy and the second was photography, the latter counting as an avocation. Such time and attention (and money) that he did not devote to the former, he devoted to the latter. After a hard day doing philosophy he would regularly spend the small hours (11 p.m. to 1 a.m.) working on his photographs. He used to say that his real motivation for accepting visiting positions at US institutions was to earn money to pay for his photography—which required significant funds, not just because he himself owned expensive equipment (which needed to be upgraded all the time) but because he would only allow the most advanced technicians to print his photographs (at least until the arrival of Photoshop and other such programs), and such people were charging £1,000 for a single print. Since it might take several prints before Parfit was completely satisfied, considerable resources were required.

Parfit's photographs, which were nearly all of St Petersburg or of Venice, were works of art, not just in the sense that they were intentional products of aesthetic value but in the sense that he changed them, first by manual retouching (done by a professional) and later electronically, so as to make the shapes of the buildings more aesthetically pleasing. He made things look the way they should have been. He also took the people (and every sign of the twentieth century) out so that they didn't distract attention or detract from the buildings.

Since Parfit's death the Hermitage Museum at St Petersburg has expressed an interest in putting on an exhibition of his oeuvre—but only if an account could be given of the relation between his philosophy and his photography. Unfortunately, such an account has proved very hard to give.

Frances Kamm has suggested to me that Parfit took up photography because he thought he lacked visual memory; photographs would serve as a surrogate for memory. His own view was that, though he had no artistic talent, he could recognize what was good when he saw it. So he found a way of producing good art, namely to take thousands of pictures and choose the best of them to put through the retouching process.

Returning to philosophy: Parfit's dedication to the subject went far beyond the norm, even among the most focused of us. He used to rise just before lunch, and then work without pause (other than for dinner) into the small hours of the morning (often, perhaps normally, with a period devoted to his photographs). He found it very hard to go to sleep and only achieved that at all by a carefully composed admixture of vodka and pills. But while he was awake he worked at a speed of which most are incapable. If you sent him a paper for comment, you would often receive those comments within a very few days, and the comments would often be as long as or longer than the paper you had sent. He achieved this partly by a simple ability to concentrate and partly by a fierce determination to avoid as much as possible of anything that would interfere with the progress of philosophical enquiry. He always wore clothes of exactly the same type: a white shirt, dark trousers, and a red tie; and he was extremely reluctant to give up time for such things as important family gatherings and unnecessary socializing. But commenting on the work of others did not count for him as dispensable interruption; it was part of what he was trying to do, not an interference in that. Philosophy was for Parfit a cooperative activity. And he assumed that others were as devoted to it as he was. All his books start with a very long list of people to whom he was indebted. All of us do this, of course, to some degree; but in Parfit's case the debt was often very significant. Before the publication of his first book he sent copies of the (supposedly nearly) final draft to very many philosophers around the world—over a hundred, I believe—saying that though they had no duty of any sort to read this material and send him comments, still he would be very grateful for anything they had to suggest. The list of those who did send him comments has fifty-six names. This was a completely new way of doing philosophy, one that only the most gifted of us could hope to practise; otherwise, nobody would get anything done.

In addition to his own work, and to commenting on the work of colleagues, Parfit had a long series of eventually distinguished doctoral students, all of whom tell grateful stories of his support. One might have supposed that someone who held himself to such high standards of commitment to the subject would have been an impossibly demanding supervisor, but in fact all reports show that he was deeply supportive and encouraging, in a way that enabled his students to become the best versions of themselves and involved no attempt to turn them into less talented versions of himself.

From mid-career onwards Parfit held a series of visiting positions at various senior departments of philosophy in the US: Harvard, NYU, and Rutgers. Even if early on his main reason for doing this was that it enabled him to pay for the expenses of his photography, he had another reason later on, which was that it enabled him to give more to charity. And, of course, he was as generous with his time while abroad as he was in the UK, so long as it was for the sake of the subject.

Amid all this concentration Parfit did find time to relax and listen to music, mainly classical (especially Bach and Wagner) but also some jazz—Lester Young and Billie Holiday were favourites.

In 2010 Parfit married his long-time companion, Janet Radcliffe Richards. He died suddenly and unexpectedly late at night in their house in London in the small hours of January 2, 2017.

Philosophical Work

Parfit's first published piece was on the nature of a person, or personal identity. Published in *The Philosophical Review* in 1971, this paper is at the foundation of much that he wrote for a long time afterwards; it is wonderfully human, idiosyncratic, and engaging—personal, even. On the first page he says:

> Some people . . . agree that our criteria of personal identity do not cover certain cases, but they believe that the nature of their own identity through time is, somehow, such as to guarantee that in these cases questions about their identity must have answers. . . . This first belief . . . has, I think, certain effects. It makes people assume that the principle of self-interest is more rationally compelling than any moral principle. And it makes them more depressed by the thought of ageing and death.

Here we see already two central strands to Parfit's thought—strands which persisted to the end. The first is the link between discussions of personal identity and ethics, which is one of the main themes of Part 3 of his *Reasons and Persons*, and which I will lay out in more detail below. The second is the practical relevance and importance of philosophical enquiry. Parfit thought that correct philosophical thought could free us from an obsessive concern with ourselves and our weal and woe, since the distinction between self and others was not as stark as common sense takes it to be.

The paper continues with a series of bizarre (though now familiar) imaginary scenarios, such as one in which I can divide my mind into two streams, neither of which has access to the other for a period. At the end of that period, I can reunite those streams. How are we to describe this scenario? If the situation persisted, and I could not reunite my streams, we might say that there are now two people in one body; but if I can reunite them, we would be less tempted to say that. Parfit's point at this stage is that there does not need to be a fact of the matter. Of a similar case devised by David Wiggins, in which my brain is divided and each half transplanted into a new body, the best thing to say is that I *survive as* two different people but not allow that I am either or both of these people. Identity is the limiting case in which there is only one person *as whom* I survive. But there is nothing so special about that and, in order not to be tricked by our language into supposing otherwise, we should give up the language of identity and with it the belief that there are important questions which turn upon questions of identity. Such questions include the question whether an action would be in my own (personal) interest.

Parfit's views about personal identity reappear in a much more advanced form as Part 3 of his first book, *Reasons and Persons* (1984). This book is as a whole much more about persons than it is about reasons. And though there is plenty of talk about reasons, the focus, at least in Parts 1 and 2, is really on rationality. The final Part 4 is about persons and value; Parfit there reveals an extraordinary set of tensions within our conception of the value of a life. As far as I can see, these tensions—or contradictions—are not themselves derived directly either from his paper on personal identity or from the previous three Parts of *Reasons and Persons*. In that sense, then, Part 4 is free-standing. The material in it was developed in and for a class which Parfit taught with James Griffin and Jonathan Glover for several years from 1968 onwards.

Part 1 is not about reasons either—unless we take the view that the notion of a reason can be expressed in terms of rationality (which I don't). Parts 1 and 2 are about rationality. So reasons don't really enter into Parfit's picture until his second book, *On What Matters*.

The links between Parfit's first paper and the material in the book which appeared thirteen years later are various. The first is that he is concerned in Parts 1 and 2 of *Reasons and Persons* with two theories about how we should act. The first of these is S, the self-interest theory: S's central claim is that each person has only one rational aim, that outcomes go, for him, as well as possible. According to S, then, we each of us have our own rational aims, which can, of course, conflict. But there is also C (consequentialism), whose central claim is that there is one ultimate moral aim: that outcomes be as good as possible. This claim gives each person the same aim, and it would seem that if one of us succeeds in this aim, others cannot be failing.

S acquires much greater force if we accept the intuitive distinction between oneself and others. But once we allow that the question "Will it be me who gets this benefit?" can be answered by saying "To some extent yes, and to some extent no", the focus of S seems to be lost, or at least to waver. Parfit does not rely on this in Parts 1 and 2 of *Reasons and Persons*. There he argues directly against S, on an ordinary understanding of the self. He produces wild and wonderful cases where acting in accordance with S will definitely make one's life go worse. It can be the case that, though I am doing what S tells me to do, it is worse for me. And if we all do what S tells us to do, it can be worse for each of us. Actually, and unfortunately, the cases don't have to be weird and wonderful, as is shown by the standard example of overfishing. We will all (and each) do worse if we all do what S recommends than if we all acted in some other way.

One central aspect of Parfit's discussion of S and C is his use of the notion of the self-defeating and the distinction between two forms of defeat—direct and indirect. A theory is indirectly individually self-defeating if it is true that, if someone tries to achieve the aims that the theory gives him, those aims will be, on the whole, worse achieved. And a theory is directly individually self-defeating if, should someone successfully follow that theory, they will cause the aims the theory specifies for them to be less well achieved than if they had failed to follow the theory successfully. A theory is directly collectively self-defeating if, were each of us to follow the requirements of the theory, we would cause the aims it gives us to be less well achieved than if none of us had followed the theory. These various forms of self-defeat make available a new range of potential criticisms of well-worn theories of practical rationality.

Like so many others, I remember reading this material with a sense of doors opening before me. Suddenly moral philosophy became exciting in a way that it had not been before; it gained a dimension. At that time, it consisted almost entirely of metaethics. We were interested in the nature of moral thought and judgement and the possibility of moral facts. In *Reasons and Persons* Parfit paid almost no attention to such issues, though they are at the core of his second book, *On What Matters*. An example of this focus (and perhaps of its limitations) is the notion of self-interest. On pages 3–4 Parfit gives several theories of self-interest, but none of these tell us what it is for something to be in my interest—to benefit me, or be "better for me". All assume that this notion makes sense; in fact it is the subject of considerable dispute, but this is all metaethics (in the sense that it concerns the nature of a certain ethical concept, that of a benefit), and Parfit was not doing that. He did not examine his tools in that way.

Part 3 builds on Parts 1 and 2 in various ways. First, Parfit lays out his conception of personal identity through time as a matter of degree—to be more precise, as a matter of the degrees of psychological continuity and connectedness between the various temporal stages of the supposed self. Then he asks what difference this conception might make to our account of rationality as self-interest. The answer is that there is a discount rate. We should not be equally concerned with all the parts of our own future; the welfare of those parts of our later selves with which we are less well connected counts for less. So it may not be irrational for a teenager to start smoking, knowing that doing so will make her later life much worse. The question is how much worse, and what is irrational is determined by whether the discount rate grounded in lesser degrees of connectedness is too steep, not steep enough, or just right. "Great imprudence is always sad, and often (as in the case of smoking) tragic. [But] we cannot claim that all such acts are irrational" (*Reasons and Persons*, p. 318). We cannot claim this because, on Parfit's account of personal identity, a teenager's adult self is *more like* a different person than we have standardly assumed. Rather, we should claim that such acts are immoral. What is wrong with the teenager who starts smoking may not be that he is treating his later self irrationally. He is treating that self immorally, and that self is more like a different person than we normally suppose. Great imprudence is morally wrong even where it is not irrational.

But if it is morally wrong, this might affect the reasons we have for interfering. Autonomy does not include the right to harm your later self—or numerically distinct selves all equally well related to you—for no good reason. Further, since there will be no point at which I begin to exist, my existence being itself grounded in matters of degree, the morality of abortion may be affected (p. 322). And someone in an incurable coma is not a person (because the degree of psychological continuity and connectedness is zero) and has no rights. So perhaps only the killing of persons is wrong. As for the morality of punishment, on Parfit's view a statute of limitations may be justified by the fact that identity is grounded in matters of degree.

These issues bring out the force in Parfit's original claim that decisions in the theory of persons can affect our moral views—in addition to our theory of rational action. Parfit also claimed that his belief that personal identity is grounded in matters of degree was liberating and consoling. It made him less concerned about his own future, and his death, and more concerned about others (p. 147). The passages in which he writes about these matters are some of the most moving, effective, and humane to be found in modern philosophy.

Part 4 is a stand-alone tour de force. Parfit lays out two paradoxes in the theory of value—paradoxes to which nobody has yet succeeded in providing any resolution. He starts with what he calls the Non-Identity Problem, which is not itself a paradox. The Non-Identity Problem concerns the question how one act or policy can be worse than another if it is not worse for anyone. Suppose we have two policies, A and B, and that different people will be born depending on which policy we adopt. We might want to compare the two policies and pronounce one worse than the other, but there is nobody for whom either policy will be worse or better. Parfit says that we need a theory, Theory X, which will answer this question. It might seem easy to provide such a theory: our answer might include the claim that if all the people who will be born if we adopt policy A will be happier than all the people who will born if we adopt policy B, policy A is better than policy B. This does not require us to say that adopting policy A is better for anybody; we can restrict ourselves to saying that the people born under policy A are better off than would be those who would be born under policy B. We don't need the notion of a benefit to say this; to benefit someone is to make something better, and that notion is inherently comparative (though what it compares is a matter of dispute). But the notion of being well off is not itself inherently comparative. So it is not clear that the Non-Identity Problem is on its own terribly hard.

But we also need to resolve two much harder issues. The first of these is the Repugnant Conclusion, and the second is the Mere Addition Paradox.

We might agree that it is better if more happy people are living than if fewer equally happy people are living. In this sense, numbers can matter. But consider cases where, as the population grows, the quality of life falls—though it never falls so far as to make the lives of those living there not worth living. We might find ourselves having to choose between two outcomes, in one of which everyone is very happy and in the other of which people are somewhat less happy but there are quite a lot more of them. Once we agree that the second world is better, there is considerable pressure to agree that a world with an enormously large population of people whose lives are just worth living is better than a world with a much smaller population of people whose lives are very well worth living. This better world is not better for anyone, of course, because the populations of these two worlds are quite distinct. But it is "better in the sense relevant to choice": we should choose it if we can. This is the Repugnant Conclusion. A fairly grim world is better than a world of general bliss.

The Mere Addition Paradox asks whether lowering the average level of welfare is itself bad. Normally that would be so, because to lower the average level we would have to lower the level of some individuals. But if we enlarge our population by adding extra people whose lives are much worse than those of the original population, though still worth living, do we make things worse? This is not a non-identity issue. We cannot hold that lowering the average quality of life is itself bad, if there is nobody whose quality of life is lowered, and if the means we take in order to lower the average quality amount to the creation of extra people whose lives are worth living. Nor does the greater inequality which we produce merely by adding more people make the new world worse than the one we started from; this is specially obvious if the new people don't know about the original population, for then there would be no issues about either social justice or jealousy. (I am not so sure about the social justice side of that.) The result is that it is always better to have an enormous population whose lives are only just worth living than a much smaller population whose lives are well worth living or even blissful. The numbers count.

We might hope that a path to the solution to (some of) these difficulties would be opened by increased subtlety in the theory of value. We might, for instance, decide that "not worse than" does not imply "at least as good as". Parfit considers some such suggestions towards the end of Part 4. But he decides that they don't work.

Parfit's last publication, "Future People, the Non-Identity Problem, and Person-Affecting Principles" (2017) was submitted to the editors on January

1, 2017, only hours before his death, and it is in fact a return to these issues, with a purported resolution. He is looking for a principle that does not encourage levelling down—in fact, for one that discourages it. What emerges is a "Wide Dual Person-Affecting Principle":

> One of two outcomes would be in one way better if this outcome would together benefit people more, and in another way better if this outcome would benefit each person more.

This principle supposedly implies that if N people exist at level 100, this is better than if 2N people exist at level 50; the benefits to each would be greater and the benefits to all would be the same. But the principle retains the idea that it is better to have 2N people at 100 than to have N people at 100. In this way the levelling-down process that drives us to the Repugnant Conclusion is supposedly stopped. My own view, however, is that this resolution is not successful. Yet again, the paradox is stronger than we are.

An alternative suggestion, which appeals to me more, focuses on the relation between values and reasons. The Repugnant Conclusion is a result in the theory of value: a large enough world at a very low average level of well-being will always be better than a much smaller world with a much higher average level of well-being. But we should bear in mind the relevance of this to decisions about what we have reason to do. Parfit himself came to accept Scanlon's buck-passing conception of value, according to which the fact that something is of value is the same fact as the fact that we have reasons of certain sorts (to protect, promote, . . ., it). And his phrase (in *Reasons and Persons*) "better in the sense relevant to choice" reveals a nascent tendency towards what one might call a deontic conception of value, since "relevant to choice" seems to mean something like "relevant to what we ought to (decide to) do". But if we reject such conceptions of value, we have room to suggest that, though a repugnant world would be better than the present smaller world, that fact gives us no reason to prefer it, to work towards it if we can, and so on. After all, the fact that a child, if I were to have it, would have a good quality of life is no reason to have that child—though it might perhaps intensify (or act as an enabler for) any reasons I do have to have that child. By contrast, the fact that, if I had a child, that child's life would not be worth living may be—probably would be—a reason not to have that child. But this need not determine our answer in the positive case.

Both of these remarks may seem peculiar because the reference of "that child" in the question how I have reason to act contains a reference to an object that does not yet exist. But we can sidestep that by saying that the fact that any child I have would have a life that is not worth living is a reason not to have a child—not to have any child. Analogous remarks on the positive case are less persuasive: the fact that any child I were to have would have a life worth living is not itself a reason for me to have a child—any child at all.

I now turn to Parfit's second major work, the massive three-volume *On What Matters* (Vols 1 and 2, 2011, and Vol. 3, 2017, comprising altogether 1,700 pages), which is dramatically different from his first, not in the stresses and strains that were involved in its production but in topic or, rather, in topics. The book derives in part from the Tanner Lectures which Parfit delivered at UC Berkeley in 2002. It has two main aims. The first is to suggest that three classic positions in normative ethics—Kantianism, rule-consequentialism and contractualism—though they appear to be rivals, may in fact, with suitable adjustments, be reworkable as three facets of a possible single position. This suggestion is mainly treated in the last sections of Volume 1. The second aim is to establish a form of cognitive realism about the normative, and this is what the book's title refers to. Parfit had long been of the view that subjectivist conceptions of ethics commit their defenders to the claim that, though some things may matter to us, indeed may matter very much to us, nothing really matters at all. All there is is what we care about, and though some carings may be more sensible than others or otherwise to be recommended, no carings are more correct than others. In this sense, nothing really matters. To say that we should care about some things is to express concern about our carings, not to enunciate some form of normative truth.

The early chapters of Volume 1 are devoted to the theory of reasons, something which, as I have said, was noticeably absent from *Reasons and Persons*. Parfit accepts Scanlon's so-called "Buck-passing Account" of value, which sinks value into reasons; to be of value is to have features that give us reasons of certain sorts—reasons to care, to conserve, to promote, etc. And Parfit offers a raft of distinctions between various kinds of reasons. In particular, he introduces a topic to which he repeatedly returns—the distinction between objective and subjective theories of reasons. Subjectivists maintain that what we have reason to do is what would most achieve what we want; our reasons depend on our desires. Objectivists maintain that what we have most reason to do is what would be best. Parfit is an objectivist, but he is alarmed by, and repeatedly returns to, the views of people he respects who are of a subjectivist persuasion, most notably Bernard Williams.

But the first main aim of *On What Matters* was highlighted in the title Parfit originally gave to the working manuscript of his eventual trilogy, namely *Climbing the Mountain*. What Parfit does is to adjust all three theories (rule-consequentialism, Kantianism, and contractualism) so that their central claims can be expressed in a single formula TT:

> An act is wrong just when such acts are disallowed by some principle that is optimific, uniquely universally willable, and not reasonably rejectable. (p. 412)

The first criterion for wrongness here is consequentialist, the second Kantian, and the third Scanlonian. Parfit's point, of course, is that these criteria need not be seen as conflicting. They may represent a difference of focus, but there is no difficulty in supposing that a principle might satisfy all three of them at once.

My immediate worry, when I first read this material, was that Parfit had carefully omitted to include the intuitionist tradition in his list of positions to be accommodated. Ross's theory of *prima facie* duties, a theory which seems to me to merit inclusion on any list of classic positions in normative ethics, gives a quite different account of which acts are wrong. For Ross, an act is right if it is one's most pressing *prima facie* duty. Showing that one could, at a pinch, squeeze all the non-Rossian theories—by which I mean theories that work in terms of absolute duties rather than in terms of Ross's *prima facie* duties—into one combined principle didn't cut all the ice for me. For Ross's *prima facie* principles don't disallow or allow, require or forbid, anything; there is no such thing as "being *prima facie* disallowed" or "being *prima facie* required". And Ross's principles do not emerge as "not reasonably rejectable" in anything approaching Scanlon's sense of that phrase.

What is more, even if we allow an evaluative shadow of Ross's apparently non-evaluative *prima facie* principles, it seems that there is no such thing as being *prima facie* good or *prima facie* bad—though Ross does occasionally suggest otherwise. An act can be *prima facie* right or *prima facie* wrong, and it can be good in a respect and bad in another respect, but being good in a respect is not a form of *prima facie* goodness; it is real, actual goodness—unlike the rightness in *prima facie* rightness, which is not a form of rightness at all.

But in the penultimate chapter of the entire book, Chapter 57, Parfit does address Ross's view directly. He argues there that there is a possible position which he calls Act-including Act Consequentialism, which holds that

> C: it would often be intrinsically bad to treat people in certain ways, such as deceiving or coercing them, or breaking promises we have made to them.

Technically this is not a form of consequentialism, since it does not mention the wrong and does not hold that all wrong acts are wrong because of the disvalue of their consequences. But it is still a view which holds that some of our *prima facie* duties are grounded in the goodness or badness of *something*, namely the goodness or badness of the relevant action; and for many that would be enough for them to think of it as a form of consequentialism. We would, of course, have to avoid the temptation to say that these acts are good because they are right, or bad because they are wrong. If this is a form of consequentialism at all, it has to go the other way round: they are right because they are good and wrong because they are bad. The question then is what sort of value we are dealing with here. Parfit says that it is a form of intrinsic value. But are we to think of this value as moral value or just as ordinary goodness? Standard consequentialism understands the right and the wrong in terms of non-moral value: the value of happiness, friendship, achievement, and so on. Act-including Act Consequentialism seems to understand the right and the wrong in terms of a new form of value, the intrinsic (not consequential) moral value of an action. Of course, we are used to moral value if it is a value that belongs to agents: some agents are morally good and others are morally bad. But this new sort of moral value is to be a value that belongs to actions, not to agents. And certainly it is a good thing that right actions be done. But this sort of goodness is not moral goodness; it is the ordinary sort of goodness that we might express by saying that this or that behaviour was welcome. So the question remains whether we can make sense of this new sort of moral goodness and badness that belongs directly to actions and is grounded in such features as deceit and coercion and charity.

Matters are complicated by the word "often" in Parfit's account of Act-including Act Consequentialism. A principle is not something that applies "often". A principle applies universally or not at all. There are such things as contributory principles; but they specify a feature that makes an invariant contribution, one that is always there and will sometimes win the day. There is no "often" about it.

One way forward would be to distinguish between intentional deceit and unintentional deceit. Intentional deceit looks as if it is a feature of the agent, and any disvalue it has will belong to the agent as well as to the action. So what about unintentional deceit? We might understand this as unintentionally causing someone to have a false belief. This is no doubt often (but not always) unfortunate and unwelcome, but it doesn't seem to be morally bad as such; and if it is bad, it will be bad because of some consequence—and we are not supposed to be appealing to the badness of consequences here.

It is hard to see one's way through this thicket, but my general conclusion is that Parfit did not manage to accommodate Ross-style intuitionism. His mountain has three sides when it needs really to have four. More generally, anyone familiar with Ross's *The Right and the Good* will be struck by the fact that none of the potential moral principles that Parfit considers are *prima facie* principles in Ross's sense. Parfit deals with Ross by proposing a further non-*prima facie* duty which is not to do with the value of consequences. (Though the word "often" in C does again give one pause.) Though Ewing called Ross's conception of a *prima facie* duty "one of the most important discoveries of the century in moral philosophy" (1959, p. 126) I don't think Parfit ever took that "discovery" on board.

I now turn to moral metaphysics, which occupies very much more space, as is appropriate in a work entitled "On What Matters". Here the question is not which things matter and how much, but whether anything matters at all. Parfit's treatment of the relevant metaethical material in Volumes 1 and 2 differs from what we find in Volume 3, which appeared six years later, but the changes are not enormously significant. His general picture of the normative, which he used to call Non-Metaphysical Non-Naturalism, is now called Non-Realist Cognitivism. I can't myself see that the change of name is any improvement; indeed, it might be a step in the wrong direction. The term "Non-Metaphysical" showed, perhaps correctly, that there was to be no challengeable metaphysics; "Non-Realist" merely avoids a particular metaphysical picture. And the term "Cognitivism" misleadingly directs our attention to issues which concern the nature of an appropriate response and away from the nature of that to which we are responding. Perhaps all that is meant is that the notions of true and false, of getting it right and getting it wrong, are appropriate in ethics and in normative enquiries more generally.

Parfit's aim here is to allow that the distinction between true and false applies to moral claims and utterances just as much as to claims and utterances in natural science and indeed in mathematics. But this can only be because the applicability of the true/false distinction is not a metaphysical one and does not depend on metaphysics. We tend to think that a true remark or thought must be one that fits the facts, and that it is the part of the naturalist to insist that the only facts are natural facts. Parfit is using a supposedly non-substantial sense of "fact" in which there are moral facts as well as natural and mathematical facts. But these moral facts do not obtain because of the existence of anything like a moral state of affairs. There is truth here, but it is not a form of correspondence to some sort of independent moral reality, because there is no such reality.

What is it then? Parfit did not seem to be interested in this question. It was enough for him to fend off the opposition (in the form of Alan Gibbard, Simon Blackburn, and others). But the rest of us might be looking for more than this. The work of David Wiggins and John McDowell in the 1970s springs to mind, especially Wiggins's "Towards a Sensible Subjectivism" (not published until 1987). The most that Parfit gives us is the term "Cognitivism", and this is a term which he does not attempt to unpack. But one would have thought that a moral belief is a form of practical commitment, and something of that sort is not happily characterized simply as cognitive, even though the main argument for what we used to call "realism" was that there is a constant fear of getting it wrong (that is, of making moral mistakes) despite one's own best efforts. Of course, the question then is what sort of mistake we make when we get it wrong.

In fact Parfit's metaphysical position is very close to John Skorupski's notion of irrealism: "Irrealism about the normative says that normative knowledge of fundamental normative propositions *rests on no receptive awareness*. The only capacity it requires is the non-receptive cognitive capacity of rationality, a capacity which involves spontaneity and regulation by the universality of reasons, not receptivity" (Skorupski 1999, p. 456). This idea of non-receptive awareness of a truth is one that Parfit might have found fruitful. But, of course, we would still be left looking for a positive account of what "non-receptive awareness" amounts to, since knowing what it is not does not tell us what it is. One final suggestion is that "non-receptive" means, or at least entails, "a priori"; on this view, our moral knowledge would emerge as a priori knowledge of particular normative truths, consisting mainly in truths about reasons. But this is only a gesture towards an adequate epistemology.

Acknowledgements

I am very grateful to John Broome, David Wiggins, Jeff McMahan, and Janet Radcliffe Richards for their help. I also wish to thank the Warden of All Souls, Sir John Vickers, for giving me access to the college's file on Parfit, from which most of the details of Parfit's time at All Souls are taken.

References

Ewing, A. C., *Second Thoughts in Moral Philosophy* (London, 1959).
Parfit, D., "Future People, the Non-Identity Problem, and Person-Affecting Principles", *Philosophy and Public Affairs*, 45/2 (2017), 118–57.
Ross, W. D., *The Right and the Good* (Oxford, 1930).
Skorupski, J. "Irrealist Cognitivism", *Ratio*, xii/4 (1999), 436–59.
Wiggins, D., "Towards a Sensible Subjectivism", in *Needs, Values, Truth: Essays in the Philosophy of Value* (Aristotelian Society Series, vol. 6) (Oxford, 1987), 185–214.

2
My Lovely Duomaniac

Janet Radcliffe Richards

The memoirs in this collection are mainly about Derek as a philosopher. That is entirely appropriate, not just because the first two volumes in this trilogy are entirely concerned with his philosophy, but also because but because for the second half of his life his work in philosophy—and to only a slightly lesser extent his architectural photography—was the essence of his life. He thought of his life in terms of what he wanted to achieve, and that is what he would want to be remembered for.

I shall not try to contribute to the discussion of his philosophy, because although I am also a philosopher, I am not really a Parfit scholar. This must sound like something earlier jurists might have called "petty treason"—the betrayal of a husband by a wife—but Derek and I agreed relatively early on that it would be better on the whole for us to pursue our work separately. This was partly because we had somewhat different interests and very different ways of working. But it was mainly because, as any student or colleague of Derek's knows well, there was no natural end to a discussion of any subject with which he was engaged. Once you had started, it was as though some philosophical Ancient Mariner had fixed you with his glittering eye and made escape impossible until the story was finished; and as it never was finished, serious engagement with his work, especially when we were in the same house, would have expanded to fill the whole of life. It was not totally avoided, of course. He would often appear at my study door or on the phone, fraught because some philosopher was disagreeing with him or misunderstanding what he had said, and then serious discussions would often start, and, especially if I disagreed with him, carry on for hours. But on the whole we worked separately.

Many people know Derek from his lectures and classes, and remember him as kind and helpful to his students and colleagues, as an amazingly quick and prolific commentator on their work, and also (as one of the obituaries said) as endearingly eccentric. But many are curious to understand more

Janet Radcliffe Richards, *My Lovely Duomaniac* In: *Derek Parfit: His Life and Thought*. Edited by: Jeff McMahan, Oxford University Press. © Oxford University Press 2025. DOI: 10.1093/9780191915307.003.0002

of what lay behind the public appearance of such a remarkable person, and I obviously have a view that no one else has. It is being impressed on me that I have a duty to posterity to make sure that what I know does not disappear.

In some ways I am as curious as anybody else. I was puzzled when I first met him, and to some extent still am. His biographer David Edmonds has found out a huge amount about his early life that I knew only in patches from what Derek and his family had told me, and it was in striking ways different from the life I knew, after he had settled on philosophy as his life's work. I wish I had known the earlier Derek: it would have been exhilarating. But he himself often said, "People don't change," and he obviously did not think he had changed. One significant element of the difference, undoubtedly, was the heavy dependence on drugs for sleeping that began when he was writing *Reasons and Persons.* It would be interesting to have a professional view of that. But I also think I now have a more general understanding of—or at least a plausible hypothesis about—how the early and later Dereks were clearly the same person. I wonder how plausible it will seem to others.

Now, more than six years after his death, I still feel this may be only a preliminary draft. There is much more that could be said. But, for now, here is an account for people to compare with those of other contributors with different experiences, and with their own impressions of Derek.

It may also, possibly, be relevant to wider ideas about men and women, which has for a long time been a professional as well as a personal interest of mine.

1 Meeting

We met in the autumn of 1983, when I was 39 and he was 40, and I had recently returned to live in Oxford. He had just finished *Reasons and Persons,* which was then in press. In fact I realized later that it was only because he had just finished *Reasons and Persons* that I met him at all. If I had appeared on the scene while he was still in the intensive period of writing and getting the book into press, he would probably not have noticed me, and certainly would have had no time or mental space for any follow-up if he had done. If I had arrived much later, when he was in the thick of *On What Matters,* he would once again have had no time to do anything, or even been conscious that there might be anything else worth doing. But now the book was in press, and, as he later said, he had space to realize that there were some things missing in his life.

As it happened, it was also a significant time in my own life. I had at last, after many vicissitudes perhaps characteristic of women of my generation, succeeded in sorting out what I saw as the essentials of life. I now had a proper job and was buying a house; my first book had been a surprising success and I was a bit famous, with interesting approaches from all kinds of directions. I was also free and happy, and ready to embark on a new phase of life; and I had returned to Oxford, where my parents had lived since the sixties and where I had done my graduate work, to do just that. I was at the time in the philosophy department of the Open University, and although I had continued to teach some graduate seminars in Oxford, I had generally lost touch with the people there. To get things going again I went along at the beginning of the Michaelmas term to the new series of the renowned seminars in the Old Library at All Souls—widely referred to as the Star Wars—run by Ronnie Dworkin, Amartya Sen, and Derek. (Gerry Cohen joined them the following year.)

I knew the others, but Derek I had not yet met. I did not notice much about him; he did not radiate the general bonhomie of the others. I do remember his starting by announcing that he was going to deal with the mistakes he had now found in the section on Mistakes in Moral Mathermatics forthcoming in *Reasons and Persons.* He seemed to need to adjust his temperature frequently, as he kept taking his jacket off and putting it on again, while not letting up for a moment in his concentration or his somewhat set expression. He also kept taking sips of water from what I realized later, but could not see then, was a vodka bottle.

The next week I noticed that he seemed to be looking at me rather a lot. Then, a few days after that, there appeared, out of the blue, a letter from him. This was long before the days of email. It was about my book, which I was surprised he knew as it was an analysis of controversies in feminism. It was very complimentary but curiously formal and with several capitalized words (I remember he mentioned my "Cause"). He told me later that he had seen Amartya come up to greet me at the end of the seminar and had asked him who I was. Amartya had filled in some background, telling him about my book, which I suppose he then bought as a kind of audition. Amartya had apparently also said that I had the previous year left an unhappy relationship, and Derek wondered whether he had ideas of matchmaking.

Then a little later I had a phone call from Derek, whom I had still not met, inviting me to a private discussion group in All Souls and college dinner the same day. To be approached by such a distinguished philosopher so soon after my return to Oxford was seriously exciting, and of course I accepted.

Since we had not met, I said I would introduce myself at the next seminar, even though I was pretty sure he must know who I was. I did that, but was somewhat dampened by the cool way in which he responded with a mere "Yes, I know," without any attempt to extend the conversation. I concluded that the dinner invitation must just be a standard courtesy to someone who was about to join the group.

I went to the discussion group, and then came back in the evening after the first meeting to join him at dinner. He was much more friendly than I expected, and also seemed rather more striking than he had done before, when he had been deep in philosophical debate. It was a very pleasant evening, though slightly strange in many ways. Over dinner he talked freely about himself and his family and his background. His doctor parents had been medical missionaries in China, until they had to return because of the outbreak of war. He had been born in China—on the slopes of a sacred mountain, he told me, though it turned out later that the mountain in question had been several miles from where he was actually born. His parents had lost their faith, but Anglican worship had been taken for granted at his prep school, and he as a child had earnestly tried to persuade them to go back to church to avoid Hell, until at the age of 7 he realized that the idea of Hell was morally outrageous and himself abandoned religion. He had an older and a younger sister, and was sorry to say that in his unenlightened youth had often described himself as the meat in the sandwich. His younger sister had wanted children but not found a husband, so had gone ahead anyway without one. He had loved school—the Dragon in Oxford, followed by Eton—which he had regarded as real life, with holidays as unwelcome interruptions.

He also talked about more personal matters such as his severe problems with insomnia during the recent book-writing process, saying that he was sometimes awake for thirty-six hours at a time and felt that if he had had a gun to hand he might have shot himself—not because he wanted to die, but because he was desperate to lose consciousness. He had eventually been recommended to try a sleep regime and calming drugs that had solved the problem, and when I commented that I also had problems with sleep, he immediately suggested I should try his methods too. I discovered later that whenever he came across some technique he regarded as providing a major life improvement, he would proselytize it far and wide.

After Hall we went briefly for coffee, and I was disappointed to find that he did not intend to go on to dessert. I had not been to All Souls before and would have liked to see everything. I later discovered that Derek had been the first person at All Souls to start skipping dessert and was rather proud of fact that others had been encouraged to do so too, and that he had broken what had been a rigid convention.

However, he did not intend that to be the end of the evening. He headed for his rooms, passing through the wonderful Hawksmoor Quad with its view across to the Radcliffe Camera. It was my first proper view of this, and at the same time my first glimpse of Derek's obsessional love of architecture. He said that he had been afraid when he moved into his rooms that he might get tired of it all when it became familiar, but that he never had done: it struck him in the same way every time he saw it. This was another thing I later saw often. He never tired of the things he most valued.

His set of rooms on the second floor overlooked this view, and his sitting room was a work of art in itself. It was a fine eighteenth-century room with windows in two directions, which—it is worth saying for anyone who saw it only later—was perfectly presented. He had added a magnificent carved wooden fire surround, bought, he said, in 1962 at a sale at Syon House, I think for £5. (It is appalling to think of what must have been demolished to make it available.) He said he had bought another similar one there too, and lamented the fact that also at that sale had been the marble façade of the original London Mansion House, which it had seemed impossible for him, then at least, to take and use. It is as well that that was well before my time, or it is conceivable—irrational as it would certainly have been—that we might have tried. He had flanked the grate with large mirror-image prints of an exquisite Rembrandt drawing of a woman. There was a comfortable and stylish modern suite, of a design with enormous brown and beige apples (which I later decided he probably found somewhat erotic) and modern lighting, including an Italian lamp arching over the sofa. There were also two or three art nouveau vases, with elegant nubile ladies twined around them.

There he introduced what turned out to be his other obsession: his architectural photography. He showed me his photographs of Venice and St Petersburg, which were framed around the room, and individually spotlit. He said that he had no capability for art, but he had for art criticism, so he had turned to photography. He went to Venice and St Petersburg, his favourite places, with the intention of finding the most beautiful buildings, waiting for the best lighting and weather conditions, taking hundreds of slightly different shots, and choosing the best among them. He then refined the prints by employing a brilliant toucher-upper, and he pointed out in great detail the changes he had made. These included removing telephone wires and other unpleasing distractions, and also such temporary obstructions as scaffolding and, I gathered, an army lorry in front of the Winter Palace. In a picture of the

Redentore (one of my favourites), he had replaced the moon with a slightly larger one copied from another picture, and enhanced the details of its surface. He also pointed out that in a picture of San Marco, which had also been obscured by scaffolding at the time, his toucher-upper had put a niche with mosaics to match one visible on the other side, though it was actually not there. People would also be removed or, in one early photo, have their clothes changed so that they were all wearing red and black.

He then showed me his IBM computer, which was one of two identical devices he had bought from Ronnie Dworkin. This was a long time ago, and hardly anyone had personal computers. My own book had been written using the excitingly advanced technology of a second-hand IBM electric typewriter, when operations like cutting and pasting were still literally just that. These computers were the kind with a green CRT screen and about eighty characters to the line, with saving on to floppy disks that held almost nothing. Derek said how excited he was about this new way of working. He would sit at the desk in front of the computer feeling like a pilot in charge of an airliner. He recommended that I should try the same and made the slightly startling suggestion that I should *rent* one of the computers from him. I was certainly interested, but what kind of arrangement would this be? What was the going rate for renting a computer? Would it be compatible with my recently acquired mortgage payments??

During the conversation that followed, Derek lamented his inability to learn poetry by heart. He said he had attempted to learn Matthew Arnold's "Dover Beach" by trying to repeat it to himself every night for a year, but was frustrated by still not being able to do it. He didn't say so then, and I could not have known at the time since *Reasons and Persons* was still in press, but the poem catches the essence of his main philosophical purpose: working on the foundations of an ethics to take the place of retreating religious certainties, and contending in that way with the problems of a world with no underlying moral order. It also suggested he wanted a companion on the darkling plain while he confronted the nocturnal clash of ignorant armies.

Then finally he wanted to listen to music. It seemed as though the same thing had happened with music as with art. He said he couldn't play an instrument but that he could play the gramophone (still vinyl records and a turntable, of course), which I took at the time to be a rather weak joke. That was fine by me (though he didn't ask, as far as I remember), and I sat on the sofa while he chose the record and started it playing. Then I was slightly startled, for the second time that evening, by his switching off the lights. Surely this was too soon? How should I react? But he simply sat down next to me on the sofa, and we listened to music in the dark, until, quite late, I left and cycled back to my house in St Clement's.

That first meeting turned out to be a pretty accurate reflection of the essentials of his life: philosophy at his computer, painstaking production of beautiful photographs, a deep love of art, architecture, music, and poetry, and a devotion to the very best of it.

But I didn't feel that I understood him at all.

In particular, I couldn't tell what his attitude was to me, and this continued through various interactions over the next two months. I returned his dinner invitation, and as he left my house at the end of the evening, he gave me a slight embrace and said he hoped I would stay in Oxford. But a few days later, when he called to tell me that there was going to be a television programme with Glenn Gould, it was an abrupt, informative call, not prolonged in the way that would indicate a courtship move. The same thing happened the following week.

Then he came to my house and installed the spare computer (with no more mention of rent). I picked him up in my car, and was struck by how extraordinarily well dressed he was for such a job. He told me later, with charming ingenuousness, that he had just bought three new suits. (On another occasion, when I commented on the lovely perfume he was wearing, he immediately told me what it was and said that he had read that it was the one most liked by women.) It took some time to get the computer to work, but eventually it did, and he briefly took my hand in excitement. But when after a week or so I started to run into problems, as I inevitably did, I felt really uncomfortable about the prospect of having to ask him to deal with them. I still saw him as a rather distant, distinguished man and felt that this would be an imposition on him. I certainly had no feeling that he would be pleased. Still, it had to be done as I had no other recourse, and he came round again to deal with the matter. Then he invited me round in the evening to listen to music again.

Although it seemed clear that this man was interested in me, and I was well disposed to him, I still didn't feel I knew him or what was going on. It had been obvious from the very first meeting that this was not someone you took up with if you were looking for an ordinary domestic life, but as I knew by then that I wasn't, that was not an issue. But what, as our grandmothers might have said, were his intentions? He was not at all shy or awkward—indeed extremely confident in a way, as you might expect of Eton and All Souls, though without anything resembling an Eton swagger—but I had never encountered anything like this before. It is hard to describe the nature of the strangeness. A curious detachment? There was friendliness and a sort of openness, but no warmth, no hint of increasing intimacy, let alone flirting; no semi-accidental touches, jokes, looks. It happened again, several times. He started inviting me to come round in the evening to listen to music, and we sat on his sofa listening to Mozart or Wagner or Bach, not exactly formally, but something like it—though he did eventually start putting his arm round my shoulders. I even began to find myself wondering slightly whether this was the kind of old-fashioned courtship where the first move might be a proposal of marriage. At any rate, it was all so far from anything I recognized that it seemed clear that all the running should be left to him; and I settled back, almost as an observer, to watch the course of events.

The computer did eventually give him his *point d'appui*. One day at midnight, after an evening of music in All Souls, he suddenly said there was still time to go and sort out the latest set of computer problems. And even though this was an odd time to start, and even though as we prepared to leave he thrust into my arms the scores of the complete keyboard works of Bach, I still thought that that was what he meant. As it happened, it wasn't.

Here, of course, we draw a veil; but the essential upshot was that I saw for the first time an expression of real warmth and engagement—pupils dilated—and from my point of view, that was it. If this brilliant and immensely knowledgeable man, with impeccable taste in art and architecture and music, who was making waves in moral philosophy, was also capable of real personal engagement, that was enough to go on. It was still clear that this was a very strange man, and that some things would certainly always be missing, but, for the first time in my life, I felt seriously hooked.

He appeared the next day with a pair of antique silver candlesticks, presumably from the silversmith on the High Street near All Souls, "for us". He suggested—announced?—that he should—would?—come and spend two or three nights a week at my house. The next day he said, "We must decide whether to get married and have children"; and although it seemed much too soon for that, and anyway I had no plans for children and thought it unlikely that he did either, the two or three nights immediately turned into his appearing every day and settling into a pattern—not exactly secret, but certainly not generally known about—of his being at my house in St Clements at night, and then, after getting up at about eleven, back to All Souls for lunch.

A week or two later I told my sister I was in love. She was amazed. She had never heard anything resembling that from me before.

So began thirty-five years of our connection in its various forms; and even longer of my trying to understand both it and him.

2 Early Impressions

As I had come late into Derek's life, it took some time to piece together the background, though it was obviously impressive and apparently privileged: Eton, Balliol, and All Souls. But his family was not particularly privileged, in the kind of way that made thinking of sending their son to Eton automatic. After they returned from China they eventually moved back to Oxford, where they both now worked in public health. They had been determined to get as good an education as possible for their children, and they sent Derek to the Dragon, a highly reputed prep school in Oxford. But from there on he progressed on his own merits, going to Eton as King's Scholar, then with a scholarship to Balliol, and now All Souls.

He said he had loved school, and over the years he related many affectionate anecdotes about it, but as he had consistently come top in all the frequent rankings, it was perhaps not surprising. His success had entitled him to become Captain (what in more ordinary schools would be called Head Boy); but to the extreme disappointment of his father, who had been to a very minor public school and would have been ecstatic to have his son Captain of Eton, Derek refused to stay and take it. Instead he filled in the time before Balliol by going to work at *The New Yorker,* which published a poem of his. At Oxford he had obviously thrown himself into all kinds of activities, such as editing the student magazine *Isis*, and on one notable occasion had managed to impale himself on spikes (consequently removed) on a drainpipe by which he was trying to get into Balliol after hours. He pointed out the drainpipe to me. He had obviously experimented with all kinds of things, and travelled a good deal, but by the time he met me he was a fully focussed philosophy and photography duomaniac (his word). Quite how fully focussed, it would take me some time to discover. In the meantime, I gradually got to know more about him.

The love of architecture had been obvious from our first meeting, and it was always apparent, anywhere we went, as he pointed out or commented on what happened to strike him. His attention was always caught by buildings, to which it kept turning to the detriment—as I gradually discovered—of his driving, and which was one of the many causes of falls from his bike. The commentary was by no means continuous or concentrated on significant beautiful buildings in the manner of a tourist guide, but about all kinds of things. I would not—pre Derek—have noticed or thought twice about the jumble of styles in the Bodleian tower, showing the influence of classical architecture but still too early for Palladian principles to have been properly established; or the porticos in Bloomsbury (I think I remember the occasion but haven't been able to track them down on Google Street View) that committed the solecism of having a central column; or that the Brasenose tower had spoilt the vista along the High Street. Nor would it have occurred to me that Magdalen tower, with one corner swollen to accommodate the staircase, looked like someone with toothache, or that the proportions of the Sheldonian were like a man with his trousers pulled up to his chin—though I think he attributed that idea to Anthony Quinton. Or (later) that the not-quite-matching chests on chests in our bedroom were like the towers of Notre Dame.

There was a background, I gradually realized, of a huge amount of knowledge and theory, and a large library. Derek often said he had no visual images, as if it were a striking limitation. I have never been sure about that claim and wonder whether he may have had a mistaken view of what other people could do—thinking that they could summon up internal pictures of things they had seen, and describe them by reading off the details?—but he had a remarkable knowledge of buildings and could describe them in detail from memory. He would recognize buildings in films and pictures, and often know who the architects were. When we were going to see houses and cathedrals, he could always tell me about them in advance and often make comments about the ways in which they had been modified or left unbuilt for structural reasons: the reinforcements across the nave at Wells, or the omitted pinnacles on the central tower at York. The same was true even in Europe, and in imaginary landscapes in art he could often point to the original buildings that were used as their basis. He knew the history of how they were built in the first place and the pressures that determined whether they were kept or destroyed. Lying around his room were books like *Unbuilt Oxford*, about plans that had never been realized, and *The Sack of Bath,* which I could not bear to look at.

I had also for many years gone around thinking of what I would do if I were aesthetic dictator, though on the basis of far less knowledge, so we both routinely commented on what we saw. Fortunately our judgments were similar, though interestingly different in emphasis. After a while Derek said we should have numbers for our most predictable comments, for shorthand. He said he went around mentally triaging buildings, into ones that must be kept at all costs, ones that could be allowed to stay until something better could be built, and ones that should be demolished immediately. His prime example of the third category was the Oxford Telephone Exchange, which most people have probably never noticed. Soon after his death there was a proposal to demolish it, though on grounds of road changes rather than aesthetics. Maybe if Derek had still been alive at the time he might have involved himself in the issue.

He was in fact concerned about, and actively involved in, various matters about the appearance of Oxford. He was one of the very few people I have heard of who was in favour of the proposal of putting a road through Christ Church Meadow, because he thought the High Street so beautiful that clearing it of traffic was much more important than preserving a not particularly attractive field. That was in the 1970s, before the city took serious efforts to improve the situation by closing the High Street to most traffic, though when that policy was first attempted Derek thought the litter of signs and obstructions and road markings was nearly as offensive as the traffic had been. That was later improved; I don't know how much he engaged in the debates. But he was for many years on the street-lighting committee, campaigning fiercely against the hideous (but energy-efficient) low-pressure sodium lighting so widely used at the time, and he was much concerned with the design of street lamps. He paid for the prototype of the Windsor lanterns now in Beaumont Buildings, decades before he knew he would one day own a house there. And he did actually design the lamps that are now throughout the centre of Oxford (with technical drawings by my sister's partner, Richard Lewis). I saw the two designs that were under consideration before he came up with his, and I think Oxford had a lucky escape. I hope that one day there will be a plaque acknowledging him.

The architectural styles he most liked were Perpendicular and Palladian. He was very disappointed by the fact that domestic architecture in Oxford had not taken off until the dons had been allowed to marry, in the late nineteenth century, by which time architecture had gone disastrously downhill. He used to comment that the decline of architecture happened at the same time as the discovery of anaesthetics: a new source of pain just as another was ending (or a relief for an old pain to compensate for a new one's beginning). I don't know whether that observation was original to him, but it might well have been. He liked very little that had been built since then, though he did admire several Edwardian buildings. He hated some of the precepts of modern architecture ("form follows function", intended normatively) and probably most modern buildings, but he was not against later styles in principle. He was positively exhilarated by New York, whose buildings he probably knew nearly as well as those of Oxford. He also objected to the fashionable contempt for pastiche, and thought it far more important to build what would look best in any place, especially architecturally sensitive places, than to be "authentic" by being modern. He was also prepared to be heretical about materials. York Minster did not have the pinnacles on its central tower that had been in the original design, because the structure turned out not to be able to support the weight. He would have liked to use modern lightweight materials to make it look as originally intended. And conversely, he thought the use of Bath stone in buildings to replace demolished terraces in Bath did nothing in itself to make them architecturally acceptable. Fortunately I was in full sympathy with all of this.

I also became gradually more aware of the way music fitted into his life. I had seen something of that at the outset, of course; but again, it took some time to recognize how much background there was. When he commented early on that he wished he had a recording of a particular piece by a particular musician (Gould? Bach?), I helpfully went to try to find it—of course without the aid of the internet, which was still a long way off—and couldn't. Derek, of course, knew that such a recording had never been made. He knew of all the recordings of his favourite works. He loved jazz as well as classical music, and particularly admired Billie Holliday and Lester Young.

He had played the piano in his childhood ("especially Bach sarabandes") and jazz trumpet at Eton ("What key does Parfit know it in?"), but had given it all up, no doubt on the grounds that it was not worth doing when he could listen to the best recordings. What he meant by being able to play the gramophone, which I had taken to be a weak joke, was that he had already made judgments about the best works and the best performances to play for other people. He had a huge collection of records and was always buying more; and, much as with his photographs, he gradually settled on the best of the best to listen to over and over again. He saw no point in going to live performances, since they would never be as good as the best recordings. He had clearly read everything on the sleeves as well, and read more generally about the history and composers. I had always done a lot of playing (also not far beyond the Bach sarabande level) and singing, and knew a great deal of music through that, but I had nothing like his access to or knowledge of recorded music.

I also began to see something of the extent to which music actually pervaded his life when, in about the second week of his being in my house overnight, I was suddenly woken up by the Goldberg Variations. The record player was next to the bed, and it apparently had not occurred to Derek that being with someone else might be a reason for not playing it in the middle of the night. He was in the habit of playing music whenever he woke.

His feelings about music were strong and universal, and he frequently quoted Nietzsche's view that without music life would be an error. He lamented the decline of classical music in the West, and was glad that it had been adopted so much in the Far East, and that so many musicians were now being produced there. He thought that classical music composition had not gone well, once pointing out that the Strauss *Four Last Songs* were the most recent music we listened to, and said he thought there should be two music academies in America, "one on the East coast and one on the West", where the students studied and listened to music only up to a certain date (was it a different date in the two academies?), and then were left free to see how their own compositions would go if they were uninfluenced by more recent musical fashions. He was struck by the way composers continued to improve over time and thought the early deaths of Mozart and Schubert were cosmic tragedies. When I asked him whether he would be willing to die now to give Mozart another thirty-five years, he did not hesitate to say he would, and I have no doubt he meant it.

He had tried writing poetry too, obviously with some success, since as well as having *The New Yorker* publish his poem, he had won a national young poets' competition when he was at school. He said he gave it up when he found he couldn't produce the effects he had been aiming for—and then gradually came to realize that Keats and Tennyson hadn't done so either. He again lamented his inability to remember poetry, and also prose. He had played Sir Toby Belch when he was at the Dragon, but said that when he had looked recently at *Twelfth Night,* the part did not even look familiar. He was amazed as he gradually discovered that I learnt poetry very easily and knew a good deal by heart. He would occasionally ask me to recite poetry to him and several times said he would exchange his general knowledge for my memory for poetry. That was not true, of course, or should not have been, but it was an indication of how much he cared about it. It was a surprising gap, given his other abilities. Maybe it was partly because he read so much and so quickly.

Of course, I also began to understand better the second main purpose of his life, the photography. This was a direct offspring of his interests in art and architecture. He had no interest whatever in taking the photographs most people take, of people and occasions. His purpose was to produce works of art, catching beautiful buildings in the best circumstances, and where appropriate removing anything that spoilt the picture. It was his way of putting his aesthetic dictator impulses into practice.

He had started by deciding which places would be best for his purposes, and settled on Venice and St Petersburg. He limited himself almost entirely to those, and then mainly to the parts that he thought were best, and then only in particular kinds of weather and light. He had no interest in presenting anything like an overview of either city, let alone showing how it actually appeared most of the time and in real life. He went to both places every year, and to Venice often more than once. He went specifically at times most likely to give him the pictures he wanted: snow and grey skies in St Petersburg, to show the colours of the buildings, and mist or low-level sun in Venice. He often deliberately went to Venice in midsummer, because dawn on Midsummer's Day was the only time that he could catch sunlight on the front of the north-facing Redentore. He would stay for hours on the Punta della Dogana, waiting to catch his Palladian churches, the Redentore and San Giorgio, in different lights and weather conditions. He said this was his favourite place on earth.

I came quite late into Derek's photography; he already had most of his most valued pictures by then. But it was obvious even before I went with him on his expeditions how much was involved in these trips. He showed me the equipment in his room, and it had a bulk and complexity hardly imaginable in these days of camera phones, when everyone takes pictures everywhere and then manipulates them in PhotoShop. There were large tripods, camera bodies, and enormous lenses including a complex rising one needed for allowing verticals to be kept vertical. He also kept a fridge in his bedroom for storing the masses of film he would take with him.

When I did go with him, once to St Petersburg and many times to Venice, the most striking thing about it all was the dogged persistence, and unconcern for personal comfort, that I imagine must characterize wildlife photographers. When Derek was out, he was hung about with a huge weight of impedimenta, which one of the colleagues who went with him to St Petersburg said made him look like the White Knight in *Through the Looking Glass.* I was struck by the fact that although he took enormous care to get the best equipment possible, he seemed to put no thought at all into the lesser matters of making it easier to carry around, or the best ways to keep himself warm and comfortable. His focus seemed to be entirely on the quality of the end result, with details like comfort and efficiency not worth any time or attention: he just took the most direct line to what he wanted to achieve. Although he normally hated getting up early, and was just about functioning by eleven in the morning, he would get up before dawn in Venice in summer without any hesitation. (He loved low light: one of his favourite films was *The Duellists,* just for its dawn shots.) He would endure hours of cold in St Petersburg, apparently hardly noticing it: his nose was once saved from frostbite only by the intervention of some local people.

Having seen all this, I bought a big New York folding shopping trolley the next time we went to NYU, to keep in Venice. I also bought some thermal underwear, which hadn't occurred to Derek, though I'm not sure he ever remembered to use it. His default way of dealing with the cold was just to add an extra couple of shirts. The only protection against the rain he ever wore, either abroad or at home, was four First World War capes from an army surplus store: the kind with a bulge in one shoulder to accommodate a rifle. These were quite good for photographic purposes, but he wore them anywhere that he bothered with anything more than an umbrella.

Then, after the trip, came the processing. All the films had to be developed and produced as slides, after which he would go through them with high-powered magnifying lenses to make his initial selection. Then he would have test strips printed, to make sure the colours were right. Finally the best ones were printed, and after that came the touching-up process, with detailed instructions written on the back of each print. These are delightfully courteous: all the instructions begin with "please". The originals must now count as period pieces.

The expense of it all was inordinate. As Derek was living in All Souls at the time—which provided all he needed for the philosophy branch of his work, and for all his living expenses—all his income must have gone on his photography. In fact it must have exceeded his income at one point. He told me that his collection of art nouveau miscellanea had at one time included a necklace he would have liked to give me, but that he had had to sell part of his collection to finance the photography.

He knew that the kind of beauty that interested him was unfashionable in photographic circles. He said he had once taken some of his photographs to a London gallery, and when he came back the gallery owner returned them, saying merely, "You must have had a very good holiday." He told this story with some amusement. He had no interest in changing his view of what was worth achieving to suit anyone else's tastes.

3 West Kennett

Our semi-detached way of life seemed to suit both of us. I had decided some time before meeting Derek, and have recently discovered I actually said in an interview, that if I took up with a partner again, it might be ideal to live in different houses in the same street, like Mary Wollstonecraft and William Godwin. That was pretty well the situation we had, so it might have continued that way indefinitely, or at least until retirement. We were both very busy and were travelling a good deal.

But then there was a change in the situation. Derek's father died, and his mother decided to sell the family home in North Oxford and move into a retirement community, and to pass on the money to the children. Derek did not need his share at the time, so his mother used it to buy a flat in Oxford for his younger sister and her son when they came to visit. But his sister was killed in an accident, and the money again became available to Derek.

It was not all that much, but it was enough for me to suggest we should pool our resources and buy a house. My idea was that this wouldn't make much difference to ordinary life—none at all to his, except being in a different place overnight—but would be a sensible retirement plan. He could remain working and officially living in college, and I could beautify the house in the meantime. I was thinking of an Oxford house bigger than my little house in St Clement's, pretty though that was by then; and his mother, a highly intelligent and competent woman whom I liked enormously, was positively keen to have her decidedly impractical son sorted out in the long run. She even wanted to give the money to me, rather than Derek—probably thinking it might otherwise vanish into photography without his noticing, and that I was a better long-term guarantee—but her solicitor insisted that this would be injudicious.

Derek was not against the idea, but not really enthusiastic. He had no positive motive, as he was not at that stage giving any thought to retirement. Anyway, there was the problem of Oxford domestic architecture. Very little came up to a standard that might excite him. We did start to look at the few architecturally passable houses available, but without much success. We found one in Park Town that I thought might have done, but we missed it through indecisiveness: Derek was really only moderately interested. But then, in the college common room, he came across in *Country Life* an advertisement for a Georgian house in Wiltshire and quite simply fell in love at first sight.

He had told me that he sometimes dreamed (literally) about coming across a Palladian house that nobody had known about, just waiting for him to take. This one was hardly unknown, of course, but it was available. It also happened to be surrounded by open chalk downland of a kind that he also particularly liked, full of ancient tumuli and beech clumps. He had often talked with interest about his aunt's house, a thatched cottage in the Vale of White Horse, and we had gone for a walk on the Downs at his suggestion, early in our relationship. We had also visited the village of Avebury, which lies in an amazing stone circle and earthworks, and which turned out to be just behind the advertised house, less than a mile away across open country. Still, the façade alone would probably have been enough.

I didn't want to go for it. I had always dreamed (figuratively) of a Georgian country house as well, regarding the idea of living in one as close to heaven on earth, and this one did indeed look delightful; but it was miles from anywhere either of us had any reason to be. It also looked like a much bigger project than I had ever taken on. The house itself was not much more daunting than an Oxford one would have been, but it had 3 acres of garden and paddock, with a coach house block and a 40-foot greenhouse. Neither of us had ever been a gardener, or had any experience of country living. It was also close to the old London to Bristol road, the A4, and although most of the traffic had now been taken by the M4, what remained kept interrupting what would otherwise have been blissful rural calm in all directions—which was, of course, why we could think of affording it. And, even so, I didn't think we really could afford it.

Still, Derek's heart was lost. He seemed not to notice or care about any of these drawbacks, or my doubts. He was in love with the house and I was in love with Derek, and I cannot be the first woman in love to have gone along, against her better judgment, with something her man really wanted. There was another potential buyer, and a nail-biting bidding war that ended with sealed bids. Derek in his anxiety sat up most of the night, trying to decide how much he dared offer and watching a video of Mitsuko Uchida talking about Mozart, and won.

His family and friends were torn between amusement and incredulity. How could he think (as he had told one astonished friend) that he would afford this house by refraining from buying CDs? How would he adapt to living in the country, when he had always been in university cities? How would someone who had always lived in institutions cope with being a householder? As his brother-in-law said, Derek would have to learn about the world of Things.

Eight years later, it was clear that this scepticism and my doubts had been justified. Derek said, looking back, that his family's gift had been a poisoned chalice, and that he had been like a man falling for a pretty face. But that had not been clear at first, and it was not clear for some years. The problems, as they came, came gradually, and did not arise from living together but from my being so far from anywhere while Derek became more and more absorbed in his work and was so often away. Although the decision to go there turned out on balance to have been a mistake, and I wish I had had the confidence to resist it, something very good would have been lost if we had not done it.

Anyway, the die was cast. We sold my house and bought a smaller one nearby in Oxford, to let to tenants while keeping a room for ourselves when we stayed there, and went off to live in rural Wiltshire. We still, of course, drove often to Oxford, every week in term time; and I did the two-hour drive to Milton Keynes when I had meetings, usually staying overnight there. But as work for both of us was mainly writing, it was in West Kennett that we were going to spend most of our time.

Derek was really excited. When he found that the house was listed in Pevsner's volume on Wiltshire in *The Buildings of England* ("West Kennett House: Georgian, red brick, five bays and two-and-a half storeys. Porch"), he said he felt like Sir Walter Elliott in *Persuasion*, who kept looking at the page in the *Baronetcy* that listed his own family. And he was full of plans. He would make a photography project of the Downs, we would restore some eighteenth-century features of the house that had been removed, and we would go to Bath and Wells and Winchester and look at nearby country houses (all of which he knew about in detail already, of course). And, looking at the expanse of land, he announced that he would get his exercise by mowing the lawn with a manual mower.

That last suggestion is perhaps enough on its own to indicate how well Derek understood the scale of the enterprise. There was more than an acre of lawn, and he went out and bought a manual cylinder mower with a 15-inch cutting width: the sort of thing that might do for a suburban front garden with an energetic gardener. He abandoned the idea halfway along the first cut. But he entered enthusiastically into getting the house organized in a preliminary way, and I even have an unlikely photograph of him putting up curtains. We spent a lovely couple of weeks settling in and exploring the neighbourhood. We went to Marlborough, the main coaching stop on the old Bristol road, which would be our local shopping town. We went for a country walk to look at the house from a distance, during which Derek took a few experimental photographs and I rolled over three sheep that had got stuck on their backs. Our totally experimental new life had begun.

The house was of classic doll's house design, originally only one room deep and with all its windows on the front, perfectly proportioned and obviously designed to look much grander than it really was. The windows overlooked—beyond the road—some old farm buildings, then open country and West Kennet Long Barrow. Our studies were the two rooms on the top floor, each with two windows, and Derek said that we should put windows in the back of the rooms as well so that we could see the even better view in that direction, over a hill with a tumulus and beech clump, and the beginning of the ancient stone avenue leading to Avebury. Our doors were opposite each other next to a windowed landing room that I started to make into an extra library. Derek was delighted and even excited by the arrangement. When he noticed that I had put his print of Newton by the top flight of stairs, he declared that it showed this was where the serious work of the house started.

We settled into our new routine, and I could now see in detail how Derek spent his day. I knew already there were several fixed elements that remained unchanged wherever he was. Here I could see them structuring his daily round with a near Kantian regularity.

He would get up at about eleven, as I already knew, and after he had very quickly shaved and dressed, his first purpose was to make for the kitchen and strong coffee. In college he had made this with instant coffee and water from the hot tap in his room: he could not wait until college lunch for his first shot of caffeine, and it never occurred to him to get a kettle. In my house he had learned to make a concession to the kettle because it was quicker than waiting for the hot water to come through to the tap, so he did the same here. But he could never be persuaded to prefer ground coffee, or to think of it in terms of enjoyment. Rapid caffeine intake was the only purpose.

Then he had a simple breakfast, of grapefruit juice, cereal with water and yoghurt, and fruit, to replace his college lunch and last until dinner time. He automatically got it for himself. It didn't occur to him then, or at any time, that I should do anything for him. If I did have his coffee ready when he appeared in the kitchen, or if I made freshly squeezed grapefruit juice for him instead of his usual sort, he would express great appreciation and regard it as a luxury. But he certainly didn't expect it or, probably, care much. It also wouldn't have occurred to him that anyone might think of breakfast as a social event. I would anyway have been up for some time and didn't really do breakfast myself, but he wouldn't have wanted to talk. As he ate, very quickly, he would read intently on his laptop, while also playing music. Finally, as a concession to luxury as well as an extra dose of caffeine, he would finish with coffee ice cream. He liked to finish every meal with ice cream.

Then he would immediately head for his study. It was very light as well as overlooking the wide landscape, and in mine, which was identical to his, the desk was by one of the two windows and the armchair by the other, because I loved to look out and I loved the light. But when it came to the point, the landscape he had so admired turned out to be wasted on Derek, because he immediately closed the curtains, and kept them closed. They were not very thick, so the room was not actually dark, but they completely hid the view. He had done the same in his little study off the sitting room at All Souls, to keep the light from behind his desktop computer, but technology had now reached the stage of the early laptops and I found no problem whatever with the light. He was struck by the way I always headed for windows or outdoors, and called me a heliotrope. He seemed to prefer the gloom, and was untempted by any need to look out. I don't think I ever saw him open the curtains, and the idea of windows in the back of the rooms was never mentioned again.

Derek's first activity each day was an extended period of tooth cleaning, with reading. It is not accidental to give the tooth cleaning priority here. It was the first thing to be done after breakfast, and reading happened to be the part of his work that did not require the use of both hands. It was not negotiable, and immediately followed each of his two daily meals, though it would also be resumed at any time in his study when his hands were not otherwise occupied. He absolutely refused to eat or drink anything except water between meals, because, he said, it would leave his teeth itchy. Itchiness, however, could presumably have been disposed of in a thorough couple of minutes: Derek's tooth cleaning seemed to be an end in itself. Most people will never have seen toothbrushes in the totally flattened state his reached after even a day of his scrubbing, and he used to express incredulity at dentists' recommendations that toothbrushes should be changed at least every six months. Everywhere he had been sitting and working there would be a detritus of dead toothbrushes and twisted interdental sticks, along with festoons of floss. When he was eventually forced by age and Oxford rules into retirement, I found eight electric toothbrushes in his college bedroom, most unused and the others barely touched. I presume a succession of dentists had told him that he should be using an electric toothbrush, and that on each occasion he had bought a new one, forgetting that he had so many already, or perhaps deciding it was easier to buy a new one than to look for the old. Anyway, the electric variety obviously could not do the extended and energetic job that he found necessary for his reading session, so they were abandoned.

Still, the tooth-cleaning time was obviously productive. It seemed usually to be the time he spent on other people's papers, producing the quick turnaround and prolific comments that so amazed his students and colleagues. He read extraordinarily quickly and with great concentration, rapidly marking paper and books with hieroglyphics in heavy pencil. (After his death the Uehiro Centre in Oxford, of which I was a member by then, offered to house his philosophy library, so that is now available to anyone who may be interested in investigating these markings.)

It was never clear which of the two activities determined the length of the other, but after the tooth session he would usually get down to his own work on his laptop and type for most of the day.

Derek's technique, as he described it, seemed much the same as with his photographs and records: he would generate great quantities of text and then choose the best paragraphs to refine. He typed with great speed and force, with the result that his keyboards went the way of his toothbrushes: he literally wore out the letters on the caps of the most commonly used keys on a series of computers. And, as many people will know—because this was one of his proselytizing topics—he speeded up his text production still further with masses of abbreviations programmed into his software. When we were first investigating Macs, of which we were early adopters, we came across a little-known program called Typeit4Me that made personalized abbreviations expand automatically into whole words and phrases. The increase in speed it allowed was phenomenal. I had dozens of abbreviations; Derek may have had thousands. When eventually a similar facility became built into Word, its potential hidden under the misleading name of AutoCorrect, he advertised it even further abroad. It was certainly valuable, but what I felt about Derek's method was that even if I could have produced such quantities of text, I would not have been able to read quickly enough to do the sorting process afterwards.

There were no coffee breaks, of course, at least partly because they would have necessitated extra tooth cleaning. I found that rather sad, because it seemed to me that an obvious element of working in the same house should be taking each other tea and coffee from time to time. But he did frequently appear at the door of my study, in varying states of mind. Sometimes there was a particular reason, such as frustration at the state of some debate or someone's failure to understand his meaning. That did sometimes turn into a long discussion, but more often he was just wanting to let off steam. Sometimes he was fraught because he was being tormented by the behaviour of the computer or the software—and by this stage I understood a lot of it better than he did. And at other times, for no particular reason, he would just wander in, looking amiable, and ask if he could get me anything, or look around for something he thought would be helpful to do, like putting on music.

Work went on till it was time to pause for an early dinner. I did make dinner, but again not because he expected it, although he did enjoy it when it appeared. I have never known anyone less sexist, and in practice I had much stronger traditional intuitions about my role than he did, as he often pointed out. Left to himself, he would have lived entirely without cooking or even heating food, except toast and coffee. He also automatically went to rinse his own dishes afterwards, and was even a bit irritated when I tried to get him to leave them for me to put in the dishwasher—which was going to be run anyway, and which would, of course, get them much cleaner. Goodness knows I am no model housekeeper, but I was automatically in charge of such things, and so, far from wanting to leave them to me, Derek's immediate impulse was slight annoyance at having his habits interrupted.

After dinner work resumed, starting once more with a session of tooth cleaning and reading. Then at nine or so came the beginning of his evening routine. This started with his anti-insomnia drugs, and this was another non-negotiable fixed point. He was adamant about them, wherever he was, and would never consider stopping them even though his doctors, his friends, and I all tried many times to persuade him to look into other ways of getting to sleep. We were afraid for his long-term health, and for his mind; but I suppose the memory of the times when he felt like shooting himself must have made a profound impression, because he would not consider even investigating alternatives. Occasionally he would find he had forgotten to take them and then triumphantly point out that he wasn't feeling sleepy, and that, as he hadn't known he had missed them, their effect could not be psychosomatic: he obviously needed them. On occasions when he thought he might not have enough with him, he became seriously frantic. I did not try to keep track of the dosage, but it was high. Someone I knew who was prescribed the same drug, amitriptyline, took 10 mg a day. Derek had a handful of mixed blue and yellow pills, and the yellow were 50 mg.

At ten, by then I suppose already somewhat drowsy, he spent an hour on his exercise bike, with more reading. He hated this, but at some point became very strict about it. I think—I never checked—that doing it was one of what he called his "gold star" resolutions, which absolutely had to be carried out. I don't remember exactly what he said the penalty for infringement would be, but it was on the lines of having to pass a severe judgment on yourself and regard yourself as a failure. That too was a policy he must have recommended to other people, because I remember his being pleased when a former student later said how invaluable it had been to her.

He took the need to exercise very seriously, I think mainly with the aim of extending life expectancy. But his stationary cycling was the only exercise he would do, because it was one of the few compatible with reading. I thought he needed some upper body exercise, and also I would have loved an exercise buddy; but there was no chance. His bike was all he would consider. Sometimes, while he was engaged with that, I would go out to Avebury on my real bike, and on the way back I might see an illuminated window at the back of the house, with a naked Derek pounding away. I don't think anyone who hadn't been looking for it would have noticed, or recognized what it was they had seen if they did, but he wouldn't have cared anyway. (Whenever he came across me with nothing on, he would say, "Ah! A radiant vision.")

Then, finally, after a quick splash—usually in the bath I had just got out of—came the winding-down session that had been recommended by his sleep therapist, and his vodka interspersed with water. He didn't actually like vodka. Like the bike, it seemed an unpleasant means to a desired end. But it was regarded as absolutely indispensable, like the amitriptyline, and whenever he had been away he would call before coming home to make sure there were adequate supplies. Again, I don't know how much he drank; it probably varied. I think he just carried on until he felt himself going to sleep. It was enough to be worrying: perhaps a quarter of a litre? But there was no point in monitoring it, because, as with the drugs, there was no point in arguing.

While Derek was drinking his vodka he was consciously winding down, so we had to remember not to talk about philosophy. For some time we just continued with listening to music and reading or talking, but as the technology advanced, we increasingly watched videos. It is perhaps worth mentioning a few. I still have VHS recordings I made of some of some of his favourite programmes: the Uchida and Mozart one already mentioned, one about Ladakh that he loved for the open magnificence of the landscape and the beauty of the people, and a documentary about Fred Astaire and Ginger Rogers, of whom he was extremely fond. Then DVDs appeared, and the collection widened. He particularly enjoyed documentaries about and performances by his favourite musicians, of course. He also liked historical film footage in documentaries about twentieth-century history, especially World War 1, which he was transfixed by as an appalling and unnecessary tragedy. (He said that the person he most wished had never existed was Bismarck.) Then there were classic black-and-white films like *The Big Sleep*, *Double Indemnity,* and *Some Like It Hot;* wildlife documentaries; and Monty Python, particularly *The Life of Brian*, at which Derek literally laughed till he cried, watching favourite clips over and over again. He enjoyed historical and period dramas and films, largely because they were interesting to look at; we both got hooked on *Downton Abbey*, even though the architecture was not to his taste. When Obama was running for President, he kept watching one of his speeches over and over, once bursting out emotionally, "I love him!"

This would go on until the vodka kicked in and Derek would suddenly say he had to sleep, usually around two in the morning. He would then make sure he had available whatever source of music the technology allowed: when CDs appeared, he had a succession of short-lived portable players in bed with him, attached to a single earphone. They were followed later by the classic iPod, on which he felt so dependent that when he heard they were going to be discontinued, in favour of wireless versions that he had heard were less good, he immediately went and bought three. He fell asleep, usually listening to Bach piano music at low volume, and had it ready for any time he woke during the night.

He then slept until eleven the next morning, when he woke and headed for the coffee again. It was a life of uppers and downers.

These elements framed his days wherever he was and whatever he was doing, except that he had to do without the exercise bike on his photography trips. The timing sometimes had to vary a little, as when he was getting up before dawn in Venice, but the essentials were as fixed as the laws of the Medes and Persians.

* * *

Everyone knows about Derek's perfectionism: the endless almost identical drafts of his philosophy he would send round for comments, and the extremes of discomfort and expense involved in getting his pictures right. Now I could see more clearly the sheer sustained focus that lay behind it. I had already seen something of this on his photographic expeditions. When he was actually engaged in the photography, his concentration was on that, often for long periods of time; but as soon as conditions were unsuitable, he would go straight back to wherever we were staying, and would again be at his computer. I remember at one time feeling rather relieved when I read somewhere in P. G. Wodehouse that he was always ready to find distractions between himself and the typewriter, which meant that I and no doubt many other writers were at least in good company. Derek, however, was clearly not one of them. He was always intent on getting to his work, and he kept at it with intense concentration. If he was interrupted, his attention seemed to take a measurable time to switch (mine would switch instantaneously), and afterwards it would swivel immediately back to where it had been before. When he was not actually working, his work always seemed to be simmering in the back of his mind. He was perpetually scribbling brief and nearly illegible notes on any surface to hand: envelopes, books, cereal packets, or anything else with a surface that could be written on. He often did it when he woke in the night. I am still coming across notes in odd places.

The other side of this intense focus on what he had decided was the purpose of his life was the extreme simplicity of his life in other respects, and his unwillingness to put any effort into anything else. That may sound a bit unlikely, since he had just bought an elegant Georgian house which had for the time being become a third project, but apart from that it was true. People often expressed envy of his position at All Souls and the privilege and ease that came with it; but although he was certainly aware of that privilege, and spared no effort to achieve and keep it, the endless good food and wine that people invariably mentioned were totally unimportant.

The wine was absolutely of no interest, because until he hit the late-night vodka Derek generally did not drink at all. Just occasionally he might on a social occasion put a drop or two of wine into a glass of sparkling water, to the horror of oenophiles when the wine was good, but otherwise there was nothing. Or rather, I should perhaps add for collectors of Parfit eccentricities, there was one exception. We noticed in Venice that our nearby grocery shop sold a cheap local Marzemino (sparkling red), which struck him purely because it is mentioned in *Don Giovanni.* We took to buying it. I can't remember whether he ever drank it out of a glass; probably not. But he did put it routinely instead of water on his breakfast cereal, along with the usual yoghurt, while we were there. He was a man of extremes.

Derek was not particularly interested in the food either. He was not like Wittgenstein in saying he didn't care what he ate as long as it was the same every day: he did care what he ate, and he had no objection to variety if it appeared in front of him. He positively liked desserts, and was once rather proud of himself for ordering three desserts instead of lunch at a restaurant during one of his American visits, and having a colleague say "There's a rational man." (He was slightly disappointed when he did the same the next day without response.) But his view about feeding himself was that nothing should take longer to prepare than it did to eat, and as he ate extremely quickly, that ruled out just about everything.

The real thing he valued about All Souls, apart from its beauty, was, of course, the freedom it gave him to do what he really wanted to do, and by this time that was philosophy. As long as he had a comfortable armchair (preferably rocking or gliding), two laptops in case one failed, books, and a source of music, he was perfectly happy wherever he was, as was evident from his many stays in temporary places when he was in the States or on photographic trips. He could still do what he really wanted to. He was altogether very self-sufficient and low-maintenance—which is perhaps why I thought, rightly, he would be very easy to live with.

Another aspect of Derek's focus on the things he regarded as important, and his determination to do them as well as possible, was his extreme impatience with everything else. He moved very quickly. In the morning he came downstairs like an avalanche, often nearly falling and occasionally doing so. When we went to the local supermarket he wanted to be as quick as possible by having us each buy "our" things to save time, though it invariably turned out that this meant there were duplicates and omissions that had to be sorted out. When he was travelling and a stone got caught in a wheel of his suitcase, he would fix on the immediate need to get the suitcase to where it was going and carry on pulling, with the result that all his suitcases had totally flattened wheels. When he was popping his pills out of their packets, he would invariably drop some, and instead of picking them up he would just pop out more—which at least did mean that whenever he panicked about not having enough at any time we could avert disaster by looking under chairs and in his bags. There were dozens under his sofa when we eventually cleared out his All Souls room. He was also extremely impatient whenever he had to listen to lectures, saying he kept wanting to fast-forward them; and, as his colleagues know, he eventually gave up going to lectures altogether and took to asking people to send them to him to read instead. He didn't even come to my own Uehiro lectures, except the final one, and that only because he was coming to the dinner afterwards so couldn't avoid it.

This impatience with anything that did not seem directly relevant to his immediate purposes often resulted in problems further down the line, and this led to outbursts of what he called the Parfit Irritability, which he said was characteristic of the males in his father's family.

It showed especially in his attitude to computing and technology in general. Derek had been very excited about computers when he first realized how much difference they could make to his work. He was also excited when we discovered the shortcut programme, and he put the effort into defining his abbreviations because the pay-off was so immediate and palpable. But as long as he could keep going, that was enough. He had no interest in the finer details, and never really learned even to sort out folders and files properly. He never wanted to update the version of Word he used, and this, as a lot of people will know, led to innumerable problems as others updated theirs. He never had any clue at all about things like styles and templates in

Word: if something wasn't working the way he wanted it to, he would just take the quickest route to what he wanted by any means he could think of ("Parfit prodding", I came to call it), such as adjusting individual font sizes and spacing manually, and then being infuriated by the way they would all be wrong when there was a software update. At one time, I don't know how, all his new documents started on p. 63, but he was not concerned enough to find out why and just carried on regardless. When changes were forced on him, he would appear in my room demanding indignantly, "Why do they keep making it worse?", as if challenging me to defend Microsoft. I would try to deal with whatever problems he had, but if I did not have the answer immediately and needed to look it up, or if time was needed to put it right, he usually would not wait. He just went back in a state of irritation and got on with things as best he could.

He was also endlessly irritated by not being able to find things, and panicking because he was sure he had lost them. That is true of a lot of untidy people, of course, and in some ways I am even worse, but I do try to have an underlying order to which things can be restored. Derek's few gestures in that direction only seemed to make things worse. He used to carry everywhere a large computer bag with dozens of interior compartments, but he never decided which of the compartments should contain what, let alone put anything where it might have been supposed to be. This meant that whenever he needed to find anything he had to look though all the compartments, and still might miss what he was looking for. My first experience of Derek and photography was when in January 1984 he set out for St Petersburg with his friend Bill Ewald on an expedition he had planned before we met. On the day he was supposed to have gone, I was surprised by a ring on my doorbell at eleven at night. It was Derek. On the bus to the airport he had suddenly been afraid that he had not got his passport, started scrabbling through his bag to try to find it, and failed. He got off the bus at the next stop to return to college, with the intention of going to Heathrow on the next available one, but he did not make it in time. His passport had been with him the whole time. It was certainly a common phenomenon for him to panic because he could not find his credit cards in his bag, and then would later discover that they had been there all the time. "I underestimated myself," he would say when he found them.

There was also the amazing way he seemed to manage (or not) his record collection. It was huge, covering a whole wall of one of our rather big basement rooms, and I began to discover that the sleeves provided only a moderate chance of identifying their contents. In the first place many of the records were doubled up in a single sleeve: he had bought most of them in

America, where he regularly browsed in Tower Records, and he had thrown away a lot of the sleeves to save weight on the way home. And then his procedure, when he was listening to music, turned out to be to put the record he had just been playing into the sleeve of the one he was just about to play, so that the whole collection was thoroughly shuffled. It was as though he thought entropy could not manage without assistance. When CDs came along, the same thing happened with that collection. How he knew where anything was I have no idea.

He recognized that his inefficiencies caused problems in the long run, of course, but was not willing to do anything about them; and actually I don't think he could have done even if he had wanted to, as it was just the other side of his focus on making directly for whatever his immediate purpose was. And although he was often slightly irritable, his irritability was always directed at things rather than people, unless you count Microsoft as people. If he sometimes felt the irritation had displaced itself from Microsoft to me, he would immediately reappear and apologize.

Another aspect of this speed and impatience was that Derek hardly ever seemed to want to linger over anything. He was struck by the beauty of the landscape around, but I don't think I ever saw him just pause and look at it. Even when we were specifically looking at things he wanted to look at, like cathedrals and galleries, he moved through them at astonishing speed. (The only time I ever saw him linger over anything was the Tintoretto *Crucifixion* in the Scuola Grande di San Rocco—which does take some absorbing. He was probably thinking about the bad thief who was not promised paradise, who had been on his mind since he had first recognized the injustice of Hell.) Maybe this was because, as with his reading, he could absorb everything so quickly. Even when he was looking at his art books—another large collection—he seemed to turn the pages very quickly, but I was often struck by the detail in which he seemed familiar with their contents. When I was looking through his books of Rembrandt drawings, he immediately told me which ones to look for and what to look for in them. (One of them was a couple making love in a curtained bed, where one of the partners had three legs.) Once when we were going to the National Gallery, he commented in advance about a relatively inconspicuous *Entombment* by Dieric ("my namesake") Bouts that many visitors might not specially notice, but which he wanted to see because he had been so struck by the quiet sadness of the faces. But again, although he seemed to know so much about them, he never seemed to linger over them. It astonished me that he could have such clear conceptions of everything and still insist he had no visual images.

Above all, his nature seemed to abhor a vacuum. At any time when he was not totally engaged in output—writing or talking—he seemed to be set on input. While he was having breakfast he would be reading on his laptop and listening to music. When YouTube arrived (later than this, of course; at this time there was still no internet), he was delighted to find the way it led him to other performances and related works, and followed them up as he read and absorbed coffee. He had books everywhere, piled up by the exercise bike and in bathrooms and at the bedside; he even had one open on the dressing table for reading while he was putting on his socks. I would not have been able to get the words into focus in that time. He always had books to hand when he was travelling; in every moment spent in an airport queue or on a bus or train he would be reading. He seemed instinctively drawn to any words that were around. When he came into my room, he would automatically start reading papers on my desk and text on the screen, and he would pick up books and often just go off with them, without thinking or asking. If there was nothing else, he would read labels on packets and bottles. I suppose the insatiability of this appetite was much of the reason for his enormous range of general knowledge.

Then, if the inputting and outputting appeared to leave any space, that would also tend to get filled. Even though Derek spent so much time sitting, there always seemed to be activity going on. He never seemed just to sit and think: he was always typing or reading. And he never even sat and read in in a relaxed way: there was always an intensity and concentration about it. As he was reading, he would always be marking margins with pencil and scribbling notes, or, if his hands were free, resume the tooth cleaning. When he had a rocking chair, he would rock energetically, regarding that and leg jiggling as forms of exercise. Whenever he did not need to concentrate intently, there would be music, usually Bach piano music, of which he never tired. When he visited his mother, he even joined her in taking up needlepoint to occupy his hands while they were talking; and once when we went to an auction sale in Oxford, in pursuit of a pair of nineteenth-century French sofas, he needlepointed away while sitting on one of them (presumably as a way of reserving it) and waiting to bid. It was all activity of some sort. He could not sit and just think; he could not linger over contemplating beautiful things; he could not dawdle or maunder. No wonder he needed his winding-down time.

***

So what was life in West Kennett like? Why did it last eight years, and why did it eventually end?

It went very well for a long time. We soon got used to the travel to and from Oxford, and I to the longer but less frequent journey to Milton Keynes. But most of the time we were there, and it really was a delightful place to be. We both loved it. Living together also turned out to be very comfortable. Neither of us turned out to have any domestic habits that irritated the other, and life was affectionate and good-humoured and often fun. Derek certainly was surprised to discover pleasures of domestic life that had not even occurred to him before, and it was a great pleasure for me to see so much more of him, particularly at times of day when he was not either going under or emerging from the drugs that made him drowsy. There had been relatively little of that in our semi-detached life, since most of our time together had been in the morning or late evening.

We did make the planned expeditions to places like Bath and Wells and Winchester, and started on the few things we intended to do to the house. Derek got particularly interested in trying to find a fire surround appropriate for the period, while I looked for appropriate cornices and replaced modernized doors. We both enjoyed the local auction room, which was next door to the supermarket and provided some consolation to Derek for the chore of grocery shopping, and in general looking for architectural antiques, furniture, and pictures. Derek's interest in all matters aesthetic also meant he was easy to engage with fabrics and even jewellery, which of course pleased me.

We also joined in the local conservation efforts. Avebury was under threat from someone who wanted to turn Avebury Manor into a theme park with fun runs round the great henge (horror), and to build various blots on the landscape. I became quite thickly involved, Derek more peripherally, and we got to know some of the local people.

It was also a time when our work overlapped to a considerable extent: I was writing an Open University philosophy course on equality (later commissioned as a book by OUP, but alas not yet written) at the same time as Derek was working on *Equality and Priority*. I also wrote an article for the volume in which that first appeared. It was all very productive.

After some time Derek announced emphatically, "This life suits me." And this continued for a long time, with no significant problems.

However, as the sceptics had recognized, there were instabilities built into the situation, and it is probably not difficult to infer from what has been said already what they must have been, and how their effects developed over time.

The problems, as they began to come, were mine. Or rather, they were mine given that Derek was Derek.

One general problem for me was, of course, the size of the project. Derek's simple and self-sufficient way of life meant that he himself was no kind of burden, but the backdrop of his life had always been not only beautiful but miraculously kept going by fleets of porters, bursars, manciples, scouts, gardeners, and handymen, of whose work, and of whose organization, he of course knew nothing. Those areas were obviously going to be my department. That was not because Derek thought they were women's work, but household arrangements were something I was much more interested in, and anyway I would have been managing them wherever I had been. But he had absolutely no conception of what they would involve. He vaguely presumed it was all just a matter of paying to get other people to do whatever needed doing, and of course it was, in a way; but such people need to be found and managed and supervised. And as I soon discovered, the place really needed at least one full-time person for the grounds alone. That was far beyond anything we could afford, so I had the task of trying to find and manage an assortment of local odd-job people that Derek began to call my "retinue".

All this, of course, meant that in ordinary life, while Derek was concentrating on his work in his study, I was up and down stairs every twenty minutes to make sure the retinue was happy and doing the right things. It wasn't the kind of retinue you could just leave to its own devices, and all the individuals (of course) had their own personal problems. Again, some version of this would have been happening wherever I had been, but the scale of this was much bigger, and the people were more miscellaneous, so I often found things stressful as well as time-consuming. The grounds soon got completely out of hand, which was rather upsetting. This was not an intolerable problem: I just took it all as part of what life there involved. But it was a big job.

I had no resentment at all that Derek was not more involved: I never expected he would be. But what I had not understood by then was quite the extent to which his work filled his whole life. He had said he was a duomaniac, and I understood that as meaning he concentrated all his work on his two chosen areas. But I had no idea that the mania implied that those would occupy his time to the exclusion of almost everything else, which, after the first excitement of moving there, turned out to be more and more the case. He loved the house, he loved owning it, he seemed to love our living together, but he had no real interest in making use of the house or in where it was. While he was there, he increasingly wanted to do nothing but philosophy, with this as another beautiful backdrop and, occasionally, something to show his friends and family.

I was there to work too, of course, but it had not occurred to me that there would be almost nothing else. I knew Derek loved the Downs, and early in our relationship we had gone for a walk there at his instigation, so I took it for granted that when we lived there we would go for walks and cycle rides. But that early walk had been in the brief, uncharacteristic period when he was relaxing a bit after *Reasons and Persons* and engaging in courtship. It turned out that the walk we did in the first week, while he was still considering the photography project, was the only one he would ever willingly do in eight years. I pressed him into going for one other, just before he was about to go off on one of his American visits, but he made it clear throughout that it was under protest, and I never tried again. He never came for a single bicycle ride. In fact he turned out to have no interest in the countryside at all. He was interested in buildings, of course, but after a few early visits to cathedrals and a couple of houses, he never wanted to go again except when we had visitors.

It is perhaps best summed up in his astonishing refusal to go and look at the bluebell woods. Derek thought bluebell woods were amazing, and one of his laments about global warming was that we would lose them. For anyone who has not seen them, it is not enough to know they are woods with bluebells, or even to see pictures of them. At their best they are quite breathtaking. They are in flower for only a couple of weeks a year, just as the beeches are starting to come into leaf—presumably catching the warmest weather before the leaves cut off the light—and the combination of the sun filtering through the pale beech leaves and masses of bluebells in a perfumed, purplish mist on the ground is overwhelming. We had two such woods within ten minutes' drive, but Derek did not once go to look at them. He enormously valued their existence, but would not spend a single hour to see them.

I also remember one striking occasion when I called him to look from a back window at a particularly spectacular sky over the hill and beech clump behind the house—the landscape he had wanted back windows for—which he could have done in literally one minute, but he would not.

In fact he turned out not only not to want to go anywhere but to have no interest in being outdoors in our three acres at all. I didn't try to take to gardening (the challenge was too big even to consider), but I loved being outside, with the vista at the back of the house. I would sit out there with my computer when the weather allowed, and watch it through the French windows in the kitchen and sitting room when it didn't. It was always worth looking at, and I was fascinated by the animals and birds. Derek, of course, was at least mildly interested in them and was involved whenever we needed to eject them (jackdaws, field mice) or rescue them (rooks, rabbits), and he liked seeing them when he was in the kitchen for dinner, but he was not interested enough to spend any time watching them or getting to know them.

More generally, I was discovering the extent to which Derek did not seem to understand or be interested in what I think of as ordinary companionableness: the kind of thing that might involve the maundering and dawdling he never did. I took it for granted that part of living in such a lovely place would be just sitting or strolling and enjoying it from time to time: in the kitchen with a glass of wine (or whatever) while getting dinner ready, or sitting outside on summer evenings, or in front of the sitting-room fire in the winter, with our laptops, just for the pleasure of being together in such a beautiful room. But Derek had no interest at all in things of that sort. Of course we had plenty to talk about, and of course dinner-time conversations would often naturally extend far beyond dinner, but the idea of just settling down deliberately to enjoy even a little time doing nothing in particular and chatting was totally foreign to him.

All in all, although he loved everything about the house and its situation, and liked having my study nearby for frequent droppings in, most of the time he was there, with his curtains closed, he might have been anywhere in the world.

What I suppose I was gradually discovering was the extremity of the extent to which Derek lived in his mind. His concern was with what he could achieve and what existed rather than what he was experiencing. It is difficult to find a succinct way of expressing the different elements of this, but it is worth a try.

As regards achievement, nearly everything that other people might count as comfort or leisure or enjoyment was sacrificed to his perfectionism in both his philosophical work and his photographs. He wanted to achieve things that he thought had real value in the advancement of knowledge and the production and preservation of things of beauty. Once he had settled on these purposes, he was obsessive about achieving them to the best of his ability and devoted everything to them. It showed in the endless rewriting of his drafts and the huge expense and trouble and unconcern for comfort shown in his photography.

As regards beauty, he was again concerned more with what there was and what there might be than anything he would experience. He wanted the bluebell woods to exist, even though he would not spend any of his knowledge-advancing time in going to see them. I don't think I doubt that he was sincere when he said he would die to give Mozart another thirty-five years, even though *ex hypothesi* he would experience none of the results. (Though I do wonder whether he would have felt that later, when he was deep in *On What Matters* and regarded it as of crucial objective importance to prove his thesis right.) Mozart also appeared during another discussion we had about the beginnings and ends of universes and Derek was lamenting that even if another universe came into existence when this one ended, there would be no way of getting Mozart over the divide between the two. He was thinking not just globally but universally and timelessly.

And when he did take time for the enjoyment of the things he cared about, he usually wanted them in their highest form rather than in real-life experience. With music he wanted to listen to the very best recordings of the best works. He was no longer interested in spending his time playing instruments—I presume because he himself could not reach those standards—whereas I had loved doing it even though I couldn't reach them either. (I gave up playing and singing almost completely when I was with Derek. That was a serious mistake.) He was not interested in live performances for the same reason. He was fascinated by the beauty of the natural world (he said, "God is an aesthete, not a moralist"—I once again don't know whether that was original to him but haven't been able to find it attributed to anyone else), and he loved watching wildlife documentaries; but he was not so interested in watching our animals in the flesh, presumably because the documentaries had selected what was most worth seeing, and anyway he seemed to have no interest in interacting with them. He loved the Downs, but as soon as he had given up the photography project of turning them into beautiful pictures, he was happy for them to exist without his looking at them. And on the whole he could get more out of his art books than by going to galleries. The whole thing is probably well summed up by his willingly going for only one country walk in eight years, and by our having only two proper holidays, planned as such rather than incidental to some other purpose, in thirty-five years.

Of course, his spending his time exactly as he wanted was quite reasonable in itself. He made no demands of me, and I was free to do as I liked. This self-sufficiency and independence were what made me think that our sharing a house would be no problem, and I was right. If we had been living in Oxford, it would not I have mattered, because there would have been plenty for me to engage with independently of Derek. But although Derek's life continued in pretty well the same way as it would have done if we had stayed in Oxford, mine could not. My Open University job was in itself rather isolated—the work was mainly writing and involved hardly any in-person teaching—and my colleagues were scattered all over the place. I was separated now from all the things and people that would have been close at hand in Oxford, and marooned in a way that obviously had not occurred to him.

This was, of course, disappointing, though not enough to spoil it completely; it was still good, even though less good than I had expected. I really did love, and enjoy, the house and the surroundings. But worse was the fact that there was so much time when Derek was not there at all. When we first met, I was also going for semesters to the USA, often at the same time as his visits. But my work allowed for fewer and fewer of these times away, while Derek's overseas commitments increased. I usually went with him to Venice, but his Venice visits eventually stopped, and there was no point whatever in my joining him for his three-week stays in a sparse apartment in St Petersburg, vainly waiting for snow. So increasingly towards the end of our time in Wiltshire, I was simply cut off from all academic contact in the middle of nowhere. I wasn't exactly lonely; I did know a few local people, and I am not prone to feeling loneliness. But I certainly was away from ordinary interpersonal intellectual stimulation, and this became a serious problem for me in ways that Derek obviously had not anticipated at all.

It was during these absences that, late on, things began to get tense, and I did actually begin to be more than disappointed and feel that I was being treated badly. I think the beginning of that was an occasion when he returned from one of his absences in the States, when I was, of course, looking forward to having him there again and found that he was planning to leave the next day for a photographic trip. He had not told me in advance, presumably because he knew I would be upset. I had never tried to dissuade him from anything he wanted to do, but he hated any kind of confrontation or tense interaction, and he just did not want to experience my disappointment. He had no intention of changing his mind, so he just left telling me until it was too late to do anything about it. It seemed not to have occurred to him that our having taken the house on as a joint project was any reason at all for his changing anything about what he personally wanted to do.

In general, it was clear that Derek did not want to adjust any aspect of the way he had always led his life, and the situation was obviously absurd for me. His frequent travels would not have mattered if we had been in Oxford, but they began to matter very much when I was alone in Wiltshire. We did not quarrel, and neither of us ever went in for recriminations or even passive aggression, but we were both aware of growing tensions over the phone during the times he was away. It all became rather unhappy. It was eventually clear that the project had to be given up.

I thought at first that as the whole essence of the difficulties had been my isolation in combination with his total focus on his work, we should go back to what I had originally intended: buy a house in Oxford and return to the kind of semi-detached life we had had before. But things had gone too far. Derek was clearly set on getting back to a way of life that was not even slightly interfered with by the need to think about anybody or anything else.

Anyway, I had already, for other reasons, been looking into a change of career direction and was actively investigating several possibilities, all away from Oxford. I also knew that, after such a long semi-isolation and the growing recognition of the extremity of Derek's duomania, I needed to re-think everything.

It took some time to work out, but the eventual upshot was that Derek bought a house in Oxford, to let until it was needed. I bought one in London and moved from the Open University to University College London.

But it was another thing that happened at about the same time that really started to change the way I thought about it all and convince me that radical change was needed.

4 Rethinking

Shortly before we left West Kennett, Derek had been reading Oliver Sacks's book *An Anthropologist on Mars*, which had been published in 1995. It was a set of studies of people who would now (not then) be called neurodivergent, and Derek had always been fascinated by unusual minds and abilities, from idiots savants to Mozart. The woman who described herself as feeling like an anthropologist on Mars, the subject of the first essay, was Temple Grandin. She was an autistic woman who had become well known because, although she had had difficulty in interacting with people, and even with dogs and cats because they were too much like people, she had an extraordinary ability to understand cows. She was in great demand with managers of holding pens and slaughterhouses, because she could see directly what distressed the cows and made them panic, and could show how to arrange everything in ways that would keep them calm and easy to manage. We had both admired her for a long time because she made things so much better for the animals. The essay was a description of Sacks's meeting with her.

I read it some time after Derek did, and I found it fascinating too, but partly for a rather different reason. Right at the beginning Sacks describes his first meeting with Temple Grandin. He arrived tired and thirsty after a long journey, to find that on opening the door that she launched immediately into the subjects they were going to discuss. There were no enquiries about the journey or how he was, and no offer of refreshment. When he eventually decided that he really must ask for coffee, she simply went and produced it, without any apologies or expressions of concern for not having done so sooner, and carried on the conversation. I was stunned. He might have been describing a meeting with Derek. If this was autism, Derek must be autistic.

Nothing of the kind had ever occurred to me. This was all happening more than thirty years ago, and at the time I, like nearly everybody else, had heard of autism only as an extreme disability that prevented normal functioning. Disability was the last thing that would enter anyone's mind in connection with Derek, who had always been very high-functioning in a wide range of areas, who had sailed through everything he had tried in highly competitive institutions, and who was successful and confident, albeit somewhat eccentric. He was also very nice: people liked him, and many were fond of him. His colleagues and students appreciated the seriousness with which he took their work and the length of time he spent on them. How could he possibly be thought to have any kind of disability?

Since then, of course, the whole subject of autism has become a matter of ordinary conversation, and everyone is now familiar with the idea of a spectrum: of some capacity for connecting and communicating with other people that is to a greater or lesser extent missing. It is now seen as modular, rather than global, and independent of other characteristics such as the impaired intellectual and language development with which it had first been associated, and as often accompanying considerable abilities. Newton is now regarded as having been autistic, and Einstein as definitely on the spectrum; and since Derek's death a couple of people have asked me whether he was autistic. But at the time Sacks was writing, this idea had only just begun to filter through to the profession, and certainly not to the general public. I had not heard of it, and I read Sacks's account of his meeting with Temple Grandin with a simple shock of recognition.

Of course, I was and am no expert. There has never been any question of diagnosis, because whatever might be the best way to understand Derek, there was obviously no illness to be treated or disability to be managed. If he was in some way and to some degree autistic, whatever that meant, it in no way limited his functioning in what he most wanted to do, especially in the institutions where his outstanding abilities gave him the freedom to flourish. The label was not important. But for me the idea opened up a completely new way of thinking about him, and in particular about our relationship. It raised the possibility that something I took for granted might simply be missing, and might prevent certain kinds of communication in the way, perhaps, that it might be impossible to discuss colour schemes with someone who was colour-blind or sounds with someone who was profoundly deaf.

There was, of course, no denying his eccentricity. But from an early age he had lived mainly in institutions, and overwhelmingly male ones at that, which might alone account for a good deal of it. Everyone knows that places like Oxford are full of eccentric college bachelors and absent-minded professors, and Derek obviously came into this category. He had changed in many ways during the time we had been together, and I presumed that he had just been opening up and becoming familiar with kinds of interaction that he might have missed before. His mother said (approvingly) after a while that he had changed out of all recognition since taking up with me. I do not know whether his colleagues and students noticed any difference: he may have been the same as always in professional contexts. But he certainly seemed to me to have gradually become easier and much warmer in his interactions with other people.

However, maybe that had been the wrong way of looking at it. Maybe it was not that his oddities were the result of his having spent most of his life in academic institutions, but that he had flourished in those institutions because those were the contexts in which some innate characteristics, which might have been problematic elsewhere or in someone less able, were less likely to matter. Maybe characteristics that manifested themselves as endearing eccentricities in the rarified world he inhabited might be much more significant drawbacks in other kinds of environment, including close personal relationships. I had sensed from the very beginning of the relationship that some things would always be missing, but this suggested a quite different way of thinking about what exactly those might be.

What follows is a kind of autobiography of this rethinking. It is not intended as any kind of definitive assessment: just an account of Derek from my point of view, for comparison with what other people know from other times and other angles.

Obviously Derek was in many ways nothing like Temple Grandin, who was impaired in ordinary life in a way that he clearly was not. Still, Sacks's account provides a good starting point. Many people in Derek's professional world will have come across Derek's launching into substantial discussions the moment they crossed his threshold or met him at a social event, and carrying on with those discussions, thoroughly absorbed, until circumstances or other people put a stop to them. I find I have one or two photographs of him on such occasions—one at a drinks reception and one at a wedding—and in neither of these does Derek look as though he is at a social occasion: his eyes are averted from the person he is talking to, and he is totally intent on the subject he is discussing. But he is talking to colleagues, who knew him, and who would not have been either surprised or (probably) unwilling to have the discussion. And in general, in his world, his encounters would mainly be with other people who wanted to discuss philosophy with him, so an immediate plunge into substance would not be particularly odd.

These encounters would also rarely take place in a context where Derek had responsibility for being a host. When students and others came to his rooms, it was usually specifically for academic purposes. When he was clearly in the position of host, as when he had guests to college dinner, he was surrounded by staff who made sure plates were distributed and glasses filled, so any unawareness of social responsibility might go unnoticed. When he did theoretically have the whole responsibility, for instance in the relatively rare context of our having visitors at the house, he was totally oblivious of it. It was not because he thought such things were my job: as I say, he was totally non-sexist, and after people had gone he would try to help clear up. But actually looking after them as guests seemed just not to enter his head, and once he got into conversation he lost all sense of the social situation. I gather this sometimes happened in college, when he was Sub Warden and occasionally responsible for declaring the end of dinner, but was deep in conversation and had to be reminded.

Even more conspicuous, perhaps, was the way he managed, or failed to manage, telephone calls. They would usually begin with no introduction (these were the days before caller ID) except sometimes an enquiry as to whether he was interrupting, and would have no proper ending. He would always go straight into what he had to discuss, and when he took the conversation to have finished, he just put the receiver down without signing off or saying goodbye. Again, when this happened with people whose whole purpose in communicating was philosophical substance, it probably did not matter much. He had been so engaged with whomever he was talking to, and was so generally known to be nice, that it could not be interpreted as implying offence or hostility in the way that abruptly cutting off telephone calls normally does. But for other people it must have been pretty startling. It certainly was for me for some time: no wonder I did not know what to make of his telephone calls about the Glenn Gould programmes soon after I met him. My family also found it startling at first, though they soon got used to it and found it entertaining, since once they knew Derek it could not possibly be interpreted as intentionally rude. Many years later, when I was unavailable and Derek needed to fill in a form giving personal details about me—none of which he knew, of course—he made a succession of calls to my sister asking a series of questions about things like my date and place of birth, each time just asking a single question with no introduction and no goodbye.

I also discovered very early on that he actually had a horror of making calls to people he did not know, even for simple things like travel enquiries. (This was in the days when all these things were done by phone.) He always wanted me to do them and seemed surprised by how easily I could. He seemed to think I had a special skill.

With things like this as a starting point, I started to think through other odd things I had long been aware of, and which might not have been as apparent in his professional or even family contexts as they were to me. How many of them might seem to fit this way of thinking? They had just seemed an assortment of oddities, but might this provide a way of linking them?

For instance, I had always been surprised by his demeanour in public places. He had nothing like the ease in negotiating social environments that you would expect of a tall, good-looking man who would have been Captain of Eton if he had wanted to be, and who was extremely confident in his professional environment. It was almost as though he had no awareness of public places as social environments. Of course, nobody interacts routinely with people in the street, but in most circumstances people are ready to do so where appropriate: to respond to what others are doing, adjust movements accordingly, and communicate in various, often unspoken, ways. Derek was not.

This was something that had first struck me in Venice. It was not as though he pushed ahead and treated people as not mattering, but essentially he avoided them as if they had been bollards: not bumping into them, but not trying to keep the appropriate social distance. It was as though he moved about with the default presumption that strangers were just objects to be manoeuvred around. When he actually did need to interact with them, he did it as minimally as possible, and rather awkwardly, generally avoiding eye contact. He was a very nice person, but he never did things that comparably nice people usually do: smile at shop assistants, or thank bus drivers. Just occasionally when something caught his interest and gave him something to talk about, he might interact: when we were buying some handmade jewellery at a market in Italy and it turned out that the maker was called Tiziana, Derek smiled and commented, "nomen meritato". But he had to have something that interested him to talk about for that to happen. It was very rare.

This apparent unawareness of strangers as people who might need to be interacted with, or might have any awareness of him, seemed to make him totally unbothered by crowded situations. When we travelled between Oxford and London by bus, it would occasionally be so full that we each had to sit next to a stranger. I always felt a fleeting social anxiety about how to treat the person who would be next to me for the next hour and a half. Should I acknowledge them? Was I taking up too much personal space? Derek had no such concerns. As long as he could get a seat, he did not care about the crowding, and the question of interacting simply did not arise, any more than if the person next to him had been a dummy. It also did not occur to him to avoid doing things he felt like doing, like jiggling his leg or energetically fanning himself with papers. It probably would not have bothered him if the other person had done the same. He opened his book or laptop as usual, and other people were just irrelevant from all points of view.

Perhaps his waking me in the middle of the night with the Goldberg Variations also comes into the same category. The record player was by the bed, and, as I discovered, Derek had been in the habit of routinely putting music on if he awoke in the night. It obviously did not occur to him to do any differently in a different, social environment. Again, it clearly was not that he would go ahead with what he wanted to do in a self-assertive way. It seemed that it just did not occur to him not to.

He seemed in general not to have any awareness of what strangers might be thinking of him, and I found this embarrassing on several occasions. A particularly striking case was another one in Venice: we were leaving and heading for the station on a very hot day. Derek got overheated, as he often did, so he just stripped to the waist and carried on, with a set, almost contorted, expression, dragging his heavy suitcase with the flattened wheel. He looked appalling, but he seemed totally unaware not only of how he looked but also that there might be any way in which it mattered. (With his bike exercise he looked rather good with his legs bare and his top covered, but not at all the other way round.)

There was another occasion in London when he started talking about philosophy, in his normal, slightly raised, seminar voice, in an echoing, sparsely populated Tube station. It did not occur to him to drop his voice, or that people hearing him might think he was an intellectual show-off (what

John Cleese somewhere refers to as people who talk in loud voices in restaurants). Of course, he was not showing off; he was just caught up in his subject and unaware of anything else. He was rather upset on yet another occasion in Venice when a shop assistant refused to take the note he offered, because he had held it in his teeth while he was using his hands for something else. And I suppose not thinking of finding an alternative to a vodka bottle to hold water in seminars comes into the same category: he did not think or care about how strangers might interpret it.

Perhaps it is all summed up in Derek's complaining that his mother had often told him that some things were "not done". He thought that was a ridiculous reason for not doing anything.

There were all sorts of social details he did not seem to know about. One thing that had irritated me many times in the early days of our relationship was that he was always stealing my lines. It often happened that when I had made some observation or given some information that had interested him, and we were together in company soon afterwards, he would make the same observation without any attribution to me. He always got into the conversation more quickly than I did, and it did not seem to occur to him that if the person you got the idea or information from was there, you should say so. It was not that he had forgotten it came from me: when I had protested about it a few times, he started remembering to do it. It was just that it had not occurred to him as a conventional courtesy.

Another thing he did not seem to understand as a social matter was driving. As with manoeuvring round pedestrians, he seemed to understand driving only in terms of avoiding objects. If he was interested in something else, like buildings he was passing or a conversation he was having, that would be where his attention was, and his default driving technique was just to slow down to avoid colliding with whatever was in front of him. He seemed to have no idea of the need to make his intentions clear to other road users, or to try to read theirs. He was not too bad while driving between Wiltshire and Oxford, because the roads were not usually busy and there were not many buildings to distract him. But within Oxford he was a menace, and more than once I took over in the middle of a drive. On the two occasions when we went driving in Europe. I ended up doing all of it.

One thing I had heard about autism was that, because autistic people did not intuitively learn ordinary conventions of social interactions, they had to learn sets of techniques to navigate them, and I realized I had noticed this a lot in Derek. In situations in which he knew what to expect, and knew there would be none of the usual substantial topics of conversation, he was prepared. When we were travelling from Wiltshire to Oxford, we often called on his elderly aunt in her thatched cottage. Her life was centred on the local church, so Derek was invariably ready with the question of how her vicar was. By the time we were visiting her, he had also got used to smiling more warmly, and it all worked beautifully. She adored him (and rather resented me, but for whom she would never have seen him). A similar thing happened whenever he knew he was going to encounter my friend Lyn, who has now been looking after me and my Oxford family and our houses in her spare time for forty years, and of whom he was very fond. Lyn was the person he thought of when he wondered how he could possibly explain what he did, and its purpose, to people in general, and he knew he had nothing substantial to talk to her about. But her husband had health problems, and he would always be ready to ask very kindly about those, before immediately disappearing back to his study, unable to think of anything else to talk about. I recently discovered that he practised the same kind of technique even in All Souls with fellows he did not know well. He would be ready to ask questions about their individual disciplines, which apparently were the same every time he saw them.

He also had a repertoire of party pieces to fill in when he did not know quite what to do. The most striking was standing on his head when children were visiting. But he also had an assortment of interesting facts and anecdotes that could be inserted into lulls in the conversation on the rare occasions when we were having dinner with friends or family and no substantial topic had appeared. He frequently would ask out of the blue, "What's the best palindrome?" (A man, a plan, a canal—Panama!), or he would ask what people's favourite metaphor was, and then offer his ("Ice formed on the butler's upper slopes").

It was not just that he found unsubstantial talk difficult: he did not see the point of it. After he had greeted Lyn and disappeared, he was astonished that she and I could talk while working around the house for a couple of hours. "You get on so well, but what do you talk about?" he would ask in genuine amazement. And when my sister and her partner came to stay, he would go back to work immediately after dinner, while they and I would sit around till late in the evening, chatting over wine. He could see that the atmosphere was really good, but had no idea how it was achieved, or any wish to join in. Again, "What do you talk about?" He knew that most of the things he and I would talk about could not be part of it, so it was hard to see what could be happening, or how the atmosphere was produced.

Indeed, one of the things I had noticed about him early on was that his idea of talking, and writing, was entirely conveying facts or opinions and conducting arguments, and he seemed to have no sense of using words to express (as opposed to describe) feelings. I recently found among his papers an early letter from me in which I mentioned this. The letters I wrote were all right in their way, but a year later I would not have dreamt of sending them: I would have known that the insignificant information they contained would have been of no interest to him, and that he would have missed completely the oblique or playful bits. When in early 1984 he left for Rice and I for UCLA, I was excited to find a series of daily love notes arriving from him; but although it was very nice to have them, they left me cold. They just said "I love you" in a script of hollow letters that went off the page in different places. I think he must have thought in a theoretical way that love notes were appropriate in the situation, but he really had not a clue. He could understand language as capable of describing emotions, as in poetry, where he was often deeply struck by it. But if it was expressed non-literally, in some nuance of phrase or tone of voice such as irony or playfulness, he missed it. He did learn a good deal of playfulness in person when we were together, and to recognize it in tone of voice (at least in me), but never in writing.

There was also the lack of feeling for companionableness that I have already mentioned. By that I do not mean he was not good company. He certainly could be, since there were so many things he could talk about. Give him the right kind of company, or the right kind of situation such as showing people art and architecture, or talking about history, and he could entertain for hours, always dominating the conversation. But he seemed to have no sense of enjoying being with people or a person just for the sake of it, without saying anything in particular, just feeling and expressing pleasure in the other's company.

All in all, then, the idea of autism did seem to make sense. And perhaps it also explained more personal things as well. There were obviously problems for me about living, with a near recluse, so far from normal academic and social life, and that put strains on the relationship which there would not otherwise have been. But there had been other things that had puzzled me about it earlier. I felt there should not have been any problems: we seemed perfectly suited in mind and tastes; we certainly found each other attractive (no shortage of personal compliments from him, ever); neither of us wanted a family or a busy social life. But there had been some difficulties early on that we had found ways round, but I still felt I did not understand. We had discovered by experience what made our interactions work and what had to be avoided, as everyone does, but this new idea suggested a quite different way to think about it all. Maybe there were some things Derek just did not experience in the way I presumed most people did.

I had found him puzzling from the beginning. What was going on seemed in some ways to be a normal courtship, but in other ways not. It was two months before I saw a really open, engaged expression in Derek; and before that, although there was obviously interest, the signals had been mixed. When I did at last see real warmth and engagement, it was quite different from anything I had seen before in him, but I fairly soon discovered that this was not anything like normal for him, even with me. I quickly began to form the impression that, when left to himself, he would in some sense revert to type, spiralling down into himself, and that without external stirring up that was where he would tend to stay.

On one occasion very early on in the relationship, when he had been away, we met in the evening in a café in the High Street (very unusual, I can't remember why). I was, of course, looking forward to it; but when Derek appeared, he was quite extraordinarily detached, not looking directly at me, and talking in a somehow mechanical way. It is hard to describe the strangeness. It was not awkward in the way it might have been if he had been embarrassed and trying to make conversation; it was more as though he hardly knew I was there and was preoccupied with something completely different. I remember wondering what on earth I was taking on in the relationship, and thinking that I would be embarrassed for my family and friends to meet such an odd man. I gather I did actually warn my sister when she first met him that she might wonder what I saw in him. This sort of thing stopped happening as he got more familiar with non-professional interactions and began to show warmth in them: that was probably why his mother thought he had changed so much since connecting with me. But I felt there was always the likelihood of reversion, and that this was something I needed to keep in mind. I had never known anything like this.

Another curious early event happened one day when we went for a walk on the Downs, at his suggestion, not far from where we later lived. During it I suddenly developed severe back pain, so we turned to go back to the car. As we went, Derek was walking a pace or two ahead of me, with his head forward and a drawn expression, on the opposite side of the track (the Ridgeway, I think). I was rather upset. Why was he not walking close to me, with his arm round me, trying to see whether there was anything he could do to help, or at least conveying sympathy? That's what would be normal with friends or even acquaintances out together, and we were supposed to be a couple. Was he in some way angry or annoyed? I asked about it later (not at that stage complaining), and he said he was trying to get to the car as quickly as possible. I now think that was probably the whole of the explanation. I discovered later that he was always sympathetic about pain, and as he saw getting to the car as the remedy for the problem, that was what he was focussed on achieving. It seemed not to occur to him that it was pointless for him to get to the car before me, and he clearly had no idea at all that anything helpful could be done before we got there.

I did not do any further research into the autism idea, although I was pretty sure it fitted the facts, but I came across it again sometime later from a different direction. While we were in West Kennett I had been writing about the implications of evolutionary studies, first as an Open University philosophy course and then as a book, which included a good deal of work about evolved sex differences. In the course of this work I encountered Simon Baron-Cohen's book *The Essential Difference* (2003),[1] which discussed the idea of autism as a characteristic of the extreme male brain. This was a clinical study, rather than connected with evolutionary reasoning, and I have some doubts about a couple of points in his overall thesis, but it was strikingly illuminating in many ways.

First, it confirmed the idea that autism had come to be regarded as modular. I knew nothing about that when I first recognized the resemblance to Temple Grandin. Apparently, autism was originally recognized in children in connection with severe disabilities such as difficulty with language development and low IQ, and it was only recently becoming recognized as quite distinct from those characteristics, and that it could also be found in adults. It was a specific characteristic, compatible with complete normality in other respects, and sometimes joined with exceptional intelligence. That conjunction was what became known as Asperger's syndrome.

Second, Baron-Cohen explained autism as an empathy disorder. At first impression this seemed inapplicable to Derek because he was so very kind, and he really did care about people. But Baron-Cohen calls the phenomenon mind-blindness, and he explains it as an inability to recognize directly what is going on in another person's mind and intuitively sense many feelings and intentions in ways that people generally can. I suppose when looked at in this way, mind-blindness must be a thing that is relative to particular kinds of other minds. The people managing the cattle in America were blind to the cows' minds, but Temple Grandin was not, while she was blind to some aspects of the usual

[1] Simon Baron-Cohen, *The Essential Difference: Men, Women and the Extreme Male Brain* (London: Allen Lane, 2003).

human mind. That also seemed to suggest that there might be degrees of this blindness: that people might be more or less good at this direct reading of other minds. Baron-Cohen thinks these degrees are on a spectrum correlated strongly with sex, with significant autism appearing in males in a ratio of 10:1.

He also stresses—another aspect of the modularity point, I suppose—that it has nothing to do with being cold and uncaring, and that people with this characteristic were often fierce defenders of causes they regarded as matters of justice. Derek certainly was not unfeeling or unemotional: he was known for weeping easily. He had been passionate about the injustice of the idea of Hell even when he was a child, and he had been determined in his pursuit of the admission of women to All Souls, as he was in his general views about social justice. I suppose the implication is that you may be passionate about things you understand, while not caring as much about ones you cannot understand.

That also fits another story about Derek. I discovered sometime during the time at West Kennett that Derek was a vegetarian. I had not realized it because I had been vegetarian since childhood and automatically produced vegetarian food, and he had never mentioned it. He said it happened suddenly during some episode of severe physical suffering—very unusual for Derek, I'm not sure what, perhaps connected with medication—and he suddenly realized what suffering was like for animals.

So, could it be true that Derek had this kind of mind-blindness, without the idea's being in conflict with anything else that was known about him?

Baron-Cohen then goes into a description of characteristics typical of autistic individuals. As he was working from clinical experience, and the cases that reached him were generally of people whose autism caused severe problems in ordinary life, some of them would not apply to Derek. But a good many of them certainly seemed to, and others are worth thinking about. It would be interesting to know how they seem to other people on the basis of their own experience. All the following points come from Baron-Cohen, and I have on the whole put them in an order ranging from the ones other people are likely to have noticed to the ones which not many people will have seen. (These are all taken, usually verbatim but sometimes slightly rephrased, from chapters 10 and 11 of *The Essential Difference*.)

For instance, he says about autistic people:

> Their lives are often governed by routines: going to the same places every weekend or every holiday . . . having the same after work routine each evening. (147–8)

That was certainly true of Derek the whole time I knew him, after he had settled on his two main purposes. The timetable of drugs and stimulants was absolutely invariable. Normally he would not consider anything but Venice and St Petersburg for holidays, and those were definitely working occasions, with philosophy filling most of the parts that were not photography. As I have said, in thirty-five years we had only two proper holidays deliberately planned as such. He had just agreed before he died, after years of no such holidays at all, that we should go again to Venice.

> They have a clear abnormality in relation to telephones. (158)

Baron-Cohen says this is true of nearly all the cases of autism he has known, and he thinks it is a very good test of communication problems. A Cambridge professor he studied—a more extreme case than Derek—said he had always been afraid of telephones because he could not work out how to use them. "What were you supposed to say to the other person? When was it your turn to speak? When were you supposed to hang up? How were you to know how to finish or start a conversation?" Telephones are especially difficult because there is no access to wider contextual clues.

Derek eventually, gradually, came to realize that the abruptness of his telephone endings might be upsetting and often phoned me back straight away to check that he had not been too quick, but he had had to learn that. Meanwhile, I learnt that the meaning of any sudden cut-off was not the same as it would have been with other people.

> It is as if they are trying to write a manual for social interaction based on if-then rules, or as if they are trying to systematise social behaviour when the natural approach to socialising should be via empathising. (141)

> They are not interested in small talk and do not know how to do it, or what it is for. (147)

> They do not mind having a discussion (note, not a chat) on a particular issue in order to establish the truth of the matter (mostly, persuading you to agree with their view). But just a casual, superficial chat? Why bother? And what on earth about? How? For these people it is both too hard and pointless. (133)

I have already described some of this. I noticed that when Derek had to engage with people he did not know, he would always assume what I began to think of as his social face: amiable and slightly smiling, but rather vague and (to me) palpably uncomfortable. I remember being particularly struck by this on one occasion when we were meeting for him to have a hearing test and he arrived a moment or two before me. He had already assumed his social face, but he seemed to have no idea how to approach the desk and say he had an appointment: I think he was waiting for me to do it. In situations in which he was meeting professional people who were not philosophers he would do the same, and perhaps be ready to ask an anodyne opening question or two; then, as soon as any substantial subject came up, he was quick to latch on to it, after which there was no problem. He was also very happy to convey interesting information, and whenever he saw a suitable opportunity he would do that. But if nothing like that happened or occurred to him, he would be lost. He told me that one day at dinner he had been sitting next to the wife of a fellow philosopher, and she eventually said, "You have nothing to say to me, have you?"

In general he had no idea how to pick up and maintain talk about ordinary things, and no feeling for the point of doing so. One day fairly soon after we moved to Wiltshire, I invited a few people from the conservation group round for drinks with the local MP. I thought we should start to be neighbourly. Afterwards Derek was as near to anger as I have ever seen him. It was a total waste of his time to stand making conversation for an hour with people he had no reason to think we would want to know. It did not occur to him to go around filling glasses. We did gradually get to know a few people, but only when he had seen enough of them to know there were things to talk about. He had no sense at all of the value of getting to know neighbours just because they were neighbours. He was interested in company only if that company was interesting to talk to, or to explain things to.

Most people from the world of philosophy will also certainly recognize in Derek the description of conversations as "mostly, persuading you to agree with their view".

> Their few friends are also usually somewhat odd themselves. (145)

I will leave people who think of themselves as Derek's friends to figure that one out! When the Warden of All Souls asked him to invite friends to his farewell dinner, he said he hadn't got any friends. (None of his American colleagues was around at the time.) Of course, there were people he regarded as friends and many he admired and was fond of, and many people were very fond of him. But he certainly did not have friends in the way that most women would understand friends, and he did not have the typical male hanging-out kind of friends. In the time I knew him he spent willingly very little time with anyone outside professional situations.

One thing that should have struck me very early on in the relationship, but for some reason did not, was the way he kept our connection so hidden and did not introduce me to friends or acknowledge it when we were together in professional settings. Even when he came from Rice to visit me at UCLA in 1984, staying in my house and giving a paper at the Philosophy Department, we did not make it known. I gather there was some discussion there about whether we were connected, with most thinking it unlikely from what they knew of Derek. For some reason I did not think twice about this. I did not mind that it was not generally known; I thought it was rather fun having a secret liaison, even though there was nothing illicit about it. Perhaps I was still continuing my early intuition that all the running should be left to him. It was a good intuition, in the light of how uncompromising he turned out to be.

> Their lack of social awareness may even result in their not even trying to camouflage their oddities. (136)

Temple Grandin had realized that cows could be calmed by being held in a close pen, and she invented a kind of hugging machine for soothing herself. She had no hesitation in showing it to other people and explaining what it did. From her point of view it was just another interesting fact about how things worked. She did not feel any need to conceal it, in the way that neurotypical people feel they have to hide deeply personal things, especially if they are odd.

It was striking that after I told Derek I thought he was autistic, he started (in another instance of stealing my lines, though I was not there at the time) telling people that when *he* had read the Sacks account, *he* had recognized himself in it. I gather that he changed his mind later on the grounds that autistic people were supposed not to understand irony, and he thought he did. (He did not, as some of his colleagues often noticed. One of my favourite personal illustrations of this was a time, late in our relationship, after we were married, when he found the poems of Edna St. Vincent Millay in my bathroom and was expressing admiration of them. "She knew you," I remarked. "I don't think so," he replied.)

> They are typically convinced by the rightness of their beliefs . . . relentlessly trying to convince the other person to change their views. (147)

This was not something I encountered personally, because in most areas we did not have any seriously clashing views, and I was not much interested in the details of the professional disputes he was dealing with in his later work. But he certainly was deeply concerned about getting agreement from other philosophers, and his main preoccupation in the later part of his life seemed to be persuading philosophers with apparently different views that they really agreed with him, and, as everyone knows, he was nothing if not dogged about arguing his points.

He was quite genuinely concerned with reaching the truth about the topics he was dealing with: as far as I can tell, there was no element of wanting to defeat his opponents just for the sake of winning. But he did passionately want their agreement, mainly because he thought real harm could follow from widespread acceptance of conflicting meta-ethical views, and he probably also wanted assurance that he was right. He would often return from discussions in an emotional state, worrying that he had been getting too worked up and irritable in his efforts to persuade other people, and might have been rude. He would sometimes apologize to them later.

What may be my own version of this point is slightly different. You would think that with such an outstanding philosopher I would have enviable access to detailed discussion about my own work as it was going on. But in fact I did not like discussing my work with Derek, at least when it was in the early stages, not because he would disagree—by the time I had finished he would have hardly any comments—but because my way of working was so different. I found that if I tried to explain my early puzzlings about various subjects, they would be swept up by him into a framework they did not fit, but which at that stage I could not explain. The whole problem was to explain the problem. Of course, I would have been very worried about any criticisms he had by the time I had finished.

How often did Derek change his views in response to arguments? That is a genuinely open question. I found he often seemed to be struck by problems I raised about his arguments, but then seemed to have forgotten afterwards. I did not usually persist, as his later work was so different from mine, and I could see no chance of reaching a conclusion

The next quotation from Baron-Cohen I put in just for amusement, and for collectors of Derek stories:

> [Teenagers] sometimes get into trouble for pursuing unusual interests (the chemistry of poisons, the construction of explosives). (145)

I can imagine that if Derek's interests had lain in that direction he might well have done such things in total innocence, and it somehow seems relevant to an incident when the police were called to the American Embassy in London. As Derek was going through security there, his bag was scanned, it was found to contain a long, pointed kitchen knife. He had been going to collect his visa as usual and knew that he was not allowed to take his laptop to the Embassy. He also knew that he might have a long wait, so as he was leaving home, he picked up a knife to sharpen his pencil. (It had not occurred to him to ask me for a pencil sharpener, of which I had many.) He had a long argument with the policemen about the unreasonableness of his being expected to know that it was illegal to carry a knife. He did succeed in convincing them that he was no threat.

I was always impressed by his not being bothered by the risk of being stopped by the authorities in Russia—which I think he was, at least once. I connected it with his general unawareness of what was going on around him in public, and having not much idea of what other people might be thinking.

> They often admit that they would not know how to comfort someone. (148)

That was certainly true, for instance, in the case of the walk on the Downs and my back pain, but I was aware of the problem more generally. Derek did not understand the kind of expressed direct connection that could be comforting in itself. My first real experience of this was when a friend of his was devastated by not getting a job he had badly wanted, and Derek was, with great difficulty, trying to write a response. He showed me the letter he had written, and it was appalling. It was essentially an argument trying to persuade him that what he wanted did not matter much. I helped to revise it radically, but I do remember wondering at the time whether someone who could write such a letter was so alien that it was not worth pursuing the relationship.

I felt similarly, later, about the condolence letters he had written to two friends who had lost their wives, and which I later discovered took a form he had sent to more people than I realized at the time. He was using his views about Time (the next subject he had been going to pursue) to argue that the person who had died was still real. I could not see how this argument was supposed to work as a consolation, even given his metaphysics, as one of the people he had written to pointed out in a reply. He seemed not to understand that the pain of bereavement was that the person was no longer there to interact and communicate with, not about some metaphysical non-existence.

I suppose it was part of his not understanding the importance to ordinary human beings of companionableness and direct intuitive connection.

It certainly was not that he did not care about distress: it was just that he thought only in terms of finding solutions to problems, without any understanding of comforting. When his mother and sister were extremely upset about the death of his younger sister and the struggles over arranging adoption for her son, Derek saw that he could help by writing statements for the court case, and he spent a long time and a great deal of effort in doing so. He also told me that, when he had been afraid that one of his girlfriends was suicidal, he had emptied her medicine capsules and refilled them with sugar. I doubt whether he knew how to do anything that could count as trying to prevent suicide by simply comforting her. Sometimes his practical suggestions for dealing with problems (at least in my case) could be acute, and of course he was kind. But when his mother wanted him to help her to move out of the family home and into her retirement flat, his response was (of course) to say that he would pay for a mover to do it. He thought it was ridiculous for him to use his time in that way when somebody else could do the job much better. He seemed to have no conception of the value of companionship and emotional continuity when she was making such a large move, and that it was not his muscles she wanted. (I can't remember whether I succeeded in persuading him to change his mind. It was very early in the relationship. I hope I did.)

The general lack of feeling for companionableness also fits with Derek's having no interest whatever in, or understanding of the point of, significant dates. Why celebrate arbitrary days like Christmas and New Year when they were exactly the same as any other days? What was the point of recognizing birthdays and anniversaries? (He said he agreed with Humpty Dumpty that unbirthdays were better because there were more of them, but he did not do many unbirthdays either). Of course they are arbitrary, but they are important simply because tradition and convention have made them so, and they provide opportunities for coordinating social activities expressing warmth and connection. But if Derek did not feel those kinds of connection, it was not surprising that he could not see the point of the occasions. His sister had to bully him into going to her son's wedding (in America), and she really did exert serious pressure, telling him that in exchange he need not go to her funeral when the time came. The wedding meant nothing to him, and going was simply a waste of time that could be spent on better things; but he did have feelings of great affection for his sister and eventually, unwillingly, agreed. (And when he was there, he obviously did find substantial things to talk about, because he apparently delighted everybody. Get him going in the right setting and nothing would seem awry.)

It did not occur to him to go to either of my parents' funerals, even though they were in Oxford, and by the time they died I knew him far too well to think of suggesting it. He never had any idea of when my birthday was.

> They would not notice that someone was upset unless the person told them so or was showing extreme signs of distress. (148)

> When they discover that they have inadvertently hurt another person . . . they are usually shocked and cannot understand why their actions have this kind of impact. They typically find it equally puzzling to know how to repair such a hurt. (137)

This was highly significant for us as a couple. Derek did hurt me several times in the early stages, by acting in ways that by ordinary social standards were not just not loverlike but apparently expressive of unconcern or irritation, or even rude. The walk on the Downs was the first of those I remember, but then, as we saw more of each other, there were many more. Several times in Venice in the early days, when we were just casually together during the day, this kind of thing began to cause problems. People in general, when they set out as companions even in the most casual and temporary way, have all kinds of ways of establishing that they are together, even when they have nothing much to say: they adjust their pace, wait if they get separated, and have continuous interactions that confirm to themselves and others that they are together. If they are going to take off on their own, they will say so and have brief parting rituals. There are innumerable such intuitive interactions, and when people are not observing them, they are usually positively showing that they are not regarding themselves as part of the group or couple. I am now sure Derek simply had no feeling for these conventions, but I interpreted their absence in ways he did not intend or understand, as not wanting to be with me.

This is something his philosophical colleagues will probably not have seen, because when he was walking with them he would be earnestly talking philosophy, or telling them something. I did not encounter it when he was first showing me Venice and St Petersburg, and absorbed in explaining history and architecture. His family will probably not have encountered it either, because when he was with them, which was not very often, he was either specially alert to showing them attention or involved in substantial conversation, and they knew him well. But with me, as we became established as a couple, if he was not actively engaged in conversation, he would often seem to wander along almost as if he were alone. When we went to galleries, he would just disappear. Of course people look at pictures at their own pace, but if they have gone in company with someone else they will keep re-establishing contact and will make sure they know where the other is, or if they are going to different places, they will tell each other and arrange to meet: there are all kinds of ways to do exactly what you want to do while expressing connection. Derek seemed to have no sense of them.

I began to show that I was a bit upset by these and similar things, and after a while I started to exaggerate the reactions to some extent, because he missed the subtle ones. This was disastrous. I soon discovered that if I showed that I was upset about anything interpersonal, Derek's response was just to become more upset, apparently without any attempt to understand the cause.

This is best illustrated by one catastrophic episode, again in Venice, early on in the relationship, when we had gone to a concert in Santo Stefano. When it ended, Derek simply stood up, walked out, and set off home, totally ignoring me. I was amazed and, of course, upset. If people have come together to a concert, when it ends they at least make eye contact, probably talk a little, and automatically coordinate their departure. What had happened? It looked like a demonstration of some hostility or displeasure, but there had been no tension whatever beforehand or during the concert. I caught him up, of course looking upset. Who would not be? (Well—I would not when I knew him better.) His response was once again to get even more upset, and this time just call the whole thing off.

That led to a longish separation, which Derek later came to call The Interregnum. I was heartbroken and utterly bewildered. I had no idea what had happened. There had been nothing that would indicate he had gone off in a huff or anything of the kind. Had he just absent-mindedly forgotten I was with him? But then he would just have explained and apologized—everyone knows about absent-minded academics—and there would have been no problem. I now think that what must have happened was something equivalent to his putting down the receiver at the end of telephone calls without saying goodbye. By all normal convention that is deliberately rude, as this sudden departure seemed to be, but Derek apparently did not know that, and was just somehow taking it for granted that, when the concert finished, you left. As a result, I think, he saw my reaction as unexpected and totally incomprehensible, and probably as the latest in a series of incomprehensible reactions. He had no idea how to deal with it, and if that was how the relationship was going to be, of course he did not want it. But I was a long way from understanding this at the time. Baron-Cohen again:

> It is in friendship, in intimate relationships, where the situation is unstructured and unpredictable, where social sensitivity and reciprocity matter, that they struggle. (141)

I did not understand what had happened, but I was sure it was absurd to end things. It did not seem that he had got tired of me or ceased to find me attractive, and we were extraordinarily well suited in most ways. But I did sense that he felt some kind of pressure that absolutely needed to be taken off, and I concentrated on doing that during our disengaged encounters over the next few months. It seemed to work. We were both going to NYU that autumn and had, of course, originally planned to share an apartment while we were there. I suggested we could still do that and live separately in it. I was fully intending to do that unless things turned out otherwise: I still had my original intuition that things had to be left to him. But they did turn out otherwise. Somehow, without any kind of discussion or drama, and absolutely no further initiative from me, things just fell back into their original and even exciting place even before we got to New York. I can't even remember the details of how it happened.

After that we both seemed to start making adjustments, again without any discussion. We had a lovely time in New York. I understood by then that the worst thing I could do about his unfamiliarity with basic conventional interactions was to show distress and started trying to get more normal behaviour from him by means of humour—teasing about his oddities—which worked very well. In the meantime he seemed to learn the relevant social techniques to some extent. One day when we went to the Frick he started by saying, "Let's each choose eight pictures we would most like to own and compare them afterwards." I have no idea how deliberate this was, but it was exactly the right sort of thing. It let him go round independently while still framing the whole thing courteously as a joint expedition. I would not have shown upset by that time anyway, because by now I had a better understanding of what I was dealing with, but it felt much better.

We went on learning many more such things when we were at West Kennett. It was as though we were both trying to learn the other's language, to bridge the curious gap and manage the underlying connection that was certainly there. It was not quite natural on either side. I had to remember when he did not get things right that he was trying and did not intend what would be conventionally implied by things he did or did not do. I suppose he was in the same way trying to compile a manual of the strange things that seemed to bother me, or might please me, and it was often slightly wrong. But the humour always worked, and it went well.

That was all achieved by trial and error, before I had any conception of missing modules. If I had had that idea from the beginning, everything would have been much easier to cope with. We were both misinterpreting what the other intended, because a significant part of common language and feeling was missing, and I would have known it was necessary to find another way of communicating. It would also have been clear that if anything could be done in the way of planning to overcome the difficulties, it would have to be done by me—just because the problem was one he was blind to. From the point of view of the relationship, he had a different sensory system, and mine seemed to be the one with the extra element.

The idea of empathy as a continuum strongly connected with maleness and femaleness suggests that there may be many common variations of this kind of problem. To whatever extent there is any tendency for some people to recognize subtle elements of communication that others miss, that is bound to result in miscommunication of feelings and intentions. To whatever extent this is linked to sex, it is likely to result in women's not understanding why men will not take the trouble to do tiny things that make all the difference, and men's not understanding why women make such a fuss about nothing. The things in question may have quite different significances if on one side they are taken as kinds of communication but are not recognized as such on the other. But this is not the place to plunge into that briar patch.

It occurs to me, as I am writing this, that I have a comparable kind of blindness: I am bad at facial recognition until I know people well. I am always afraid that I must be offending people who think I am ignoring them, when I simply have not recognized them.

> A relationship is on their terms only. It is only possible when the other person is able to accommodate in the extreme to their partner's needs, wishes and routines. (141)

Absolutely. Our day was run on Derek's timetable, and we did together only things he wanted to do. I can't think of anything that Derek did not positively want to do but did with me because, or even partly because, I would have liked to do it. He was uncompromising in his pursuit of his own purposes.

This was obviously more significant for me than anyone else, since we were living together. I had gone to West Kennett because he wanted the house so much. I did love the place, but the cost for me—in trying to maintain it, and in isolation from cultural and intellectual company that would have been available to me in Oxford—was enormous. In the meantime Derek carried on his life there pretty well unchanged, as if West Kennett had been All Souls transposed. He worked all day and continued with all his overseas trips as a matter of course.

But other people have come across variations of the same thing. His family would always have liked to see much more of him than they could persuade him to agree to: as I said, he had to be seriously bullied into going to something as important to his sister as her son's wedding. And there is one particularly striking episode concerning friends, mentioned in the David Edmonds biography, but which I knew about independently. His friends Susan Hurley and Bill Ewald were taking advantage of a rare opportunity to meet, and asked Derek to join them for dinner in All Souls. These were the people who had sat up all night devising the conclusion for *Reasons and Persons* in time for the publishing deadline, when Derek had collapsed with exhaustion. Susan had formerly been his lover and was now dying of cancer, and Bill was about to return to America, and it was unclear when or whether he would see either of them again. He refused to join them and went upstairs to his room, saying he had to work.

So what should be made of all this? How could someone as undoubtedly kind and benevolent as Derek, who was so generous in many ways and so concerned with justice, act in ways that seemed so uncompromisingly selfish and unconcerned with the interests and feelings of people he was fond of? How might this connect with the mind-blindness phenomenon, as Baron-Cohen says it does?

What Derek himself often said was that time was his most valuable commodity, and he did not think he should spend it doing things he did not want to do just because other people would have liked him to. He was aware that this attitude precluded certain kinds of altruism, and he was both explicit and unapologetic about it. I remember his talking about an author who said in public that she was not going to spend time personally looking after her elderly parents "because she did not want to". She wanted to get on with her writing, and Derek thought she was right. She should not give up her own aims in life to do something that could be adequately done by others, just because other people would have liked her to. He thought it wrong for other people to expect her to and regard it as her duty. And in fact he quite explicitly classified everything he did into "things he wanted to do" and "duties"—things he did not want to do but felt he ought to—and he deliberately limited how much in the second category he would accept. He would do things he could see were urgent, like helping his family when the problems caused by the death of his sister arose, and he was generous and helpful in his attitudes and in many actions. But in general other people's needs, and certainly their preferences, were not to be allowed to get in the way of how he wanted to spend his time.

That is what think Derek would have seen as the essence of the matter. What he wanted to spend time doing was making progress in philosophy, and he did not want to waste it doing something as relatively unimportant as having dinners, or going to weddings, or going to see bluebells with me, just because I or others would have liked it. Such concessions to other people would have seemed to him supererogatory, and not something for which it was reasonable to sacrifice his time.

Of course, no one doubted that his work should be his main concern, or that what he achieved came from intense application. On the other hand, although there is no doubt that his mind was fixed on philosophy most of the time, and that he thought what he was doing was seriously important, it was not all he did. There was, of course, the photography, about which he was almost equally obsessive, and he did not think that had the same objective importance that he hoped his work in philosophy would. And there were also various things even Derek did for relaxation. He would watch videos or sometimes go to films, listen to music, look at pictures, read poetry or architecture books, and occasionally travel for pleasure. He was sometimes happy to go to social occasions with people he knew would be interesting to talk to. He could take some time from philosophy. But these other things were also things he actually wanted to do, and to that extent they were part of his own purposes, not interruptions of them.

I think this is where the mind-blindness comes, and where his own account of his reluctance to join in things his friends and family would have liked to do—as a reasonable limit to his willingness for altruism—does not catch the essence of the matter. The problem, from the point of us more ordinary people, was that spending time with us was not in itself something that mattered to him or something he sought out for his own enjoyment in the way he sought out music or art. It was not that he was not fond of us or did not care about us. It was just that because he had so little feeling for the value of immediate personal connectedness in its various forms, socializing as such did not come into the category of things he wanted to do for their own sake, and they therefore came into the duty category, to be allocated out of the limited altruism quota.

This needs clarifying. It was not that Derek did not value company or like people. He enjoyed company in many contexts. He certainly liked endlessly discussing philosophy; he liked taking people on his photographic expeditions as long as they did not interfere with the purpose of them; he often liked having people with him to listen to music; he enjoyed relaying interesting information; he really liked having me in the house and in the study next to him. But in all these cases the company was, as it were, the icing: something pleasant to add to what he wanted to do anyway and would probably have done alone. For most people companionableness, actually being with or connecting with congenial friends, is valuable in itself. It is something worth having in its own right, and which therefore can substantially influence decisions about whether other things are, all things considered, worth doing.

For instance, Derek liked having me and others listening to music with him, and discussing compositions and performances. But he would have listened to it whether we had been there or not, and his enjoyment of the music itself would have been exactly the same. He did not want to go to live performances because they would not be as good as the best recordings: going to a string quartet in his aunt's church came into the duty category. In contrast, I used sometimes to go to operas with a musical friend of mine. We knew that the productions might not be first-rate, but the pleasure of going out with a friend would make the occasion worthwhile nonetheless, and even the enjoyment of the music itself was actually enhanced because we were communicating enjoyment to each other and amplifying it. For people who value companionableness—the direct, intuitive awareness of other people, being with them and communicating irrespective of content—its intrinsic value can substantially affect the all-things-considered value of something that might not otherwise have been worth doing. For Derek, it did not.

So I think the root of the problem, as Derek's neglected friends and family and I would understand it, was not that he did not have any time for other things than philosophy and photography (he did), or that he did not care about us (he did). It was that he did not value time in our company as such in the expressive way that most people do with friends they are fond of. When he refused to have dinner with Susan and Bill, he probably thought the issue was simply a matter of their wanting to have dinner and his wanting to work, so of course they should each follow their own preference. If he were to give up his preference for theirs, it would be an act of altruism, of duty. He seemed not to understand that for most people spending time together was actually in itself expressive and constitutive of connection, and that his refusing to do so was actually hurtful.

So I think the problem was not just, as he thought, that he wanted to limit the things he did as acts of altruism, as matters of duty. It was the fact that he thought of time spent with those of us who were close to him, for its own sake, as coming into the duty category. We did not want him to spend time with us as a matter of duty. We wanted him to value companionable interactions for their own sake, in the way we did, and therefore as sometimes bringing dinners or weddings or going to bluebell woods into the category of things he actually wanted to do. But if he did not feel things in that way, he would not understand how they seemed to us.

I think a similar kind of thing accounts for the West Kennett situation. Although I was very happy there for some time, the arrangement turned out to be deeply unfair in its structure in that the whole project depended critically on major adaptations from me while life for Derek went pretty well exactly as before, but enhanced by this lovely extra possession. I do not think it was that he did not care about unfairness: it was just that it did not occur to him that that was the situation.

Here is another remark from Baron-Cohen about people with the extreme male brain:

> These are the people who, in the first instance, think of solving tasks on their own, by figuring it out for themselves. The object or system in front of them is all that is in their mind, and they do not stop for a moment to consider another person's knowledge of it. (133)

By the time I met him, Derek had reached a situation in life when he was self-sufficient and able to do everything he wanted to. When he fell in love with West Kennett, he made a direct line for it, almost as if it had been just another antique fireplace or addition to his art nouveau miscellanea. He was so used to making decisions on his own that I really do not think it occurred to him to try to think the matter through from my point of view, or notice my doubts (no doubt too subtly expressed). He just thought, as he said later, that as I liked Georgian architecture and beautifying houses, there would be no problem. (Other people have noticed the readiness with which Derek produced arguments to show that what he wanted for himself was actually best for everyone.) When we were there, he made no day-to-day demands of me and probably thought I was free to do just as I liked, as he was. He seemed to have no idea of the significance for me, with my isolated job, of moving to the middle of nowhere while he carried on with his reclusive life and his travels as before. He simply did not understand, for some time, the massive underlying investment from me on which the whole arrangement was based, and which made me dependent on him in a way that suited neither of us.

I think all this accounts for why it is so difficult to decide whether it is appropriate to describe Derek as selfish. He certainly did what he wanted to do with very little accommodating of other people, but it was difficult to tell the extent to which this was actually rooted in selfishness—a limit to altruism—and how much was a matter of his having different personal values from other people. If he did not value connection for its own sake in the way many people do, then giving up his working time would have seemed a greater cost for him that it would to others, and in the same way he would probably underestimate the cost of his refusal to other people. If he had understood what they felt, he might have given them greater weight, and recognized, by his own standards, that these things really mattered. It is impossible to know. My impression is that, even then, he would have done the same.

Conversely, in contexts where he appeared generous—and there were many—it was usually in contexts such as reading and commenting on philosophy, which he was anyway happy to do and could do far more quickly and easily than others could. The real costs to him were less than the benefits to others. When the costs were high, it was different. It is well known that he refused to supervise many students who would have loved to work with him, only because he so hated the appalling chore that reference writing had now become. If he could simply have given his opinions of these students, there would have been no problem, but trying to produce the kind of confection that reference-inflation now demanded, especially in America, was beyond his literal-mindedness and total misery to him. It was too much to ask.

This has all taken some time to work out, but I think the analysis is broadly right, even if the conclusion remains uncertain.

Baron-Cohen also says:

> As children they will play, but only if the game is the one they want to play. (141)

I have included this one partly because it connects with the previous point, but more importantly because I wonder whether it provides the key to how differently Derek appeared in his earlier and later life, while still being the same person. People who knew him earlier wonder what happened to him to make his reclusive later self so different from the person they knew, who did all kinds of things involving other people. But I wonder whether, even then, he ever willingly went along with things other people wanted to do but he did not.

All his early life, right up to getting into All Souls, Derek had been, as it were, playing the games he wanted to play, and while he was still experimenting to find out what his values and abilities were, there had been a great many of them. My suspicion is that, at the time before the duomania set in, the issues I have been describing simply would not have arisen. Derek liked having other people involved in his games in the same way that he wanted people later on to comment on his drafts and come to meetings in his room to discuss his work, or discuss the aesthetics of his photographs, or listen to music with him. And as he was so nice, so completely lacking in any kind of self-centredness or aggression to other people, so engaged in activities which they were happy to join in, and so knowledgeable about so many things, the missing elements just did not show.

That is something that it would be interesting to investigate further, but some of the accounts in David Edmonds's biography suggest it. It is interesting to read that when he was travelling round the States for his Harkness Fellowship in company with others, he would read up on the place they were going to go to next day, and, I have no doubt, spend that day explaining it to them. There would be no problem in a situation like that: there would have been no need for any compromise, because everyone would have enjoyed what Derek wanted to do, and his being there would have enhanced it for them. But when his focus became narrow—when he had done all he wanted to do—there was limited scope for doing much with other people.

Derek started our relationship with all kinds of plans for things we were going to do and places we were going to see that would have delighted me, but I suppose that was in the phase when he had just finished *Reasons and Persons*, and he was relaxing a bit. As the duomania intensified, these things came lower on his list of priorities, and gradually became shifted into the never-never land of things we would do when he decided he could do no more productive work. Nobody who knew him thought that time would ever come. The fact that I would have enjoyed them, or that we would be doing them together, could not shift the balance of worthwhileness even slightly.

> Some marry, but remain married only if their partner is patient to the point of saintliness. (149)

That was true in a way, but in Derek's case it was not exactly saintliness that was called for. Saintliness implies self-sacrifice, but—except for the deep mistake involved in West Kennett—he did not demand or expect anything of me. He was going to go his own way, and to the extent that I fitted in or enhanced it, that was excellent. But there was no other condition under which it was possible to have a relationship with Derek. The connection could keep going only if it did not interrupt the things he valued more. What was needed was not exactly saintliness but extreme tolerance and independence.

What took a long time to understand, because it was such an alien idea, was that he would never have minded what I did, or with whom, as long as he could carry on without having to deviate from what he wanted to do. Once I had a proper understanding of what the situation was, the question for me became whether it was worthwhile to keep the good and indeed exceptional elements of the relationship with Derek, while accepting that there was a lot missing, and that some things I wanted to do would have to be, if they were done at all, with other people rather than him. By the time we actually married I knew what was I was taking on and had recognized the non-negotiable elements.

Finally, here is a comment from one of Baron-Cohen's subjects:

> "We're like saltwater fish trying to live in fresh water. We're fine if you put us in the right environment." (180)

In the academic world and All Souls, Derek had managed to find himself a dream of a saltwater environment, where he could spend his time doing exactly what he wanted. But there are far fewer saltwater females around. West Kennett was as near to this as I could make it, but there were limits. I needed water that was at least brackish.

All this, however, was what I concluded after a long time and a great deal of thinking—which has in some ways been as intellectually complicated as working through philosophical problems. At the time of our leaving West Kennett I had only got as far as the shock of the Temple Grandin recognition and enough of a jolt to persuade me that the decision to go to London was right.

5 Finale

Once the London decision had been made, we went there together to look at houses. Derek rather liked one in Camden Town that had proper classical proportions in its front elevation, and he was unconcerned by the fact that it was next door to a pub and that the pub had at some point acquired its garden. This time I was going to find a house that was going to be suitable for living in, even if the most suitable candidate was past the architectural tipping point. We found a late Victorian end-of-terrace house that I could see had great interior potential, and that was something I was better at judging than Derek. (He liked it when it was done.) Meanwhile, he bought a very pretty house in Beaumont Buildings in central Oxford, to be used mainly by tenants until it was needed for retirement.

It was not clear what the state of the relationship was, and we did not discuss it. We still had joint bank accounts and were still the beneficiaries of each other's wills, and we were still for that matter both wearing the non-wedding rings we had bought when we moved to Wiltshire, though they were so habitual by then that I don't think either of us thought about it. But we were certainly regarding ourselves as independent. Whatever the connection turned out to be, I was positively intending not to feel in any way constrained by it, and I imagine Derek did not think about it at all except in terms of feeling he could now get back to his concentrated philosophical life without extraneous worries. He now lived entirely in All Souls, except for his regular rotation round Harvard, NYU, and Rutgers, while I began a new life in London and at UCL.

Although we were apart, however, there were some respects in which rather little changed. He stayed with me whenever he had reason to come to London, though that was not all that often—mainly just for such things as renewing his US visas. But he was in constant communication by phone, in rather the way that he had kept appearing at my study door at intervals during the day, and for the same kinds of reason: letting off philosophical steam, asking about computer problems, or sometimes just because he felt like dropping in. (In that last case he would often have one of his obviously prepared enquiries ready, to which I would usually respond by saying that my vicar was fine.) And he called again at night.

His photographic expeditions were gradually winding down. He did not go to Venice any more and felt that project was essentially finished. He said he would have liked to photograph Venice in snow, but on the one occasion snow was forecast, and I pressed him to go, he did not do it. He still made a few more trips to St Petersburg, but they were all failures for lack of snow. Technology had advanced, however, and although he never took digital photographs, he did now get his slides and prints scanned and started to learn the basics of PhotoShop. He once again bought masses of equipment: two printers, one so huge that he lent it to a company rather than try to fit it into his room (I think he made only one print on it, and it disappeared when the company went bankrupt), three professional paper cutters, one of them 5 feet long, crates full of ink cartridges, a large artist's easel for displaying the biggest prints, and several of the kinds of display racks normally found in print shops. Once again he was pursuing the very best for his photographs, with no expense spared. Working on them was now his main winding-down activity, accompanied by amitriptyline, vodka, and music or videos.

I know rather little about his professional life at this time, mainly, I think, because there was not much to know: it was essentially just pressing on with *On What Matters*, and making his regular trips to the US. The highlight was a conference in his honour at Rutgers in 2003, when he was very deeply moved by all the affection and appreciation shown to him and said afterwards that he wished I had been there. But I was getting increasingly out of touch with the direction of his work. I was not much interested in the details of the controversies that now preoccupied him. Life in this period was very much more varied for me than for Derek, and in no way relevant to what he was doing. A couple of times he did pass on enquiries from colleagues about appointments I might be interested in, but there was nothing interesting enough to pursue.

But in 2007, long after the end of West Kennett and for reasons having nothing to do with Derek, I returned to Oxford. I had met Julian Savulescu through my work in bioethics, and he invited me to join him at the Uehiro Centre for Practical Ethics in the Philosophy faculty in Oxford. I took early retirement from UCL and returned half-time to Oxford.

I was still living in the London house and was not yet ready to make any plans to move, but I now needed to be in Oxford several days a week. Derek's house in Oxford was still tenanted, and the question of reclaiming it did not occur to either of us. But he had kept a tiny room at the top of it, where he slept for two nights a week to satisfy the conditions of his All Souls housing allowance, and his tenants were by then a congenial lot of eccentric philosophers whom I already knew. So when I came back to Oxford, it was automatic that I should at least start by staying in Derek's bedroom there, in the remarkable situation of boxing and coxing with him in his single bed.

It was not a bad solution, but it quickly became clear that it was far too small a place to stay, even for a few days a week. The room was only a couple of feet wider than the bed, and there was no room to store or do anything. But after two or three weeks it became clear that nobody was using the common sitting room, so I took that over and installed a sofa bed. And late in the evening of the day I did it, to my considerable surprise, Derek called from All Souls saying "he might toddle along". I had presumed he would by now be so deep in his resumed college bachelor habits that it would not occur to him to change them. But he did toddle along, and he immediately returned to his old pattern of coming round at night and going back to college during the day. The long semi-separation had suddenly and seamlessly ended, in the same unremarkable, undiscussed way as had the Interregnum so many years before. In fact I am not sure that Derek was even aware of quite how little we had seen of each other during the time I was in London, the communication had been so constant.

The arrangement now was not quite the same as the original one when I had had my Oxford house, of course—the arrangement I had wanted to continue when I suggested buying a house in Oxford together and Derek fell in love with West Kennett—because I still lived in London. But every week he would come to see me off on the London bus, and join me again when I came back.

I could now begin to see more directly what was happening in his life, and what had happened to Derek himself. His mother had died while we were still in Wiltshire, and he now had no family in Oxford and must have had hardly anything in the way of non-philosophical company for years. He had even completely given up going to dinner in college, instead just having a bowl of cereal in his room. There seemed little doubt that he would have done what I had, early on, found myself thinking of as spiralling into himself and reverting to type. It took some time to catch up properly, as I usually saw him only after the end of the working day, but everything I was afraid of had indeed happened, and to an extreme degree.

His once beautiful college room was now a tip. During our time in West Kennett, his rooms had been packed up for rewiring and redecorating, and he had never got round to properly unpacking and rearranging them. His framed pictures had been dismantled for scanning, and the spotlights had gone. There were still half-emptied boxes, piles of books on the floor, prints strewn and stacked everywhere, and CDs all over the place and likely to crunch underfoot. He would not let the college scouts in to clean, and anyway it was difficult to see what they could have done even if he had allowed it. Derek sat in the middle of all this in his big, rocking armchair with his laptop, working as always with total concentration, until it was time to wind down with music and PhotoShop. He must have cared about the mess to some extent: it must have been depressing, given his sense of beauty. But it was obviously not worth the time and effort to put right.

I also discovered that he was now taking two shovelfuls of amitriptyline in the evening, rather than one. I presume that, as he now had nothing but his work during the day, winding down properly at night must have been even more of a problem. It was bound to be bad for his health.

Also very striking, and very distressing to me, was what had happened to him personally—though once again I had anticipated it. He must have cared about his appearance at one time. I would have expected him to, on the purely aesthetic grounds that led him to put initial effort into the beauty of his rooms. As everyone knows, he had settled early into his uniform of nearly black, white, and scarlet—his favourite colours—and my presumption was that even though he found this uniformity useful in keeping things simple, he also thought nothing would look better and saw no reason to change. He also used a bronzer, saying, in case justification might be demanded, that it would be sexist if he refrained from doing it on grounds of his being male. (He admired the black kohl eyeliner used by some Arab men.) And he was certainly proud of his hair. It was thoroughly white by the time I met him, but he said he had bleached it in his youth. He also used to like telling people that whenever the former Warden John Sparrow, in later life and past his intellectual prime, came to dinner in All Souls, he would demand of the assembled fellows, "What's the most beautiful thing in this room?", and immediately answer himself, "Parfit's chevelure".

But even though he must have cared at one time, I had been struck when we lived together that Derek was not in the least ordinarily vain, and that he seemed not to care how he appeared in general. I never saw him even glancing in a mirror, except for the rapid shaving and bronzing in the morning. And, of course, I had also often noticed before his unawareness of how strangers might think about the way he looked, except when there was a particular reason. I think the original care with his appearance must have been to some extent connected with recognition of its importance to the achievement of his early purposes—professional advancement and attracting women—and that once those became irrelevant, and once he was no longer being prodded by me, he just went on to autopilot. I remember being slightly disappointed at a Faculty occasion when all the other men were wearing black ties and beautifully smooth shirts, and Derek turned up just as usual, with a shirt that may have had contact with an iron, but only in passing. Now he had had hardly any reason to care or think about it for years, and although the uniform had not changed, everything else had done.

I saw something of this when he came to London to give a paper at UCL, and it turned out that he had nothing with him but the tatty, stained corduroys he had travelled in. I suppose at some level he must have just presumed that there would be suitable clothes at my house. I cleaned what he was wearing as well as I could, which was not very well, and it was fortunate that the lecture theatre had a lab bench across the front, so he could not be seen from the waist down. But it did look then as though things had gone downhill, and they had.

It was not just that he was scruffy, which must have been evident to everyone; it was his whole demeanour. I do not know how he seemed to his colleagues, but to see him in public, in the street, or in the shops was to me actually horrifying. He walked bent almost double, pulled down by the big bag round his neck, but not like a decrepit elderly person on a stick: he walked quickly and purposefully, with his set outdoor expression, his mouth open and his lower lip pulled over his teeth, and manifestly unaware of everything around him. On one striking occasion when we in a local supermarket, he bent over to pick up something on one side of the aisle and then moved across to get something on the other side without straightening up as he crossed. He did not just look eccentric, he looked literally crazed, as though there should be someone taking care of him. The strange half-naked person who had been dragging the flat-wheeled suitcase in Venice, oblivious of what anyone might think of him, seemed to have taken over. I suppose this was not so apparent to the people he interacted with professionally, because then he became animated and talked much as usual. But his appearance elsewhere was something he did not think about at all. Strangers were still just external objects rather than people who would notice or care about how he appeared. I was shocked to see how extreme it was.

I did not know how much he would have cared about this if I had tried to explain it. But I started to try breaking the downward spiral unobtrusively, to the extent that I could with the limited time we had together while we were still mainly living in different places. I saw that pulling his lip over his lower teeth was a habit he had developed while he was at the computer (and therefore unable to do the tooth cleaning), and I persuaded him to try to break it by getting him to use chewing gum. He did actually do that (after some irritated resistance), and his face began to relax a bit—though it did have the effect of adding chewing gum to the litter of toothbrushes and dental floss surrounding his chair and attached to his corduroys. (When he saw some photographs, long after this relaxing had started, he was distressed to see what remained of the habit. It seemed he did care; it just had not occurred to him to think about it.) There was also a gradual increase in warm expressions, as when I first met him.

Presumably also partly because of the lack of everyday stirring up, and making contact with other people, he seemed to have closed in intellectually as well. We would discuss his work and he would seem to be struck by some point I was making, but by the next day he would have forgotten it. Or he would misunderstand and respond as if what I was saying had been something else he was used to hearing from critics, or sometimes even conflate two such things and slip between them in the course of an argument. Of course, I was mainly seeing him in the evening, when he was under the influence of his horribly large dose of amitriptyline, but I began to get the impression that his colleagues were finding something of the same.

I wished I had been able to find a way to avoid the long time apart, which would certainly have prevented a lot of this. If I could probably have found a way to do it; but their work came too late.

The next three years were the ones leading up to the publication of *On What Matters.*

Now added to the writing pressure was the matter of book production, which brought in the other side of the duomania; the books as works of art became as much of an obsession as the photographs were. When Derek's passions could be diverted from anxiety about the need to prove that his opponents' arguments against the objectivity of things' mattering were wrong, they turned to how his books would look. He started early, anticipating intensive negotiations with the publisher. He started working through his photographs to find out which could best accommodate the print and titles on the covers, fine-tuning the colours and using PhotoShop to accommodate the thickness of the spines.

I did not see the details of all this, as I was still between Oxford and London, but I did see the efforts and the intensity of the emotions. He began to haunt the OUP bookshop in the High Street, looking through the books to find fonts and layouts that he liked, and so? arm himself with examples so that he could argue with anyone who tried to tell him that what he wanted was impossible. When I was sorting out Derek's books after his retirement, I found three copies of a book called *Blondel's Song*, about Richard I, none of which showed any signs of having been read. I knew why they were there. One of the arguments he was having with OUP was about the lettering on the cover of Volume 1 of *On What Matters* Derek wanted metallic gold, and the editor thought that would be unsuitable. *Blondel's Song* had metallic gold print on its cover, and I presume it must have struck him on three separate occasions in the OUP shop that a copy would be useful ammunition, and each time he forgot that he had bought it already, or did not think he would be able to find it in the chaos his room had become, or just did not want to spend time looking for it when he could easily buy another.

He won the gold argument, but there were many more to come. The cover proofs came through, but then the arguments began about the colour reproduction. Derek was not satisfied with what appeared and became increasingly agitated and distressed. He had sent his instructions in plenty of time: "Why had they delayed so long, and left so little time for getting them right?" He sent the proofs back with instructions about how the adjustments should be made; but dealing with a commercial publisher was not at all like dealing with the expensive producer of his original photographic prints, or giving instructions to Gordon, his toucher-upper. "Why can't they understand a perfectly simple instruction to make the wall less blue and more green? Why have they made it brown?", he would demand indignantly, as if challenging me to explain the absurdity, as he had done when Microsoft kept making Word worse. But this was more emotionally fraught, because here he thought there was something that could be achieved with enough effort—and payment. He persuaded OUP to let him pay for extra proofs, and then, when even those were not right and he was told that no more would be allowed, he fell into serious despair. I got involved at that point and called the editor to plead for one final run, which I promised would be the last, and (I think I remember) succeeded. The result was not really right even then, and Derek had to console himself with the thought that libraries usually threw away the dust jackets of hardbacks anyway, and that what really mattered would be the paperbacks. The emotion was seriously intense.

Everything came to a head in the first week of September 2010. This was when the final corrected text was due for handover to OUP, but it was only one element of a tsunami. That week there also arrived the unthinkable but inevitable time when Derek had to leave All Souls for the last time. Oxford has strict age-related retirement rules, and in the same week we had to move Derek's forty-two years' worth of books, photographic paraphernalia, and music into his house in Beaumont Buildings. He also had to prepare to leave for NYU, to start teaching the next week. And as well as all that, we had added to the pressure by deciding at last to get married.

It was a decision we found other couples in our position were making as they became increasingly conscious of age and mortality. Our wills had been sorted out long before, but, as we now both owned houses, being married would make a great difference to taxes and pensions when either of us died. It would also make clear that we were each other's next of kin, in case decisions had to be made in case of incapacity, and we both had strong feelings about end-of-life decisions.

The wedding was arranged for 31 August. Partly because of the intensity of the other goings-on in this rushed week, I took it for granted that Derek would think of the whole thing as nothing more than a technicality and want it done as simply and quickly as possible, so I was thinking we would just pick up a couple of witnesses from the Uehiro Centre on the way to the register office. But my sister and niece, who were very fond of Derek, thought it would be absurd after all these years to let such an event pass without celebration, and they came down to Oxford with their partners, bearing flowers and picnic supplies. We all had a celebration dinner the night before, and it was on the way to this that the exchange occurred that was described by David Edmonds in the *Prospect* article about us: as we passed a wedding shop in Little Clarendon Street, I pointed to a standard frothy wedding dress in the window and said "That's what I'll wear tomorrow!", and Derek said, "Do you mean that exact one, or just one like it?". Literal-minded as ever.

In fact I wore a red dress, which, of course, went with Derek's tie. As one of his friends said afterwards, it would have been impossible the other way round. We walked the five minutes to the register office for the brief ceremony—with Derek wanting the traditional wording of the vows—and then all six of us went off, pushing two bicycles loaded with flowers and food, to Magdalen Bridge to hire a punt and go for a picnic. It was a beautiful day, and as the photographs show, everyone, including Derek notwithstanding all the surrounding anxieties, looked really happy. If I had anticipated how much he would enjoy it, I would have suggested All Souls chapel and planned it with enough time to give his sister Theodora time to come from America. As it was, Derek told her only the night before, mentioning that he was getting married after some other trivial bit of information as though it had been an afterthought. Still, it was a delightful occasion. My sister said it was the nicest wedding she had ever been to, and Theodora later produced a lovely book of the photographs we had sent her.

After the visitors had gone in the late afternoon, we did just what you would expect a couple to do on their wedding day: we returned to Derek's chaotic room to carry on with the real business of the week—getting him finally out of college and off to the States, and his book to the publisher. He ploughed on through his texts, while I carried on with the archaeological dig through forty-two years of history (it was here I came across the eight electric toothbrushes) and getting things packed into boxes.

This continued the next day and the one after. I continued packing and Derek was frantically printing out drafts, reading them, and printing out revisions. At least, I think that was what he was doing. His room was on the second floor, and the printer was in the secretaries' room near the lodge in the front quad, so he was rushing backwards and forwards, up and down stairs, all the time, and I lost track of what was going on. So, apparently, did he. In the late evening, having just come into the room with another sheaf of paper, he suddenly said, "I can't remember what I'm doing," and stopped. He was supposed to be going to the States the next day.

He really had forgotten everything. I was not too alarmed, because fortunately I had had a similar episode a year or two before and was pretty sure I recognized this as what I had been told was transient global amnesia, which would pass. But medical advice was obviously needed, so we cancelled his flight and went off in a taxi to the overnight emergency medical service. He was doing what I gather I had done under the same circumstances, saying the same couple of things over and over again. "Have I had a stroke?" he kept saying, and "I'm lucky to have you!", poking his finger at me. But he could not remember anything. I told the doctor that he had been dealing with the last stages of getting a book to the publishers, and when he asked Derek about it, he had forgotten *On What Matters* and thought it was *Reasons and Persons.* When the doctor asked who I was, he had forgotten that we were married, and said, "She's the love of my life." But the doctor agreed with me that it was transient, and we got back to the house at about two or three in the morning.

I have never looked into the question of what brings about such incidents, but it was striking how much this case had in common with my own experience of the same thing. That had happened a couple of years before when I had returned to London from a conference in Hong Kong just before Christmas, with a family crisis to cope with. On the night of my return I was burgled, and all my computing equipment, including backup drives, was stolen. This was before the days of online backup, and I lost a huge amount of important work. As it happened, Derek was due to London the next day, to get his visa, and it was while he was out of the house that my memory went. I called my sister, sounding lost, and apparently kept saying, "Is Derek here? I've found his toothbrush", along with some nonsense about being able to find only one shoe, and having no recollection of Hong Kong, or travelling, or anything else about what was going on. What the situation seemed to have in common with what happened to Derek was that it too was rooted in a series of extreme stresses, combined with the (unusual) feeling that someone else was there who might be able to take over. That also seemed to fit the repeated 'I'm lucky to have you', and the 'love of his life' remark, when he would more usually have described me as his partner. Even though he had not remembered the details, there seemed to be an underlying awareness that something was different. It would be interesting to find out whether that is a recognized set of circumstances.

Anyway, by morning he was more or less back to normal, so we rearranged his flight for the following day. I think his NYU teaching started a couple of days later. After he had gone, I stayed in his All Souls room (no doubt illegally) for three days finishing the packing, and then moved everything into the Beaumont Buildings house. It was extraordinary for me to be in Derek's room after he had left it for ever, and to see it empty of everything except his suite, with Henry the vacuum cleaner beaming inappropriately in front of the denuded fireplace. The end of a remarkable era.

There was a lot of building work needed in the Oxford house, and I set about trying to organize that while Derek was away. But it ran into problems and took far too long, so when Derek came back we lived for a while mainly in my house in London, which was much more comfortable. Derek settled with his rocking chair into a corner of the sitting room. This was as near a transplantation of West Kennett as could be achieved on the first floor of a Victorian end-of-terrace house in London, with one of his fine antique fire surrounds, the French sofas on which he had sat needlepointing, and a set of screen-printed panels I had found in the Marlborough auction room. Something close to our life in West Kennett resumed.

Oddly enough, there was no sign of regret at the loss of All Souls. Of course, he was still welcome there, but he did not make much use of it. It confirmed the view I had reached that All Souls as such really was much less important to him than his freedom to work on philosophy as he wanted, and he could still do that. He seemed perfectly happy. He also seemed (yet again to my surprise) positively pleased that we were actually married. I had presumed he would not think it made any substantial difference, but he obviously did. He did not say so directly, but it kept coming up in unexpected ways: picking up the envelope with the marriage certificate and opening it "to gloat"; saying one day after he had passed along Park End Street that "that undistinguished building" (the Oxford Register Office) had acquired a new aspect; telling one of his friends that he thought the marriage meant more to him than to me; and commenting one day when mention of the marriage came up in another context, "Yes, that was a good thing."

In the spring of 2011, Volumes 1 and 2 of *On What Matters* appeared, and Derek was, of course, swept up in the aftermath. First there was the lead review in *The New York Review of Books* by Peter Singer, then the profile in *The New Yorker* by Larissa MacFarquhar, who came to Oxford to interview him. Later there was a profile of both of us in *Prospect* by David Edmonds, who had pointed out to the editors that on their list of the year's most significant books was not only *On What Matters* but a book by Derek's differently named wife as well. No one had known we were connected. Then, in March of 2014, Derek found he had been awarded the Schock Prize—one of the set of prestigious prizes for areas, like philosophy and mathematics, that did not have Nobel Prizes—and in October came the presentation ceremony in Stockholm.

This was, of course, a momentous occasion, though it turned out to involve a good deal of comedy (in retrospect) behind the scenes, due to typically inefficient planning from both of us. Soon after we arrived, Derek discovered to his alarm the restrictive nature of the Swedish licensing laws, which made it impossible for him to go and buy his vodka. That was obviously intolerable, so we had to resort to the hotel bar and getting a large tumbler filled with shots of vodka until Derek thought it looked full enough. I do not think Derek was embarrassed, though I was a little. Then we made two more unwelcome discoveries. Derek found he had come without his jacket, and there was a formal ceremony to come. And I discovered that I had come without some crucial medication. So the next morning, while we should have been concentrating entirely on what was supposed to be happening, we had to go into Stockholm to try to sort things out. We first had to go and get Derek a suit, which made him extremely fretful, because he wanted to work on writing the four-minute speech that was supposed to summarize what all his work had been about. He was so impatient that he wanted to buy the first one he tried on, which might have been appropriate if he had been a third of his age and set on looking trendy, and it took some doing to persuade him to look further. We did look further, however, and he calmed down and happily explained to the shop assistants that he needed it because he was being presented with an award by Princess Christina.

Then, during most of the conference that was held for Derek during the afternoon, I had to spend my time making medical appointments, finding my way to them, and going in search of pharmacies. I was able to join the conference only near the end, though in time to get a good sense of what was going on, and a few bad but telling photographs. It was obviously a striking event in many ways, not least because Derek, in his absorption in his topic, left the audience perpetually afraid that he was about to fall off the stage. He also burst into one of his striking weeping episodes, apparently at the thought that Bach had died before he could finish *The Art of Fugue*. When he was in intense emotional states, as he obviously was then, it took very little to trigger these outbursts.

Then, at night, I made the bad mistake of challenging the suitability of what Derek said he was going to put into his four-minute speech at the presentation, thereby breaking the rule that no philosophy was to be discussed during the winding-down period. We went on for hours, on the worst possible night for it to happen.

But that was all behind the scenes. The formal event went very well, in spite of all the background mishaps. It was a wonderful recognition of Derek.

By this time the house in Beaumont Buildings was liveable in, and Derek had settled in there. I was still shuttling between Oxford and London, but there was now obviously no point in keeping the London house. I was sorry to be thinking of leaving yet another house that I had beautified, but it would obviously be better to have both of us permanently in Oxford. Derek's house was too small for both of us, and we wondered about my original idea of two houses in the same street if another one in Beaumont Buildings became available, or, ideally, a larger one in St John Street where we could both live. As we both wanted to stay in central Oxford, it was a matter of waiting to see what would appear.

All that was my concern, of course. Derek was now pressing on with what would become Volume 3 of *On What Matters*, which was planned to coincide with the publication of an accompanying anthology edited by Peter Singer. He was planning other projects as well: rewriting *Reasons and Persons* (which his friends hoped he would not), and tackling Time. He was obsessed with how much he wanted to do, and how little time there might be. He had even given up the photography completely since leaving All Souls: the printers were never unpacked. But he was endlessly optimistic, saying that we might have another thirty years, and still even making the odd remark about things we would do when he could no longer do philosophy.

If he had been less optimistic, he might have paid more attention to the increasing signs of trouble looming for both of us. In the summer of 2014, which was very busy, we both found ourselves with health problems.

Derek came with me to a conference in Amsterdam where I was speaking, with the plan of staying for a few days afterwards. We did not do much. It was alarming how often he needed to sit down when he was out. Of course, he would not seek medical help: he was sure there was nothing seriously wrong.

Meanwhile, I had suddenly developed puzzling symptoms which had eventually been diagnosed as rheumatoid arthritis, an auto-immune disease, and it took some time for the medical people to find anything that would keep the symptoms under control. I was in pain and finding walking difficult, and had had to give up cycling. Travel between London and Oxford itself became difficult, but I was now in no state to think about the job of moving house. Anyway, I had to spend a lot of time in London going to hospitals.

Then in September, during one of Derek's regular visits to Rutgers, I had a call from Jeff McMahan, which began with his saying, "Derek's all right." Of course I did not know anything had been wrong, so Jeff had started with the reassuring part of the news. Derek had been staying with him, and Jeff had found him struggling for breath and had rushed him to hospital for emergency treatment which had almost certainly saved his life. Derek was amazingly (absurdly) insouciant about the whole thing, starting to talk about work as soon as he recovered consciousness. He even seemed rather proud of himself in a way, because the doctor said the X-ray showed long-standing anomalies which he would have said were incompatible with life. He also kept the shirt which they had cut off him because of the speed needed to get him on to a ventilator, and proudly brought it home rather as if he had been showing his Agincourt scars on St Crispin's Day. Later, after he was persuaded by Ruth Chang to consult a specialist she recommended for a further opinion, he was told that the situation was not life-threatening. With his usual optimism, Derek regarded this as meaning he need not worry. He obstinately refused to consult further, and was extremely annoyed when his doctors would not give him as much amitriptyline as he wanted. He had never got to know any of the doctors in his practice personally, or talked to them about his health. He just treated them as the necessary means to repeat his drug prescriptions and carried on with everything as usual.

In 2015 he was running into his familiar problems about book production. The plan was for Volume 3 to come out at the same time as the matching volume of articles edited by Peter Singer (*Does Anything Really Matter?*), and Derek was as usual putting it off, saying he wanted to add more. I do not know whether OUP realized this, but the reason he eventually agreed to publish the material he had already was that I joined in trying to persuade him, and succeeded simply by pointing out to him that if he thought of the rest of the material as a separate volume, he would be able to have another photograph on the cover. It may seem amazing, but that idea did almost instantly persuade him to agree to let the material go forward as it was and save the rest for another cover photograph. I knew my duomaniac. That was how Volume 3 appeared.

In summer, Derek pressed me to go with him to visit Theodora in her Maine holiday home, where I had not been before. He had arranged to go there en route to one of his American destinations. I was surprised, because I was still seriously unwell, with new puzzling symptoms, and about to start on another experimental medication. However, I did go, with help at the airport, and when we got there it was immediately clear why he had been so keen for me to come. He was intending to work for as much of the time as he could decently get away with, and it made things easier that I was there. I went kayaking with Theodora (which was lovely), while he spent as much time as he could indoors, glued to his screen. The biography has a picture of Derek in a kayak, but he went out only once, and I am sure he counted it as a Duty. I have some photographs of him during that holiday that would have been much more representative of his time there: working in our room and apparently wholly unaware of where he was.

When I returned, leaving Derek at NYU, it was clear that, although I had been under treatment for a year and no longer in the worst pain, I was not getting better and it was not clear why. There were tests and scans, but no one could find anything. Then new symptoms began to show more often, and one day, with Derek still away, I suddenly developed aphasia. It was difficult to get help, as I could not make myself understood over the phone; and my Lithuanian cleaner, who was with me, knew nothing about the medical services or what to do. Fortunately, at that moment Derek happened to phone from America, and he could tell her. I was taken by ambulance to hospital. It turned out not to be a stroke, which was the first idea, and by the next day I had recovered. But it did not bode well.

Then in September, when Derek was back with me in London, I suddenly found I could not move. He got me to A & E at University College Hospital, and I was kept in the neurological hospital in Queen Square for nine weeks while they tried to work out what was wrong. This is one of the main neurological centres in the world, but they could find nothing helpful in the relevant literature, and it was obviously serious. My state was variable, but I was decidedly neurologically abnormal and seriously ill, and a couple of times I thought I was dying.

This was a difficult time for Derek. Except for a trip to Oxford to argue about the proofs of the covers of Volume 3, he stayed in London all the time. I did not want him to visit just for the sake of visiting, but I did sometimes need things from home, and this must have been seriously burdensome for him, though he did not complain. He apparently had to stop and rest often on the walk from Euston to Queen Square, and on one of the stops forgot to pick up the case he had with things he was bringing for me. He was obviously not at all well and was now having to look after me, without anyone to look after him and the house. We were both worried about the other. Fortunately my sister came to London a couple of times and told me that Derek expressed great gratitude for the help she gave him (such as showing him how to use the washing machine).

Most of what I know about Derek during that time, in my confused state, comes from what I have heard from other people. Several people told me later that he seemed to have been very disoriented and agitated, uncharacteristically calling friends of mine he scarcely knew. My sister and Lyn both found him breaking into weeping episodes.

The hospital eventually got enough of a diagnosis, via a risky cranial biopsy done reluctantly, of what they tentatively called rheumatoid vasculitis. It was the third label they had given whatever it was; it still all seemed to be new to them. They decided on what seemed the most appropriate treatment, and in November, shortly after the Trump election, they let me out, still with a very uncertain prognosis. They warned me that after so long in hospital it would take several weeks to get any strength back, and that I would not reach whatever normal was going to be for a couple of years. Everything was still unsettled, and neither of us was well.

We continued to stay in London. Christmas was impending, and Derek volunteered without any pressure to come with me to my sister's family at Christmas. I think this was a real act of altruism. It went without saying that he would have a room to himself with a comfortable chair, and would not be expected to appear except at meals. Once again, he was struck by the warmth and the companionable atmosphere, but without having any idea of what brought it about or any inclination to join in. The last photo taken of us was there and shows Derek looking as though he did not know what was going on (which was the case) and giving a vague half smile while avoiding the camera, and me unrecognizable with a face swollen by steroids and whatever else it was they had pumped into me.

We returned to London. There was a nasty bug around that winter, and we both caught it. Derek became extremely unwell, but as was typical he carried on, working his usual full days, though he could no longer cope with his bike in the evening.

On New Year's Day, after a New Year's Eve that he had of course not noticed, he decided he needed more medication to try to deal with his cough, and, far too unwell to do so, he went off to the local pharmacy. He came back and dosed himself with Night Nurse, a symptom suppressant which was presumably not the best thing to have added to the amitriptyline and vodka, but he would not have thought to consult the pharmacist about that.

We went to bed shortly before midnight, and he started his winding down. Then he started to cough again, and he left the bedroom and sat in the nearby bathroom so as not to disturb me, even though I tried to persuade him to stay. He reappeared after a while, and said he had been choking. This was alarming, and I said we should go to the hospital. He refused; he said he did not need to. He obviously had no suspicion he might be in real danger. I had not heard the choking but kept very alert after that, making sure I could hear any sign of its reappearing, but it did not happen again. The coughing stopped, and he came back to the bedroom, standing by the bed, saying he was too hot and asking for a fan. I went for one—it took only a moment—and when I got back he was lying on the bed, apparently asleep. I settled down to listen to music with headphones.

But then slowly came the realization that he was too quiet, and rising panic as I could not detect any breathing. I did not know what to do. I thought of neighbours who were doctors, but could not find their number. I called the emergency services, who assured me that help was coming, and also told me to get him on to the floor and attempt CPR. I did get him on to the floor, but I did not really know what I was doing and anyway was still far too weak to do anything useful.

The emergency services arrived and started CPR in earnest, but long before they had given up I realized, and I suppose actually began to hope, they would fail. He had been without oxygen for too long; and what would be the point of keeping the organism that had been Derek in some sort of life without its brain?

As he had been arguing the last time I had heard him lecture, we are not human beings. The human beings may outlive ourselves. By the time the ambulance arrived, he had already gone.

6 Retrospect

These biographies and memoirs of Derek as a person would probably not have interested him much. He would have been deeply affected by the interest and affection shown in their production, but probably not much concerned with their content. As he once said, he did not want to be a well-rounded human being. He was deeply, essentially, an academic and aesthete, fascinated by the capacities of the human mind in advancing knowledge and creating things of beauty, and he thought of the purpose of his life in terms of advancing such achievements. But more ordinary people are interested in what makes the extraordinary ones, which is why the people who knew them should write about them.

He was indeed extraordinary. He had started with the great advantage of parents who were determined to give their children a good education, and whose relatively well-paid profession made that possible, but all that followed came from what he achieved himself. He was manifestly brilliant, and his wide range of abilities made so many choices available to him that he was able to do exactly what he wanted to do, with very few compromises.

By the time I met him he was at All Souls, and philosophy was fixed as the main purpose of his life. He had chosen an area of enquiry that he cared deeply about—that he thought really mattered—and where he judged he had the ability to make significant advances, and his time was mainly dedicated to trying to make those advances. He described himself as a philosopher's philosopher. He really cared, passionately, about reaching the truth, but he also cared about what the truth was. He thought it would be appalling if it were true that nothing really mattered.

Also, permanently in the background, were his intense feelings for beauty in art, architecture, the natural world, poetry, and music. My impression is that if he had thought he could produce outstanding work in any of these areas, he might have pursued them, but that he judged that he would not be able to achieve anything of the very highest quality in any of them and had no interest in spending his time on anything less. He decided that his abilities for criticism could be best put into practice in his architectural photography, and he threw into that nearly all the time and effort that did not go into philosophy, as well as a huge amount of money.

What he wanted to do in both areas was produce something of real objective value, which would in its particular way make the world better than it would have been without it. I am sure he hoped his pictures would always be valued, though he said relatively little about that. But the philosophy was what really mattered. He often said his life would have been wasted if he had not succeeded in his arguments in *On What Matters*. Fortunately, even people who have doubts about his success in that respect have no doubt that his life was not wasted.

Derek often spoke about how competitive his schools had been, with their regular rankings, as if this explained his drive and focus, and, from what he said, it was clear that in the first part of his life he had been seriously competitive. Brilliant as he was, he could not have so consistently come top at the Dragon and Eton without working extremely hard at it. In those settings, winning was itself his object, because doing better than other people was necessary to get him into a position where he would be able to choose what he really wanted to do.

This is shown by one or two of the rather entertaining lengths to which he sometimes went. He told me that he had sometimes in history exams invented quotations from texts in other languages (Czech?) to support the case he was arguing for; though maybe if that was based on enough knowledge to appear plausible to the examiner, it may not quite count as cheating. Another thing he told me was that when one of his All Souls appointment decisions was coming up, he suddenly realized that one of his referees had effusively thanked him in the acknowledgments to a book, and Derek, afraid that if the college committee saw this it would devalue the reference, went and bought up all the copies of the book he could find in Oxford to lessen the chance that his assessors would see it. (I have not been able to establish who the referee was.) And in general when his mind was set on some particular end, from fixing his position at All Souls to getting the colours right on the covers of his books, and indeed in buying West Kennett House, he was obsessive to the extent of ruthlessness in his determination to achieve it.

Although he could be competitive, however, it never seemed that any part of his purpose was winning for its own sake. None of the intensity he applied to his main projects seemed to have had anything whatever to do with a wish to prove himself above other people. His focus was always outward, on what he was trying to achieve. Of course he wanted other people to admire and value what he did, because that would confirm that it really was of value, but he never tried to denigrate or belittle other people or put them down, and he readily recognized and acknowledged ideas he thought were good. He seemed completely unaware of the nuances of status competition. He was dogged in argument, but never arrogant or vain. That was why so many people liked him, and many were fond of him.

And, of course, as everyone knows, Derek was, quite genuinely, very kind and universally benevolent. There really was no hint whatever of wishing anyone harm, and no malice or spite, and this was as true behind the scenes as it was in public. He was, of course, intellectually convinced that wishing even your enemies harm as an end in itself must be wrong. I was never sure whether he attributed his own benign feelings to the intellectual conviction, and hoped that reasoning might persuade other people to feel equally benign, but many philosophers with similar intellectual convictions know how hard they are to maintain in the face of strong reactive emotions. It is true that, as he himself realized, he anyway had very little cause to have such emotions, since if you keep winning all the competitions you have not much scope for resentment. It is easy to be benevolent if you have everything you want. But it did seem deep in his character.

On the other hand, all this was in a way negative. He wished everyone well, and his work was largely directed to questions relevant to how the world could be made better, but very little of his life was directed towards doing things with, or for, other people. He was fond of many people, and was often generous and helpful, but his essential focus was his projects. He was happy to do endless discussing, reading, and commenting on philosophy, and to be generous and helpful in that area, because philosophy was his purpose. But interactions with other people were rarely purposes in their own right, and on the whole he was little involved with anything that depended on cooperation, reciprocity, and compromise. He was not self-centred or demanding, but he was not positively unselfish and giving. Most of his mind was fixed on his own projects, and he was uncompromising in his dedication to them.

So, where did I fit into this? And the earlier women?

We, too, mattered far less than his real purposes. We were certainly not essential: not something he would mention if he were giving an account of his life, or no more than in passing. In that way, Derek's love was of his life a thing apart.

I originally did not plan to say anything about what Derek told me about his earlier girlfriends, because I was regarding it as confidential. But as some things have been discovered from other sources and now appear in David Edmonds's biography, it does not seem inappropriate to mention a few relevant things, at least as regards Derek.

He had been very romantically attached to his undergraduate girlfriend Mary Clemmey. He spoke of her as his first love, and he had strong and sentimental memories of that love. He particularly remembered an occasion when he travelled from Oxford to Birmingham to meet her, when she was going to be there for only twenty minutes when changing buses. He said it didn't occur to him not to. She doesn't remember it, but it was clearly deep in his consciousness as a striking romantic gesture. He wrote her real love letters as well, saying he would love her for ever. But even though I know Derek's uncompromising attitudes well, I was still shocked at the story in the biography that when much later he ran into her in Oxford, and she suggested meeting for coffee, he refused. He said they had nothing to talk about. How could those feelings have become so completely detached from the person that he did not want to spend even an hour with her?

I suppose some of the paradox may be attributed to the relationship's having happened on the far side of 1963, when the sexual revolution really did change the atmosphere as perceptibly as Larkin said it did. When sex was officially off limits, there was more scope for indulging in romantic yearnings. Derek certainly had a strong romantic streak, and I think he must have been exploring such feelings. It was also at a time before his duomania set in, and he was still experimenting with poetry and literary styles, and no doubt poetic emotions. It was also, of course, before the time of his dependence on his drugs, which may have been significant. Anyway, he seems never to have written anything of that kind later.

Derek also told me that when his transatlantic relationship with Patricia Zander started (initiated by her), he had been "blissfully happy"; but he almost never saw her (twice, perhaps?—and this was long before the days of the internet or even common international calls), and when he did see her, he would not let her stay with him overnight. He told me that when the relationship with Susan Hurley (also initiated by her, but in response to evident interest from Derek) came to an end with her engagement to another man, he was very upset. But he also said that he had refused to spend much time with her because he was writing *Reasons and Persons*, and had even rejected her suggestion that she should come and sit in his room while they both worked independently. He would not have seen the point of it. His own lack of feeling for intuitive connectedness meant he had little understanding of—or sufficient concern for—those kinds of feelings in women. He could see that they wanted these things, but would make no concessions. And not only that: he was also actively encouraging Susan to see the man she did eventually marry—one that he himself regarded as very attractive—and nevertheless was shocked as well as upset when that connection brought Susan's relationship with him to an end. Derek often commented that he didn't understand jealousy. I took to replying to that by quoting Mr Rochester: "You never felt jealousy, did you, Miss Eyre? Of course not, because you never felt love."

Putting all that together with my own experience, what did he want from relationships with women? Sex, of course. But when the women involved turned out to want more of him than he was willing or able to give, he seemed to think, with Sophocles and Origen, that it was a nuisance that diverted his attention from where it should be. The cost of a relationship, if there were the slightest encroachment on what he wanted to do or the slightest sign of incomprehensible interpersonal stresses, was too high. He did once say, in a time of tension, that he should have been castrated at birth.

But he did also appear to want a real connection, and that was where the romanticism seemed to lie. He said early on, "I was afraid I would die alone", and those feelings were also suggested by his having tried so hard for a year to learn "Dover Beach". As I said before, that reflected his general feelings about the need to establish a firm foundation for secular ethics and a purpose for life to replace receding religious certainties, but it also suggested he wanted a fixed romantic love to cling to while he did it. I suppose that was borne out by the permanence, through various permutations, of the connection with me. After both the gaps in the relationship, I was responsible for the relevant changes in geography, but it was he who initiated the reconnection.

What was lacking, however, was the module of directly sensed connection and intuitive recognition of reciprocity where real love, and indeed real friendship, lie: the empathy that Baron-Cohen says is missing in one kind of extreme male brain. With most women this in itself must make for mutual incomprehension, and inevitable tensions, even with such an intrinsically kind man.

But what was there instead? What was it like to be Derek? I suppose to whatever extent Derek could not read what was going on in more commonplace other minds, they must have been correspondingly unaware of what went on in his. That is where, inevitably, there must be a limit to which I can be certain I understood him. Most of the time, there is no doubt, his mind was on philosophy and matters of the mind, but he was not in the least unfeeling or unemotional. As everyone knows, he wept easily. But what exactly connected the weeping episodes? What was there in common between the outburst about Bach and the unfinished *The Art of Fugue* and similar breakdowns that I was told happened when I was in danger and in hospital for two months? And why did it mean so much to him when we actually married? He was manifestly happier when we were together, as long as I could keep incomprehensible stresses out of the way. He really did love me, even if not in a way I fully understand.

So what do I think of it all now?

I wish I had had the confidence not to go to West Kennett. At least, I suppose I do. There would have been a great loss, as our domestic life was very happy in itself and I really did love the place (more that Derek did). But it turned out to have been an enormous waste of time and opportunity for me, as well as a great source of sadness and distress when it eventually had to end. I also find it particularly poignant to realize that if the Oxford house where I now live had been available when we were first looking, Derek would unquestionably have wanted it. West Kennett, with its consequent and subsequent upheavals, need never have happened. The course of life would have been significantly different, and almost certainly better, for both of us.

I also wish I could have read Sacks and Baron-Cohen earlier, ideally in 1983. That was impossible, of course, since they were not writing until much later, when the relevant ideas were only just becoming known. If I had had that framework for understanding the situation I was dealing with, I would have been able to work out much sooner how to manage the perception gap, rather than finding out how to do it by trial and error and heartache. Derek had neither the understanding nor the motivation to find such a framework, but I could have done it, and to a large extent, eventually, I did. It would probably also have been possible to avoid the long semi-separation while I was in London, during which Derek manifestly did spiral inwards and seriously deteriorated in ways that seem to have damaged his health and even narrowed his mind. It would have been much better for Derek as well as for me, philosophically as well as personally, if we had gone on living together, even though—or perhaps because—we did not spend much time talking about his philosophy.

I also wish I had not unnecessarily curtailed my own life in the way I did, through my rather standard views about what couples did together and relationships rooted in reciprocity. Derek did not need such adjustments, but I did not understand that then.

Oh well. *Si jeunesse savait, si vieillesse pouvait.*

But even if I had understood all this from the very beginning, I don't think I would have given up altogether. Derek was never anything other than supportive and admiring, and once I had stopped looking for things that were simply not there and working on the very many things that were, it was an easy and a very affectionate relationship. We both eventually had a clear understanding of what was going on and learned to treat the differences as humorous. When he said he loved me, as he often did, I would look arch, and he would say, "I have a funny way of showing it?" Then he might say, "I have loved you in my fashion," (quoting Poe). "Would you rather I loved you in someone else's fashion?" To that I would say, "Yes, of course." But who knows? I certainly wanted more from him than there was to be got, but on the other hand if the missing module had been there, could Derek still have been what he was in other ways? Probably not; Baron-Cohen quotes Asperger as saying, "It seems that for success in science or art, a dash of autism is essential" (169). If you really are to devote your life to the pursuit of the sublime, it is as well not to be distracted by normal interpersonal emotions.

Anyway, I was not deterred, even though—or perhaps because?—I realized very early on that I was a relatively small part of his life. I remember telling someone that I was "his other . . . quarter". I did not want a normal domestic life, either. I would have managed my own life very differently if I had understood Derek earlier, but I don't think I would not have stayed with him. I could not have married anyone else.

The fact is, he was the love of my life, and it is rather hard to explain why in any further terms. I am materially better off than I would have been if our incomes had not been joined, of course, but that was never any kind of issue: I was happily independent when we met and could have remained so. There was nothing gained in the way of reflected status, since for many years most people who were aware of either of us did not know about the connection with the other; in fact, I think that in the eyes of some people who were aware of it, my philosophical standing was if anything diminished, because in Derek's circle I was merely his partner, and barely known otherwise. He did not open up new opportunities for me; on the contrary, I rather dropped out of public view when we lived together. He did not widen my social circle, because he did not have one; in practice (not deliberately), he severely contracted it. He was of little use for anything recreational, because we did together only what he wanted to do, and soon after I met him most possibilities of that kind were perpetually over the horizon. He did not in any way advance my career: he was neither my teacher nor my referee, and I had started to establish my terrain—very different from his—before I knew him. I learned an enormous amount from him, of course; but I did not often find it helpful to discuss my work with him. Even my eventual return to Oxford had nothing to do with him.

As he never seemed a means to any further end, therefore, I presume he must have been the end in himself. I once found myself saying, "Women will put up with a lot for a high enough calibre man." Maybe I was right, at least in a rare case like this, where the high calibre comes with undemandingness, kindness, and manifest appreciation and affection.

Like my cat,[2] Derek did simply what he wanted to do. He had, of course, Reasons for what he wanted to do, and those reasons led him to seek out and establish himself in surroundings where he could thenceforward pursue his purposes without hindrance. Like my cat, he was pleased to have me around and in his house. He would purr appreciatively when I did things that he

[2] Readers of *Reasons and Persons* may remember the first sentence of its Introduction: "Like my cat, I often simply do what I want to do."

liked; he would play the occasional game he wanted to play and even learn new ones; and he would be very affectionate whenever he was not wholly absorbed by his feline purposes. But, as with other cats, it was on his own terms and in his own fashion. We may well wonder why we bother with cats, but for some reason some of us seem to.

He was remarkable, he was lovely, and he is totally irreplaceable.

3

To Derek, with Love

Larry Temkin

In 1977, two chance conversations changed the direction of my philosophical life.[1] First, a fellow graduate student at Princeton, Milton Wachsberg, convinced me to attend a course led by a visiting professor—someone of whom I had never heard. Milton claimed that some people regarded the professor in question as the smartest living philosopher—which, in a department that included, among others, David Lewis, Saul Kripke, Tom Nagel, Tim Scanlon, Dick Rorty, and Gil Harman, was a bold claim. The course, given by Derek Parfit, did not disappoint. It covered much of the seminal work later developed in *Reasons and Persons*,[2] and it was *easily* the most fascinating course I ever took. Later, another fellow graduate student, Eileen O'Neill, and I were

[1] Most of this essay is based on first-person memories. In certain cases, where I have quoted Derek Parfit, our conversations were indelibly etched in my brain, and I am confident that I have quoted him verbatim. However, as some of our conversations took place decades ago, I grant that in some cases I have put an exchange in quotation marks mainly for literary effect, and I am taking poetic license in doing so. Still, I want to make clear that in no cases have I fabricated a story about Derek. More particularly, I am confident about the content and tone of any "quoted" material, even if my memory may have failed me as to the *exact* words used at the time.
Some of the stories conveyed in this essay have been told by me on other occasions. One such occasion was a three-hour interview with me by Larissa MacFarquhar, in May 2011, when she was gathering background information for her excellent *New Yorker* article on Derek, "How To Be Good" (September 5, 2011, issue). Another was at a special meeting of the Rutgers Philosophy Club memorializing Derek, in the spring of 2017. I am most grateful to Larissa MacFarquhar for providing me with a transcript of our interview, and to Daniel Cappell for transcribing a recording of my Philosophy Club talk. I drew on both of those transcriptions in preparing this essay.

I would like to acknowledge a debt to both my wife, Meg Temkin, and my son, Daniel Temkin, for providing me with a few details included in this essay. Meg also gave me valuable editorial comments on the essay. Unfortunately, a few details came from sources that I don't recall, for which I apologize. Jeff McMahan and I began talking about writing a memoir of sorts, honoring Derek, within days of his death. We assumed that any memoir would also include contributions from others, such as Ruth Chang, Janet Radcliffe Richards (Derek's wife), and Theodora Ooms (Derek's sister). I am most grateful to Jeff for carrying this project forward and for all the other extraordinary work that he has done on behalf of Derek. Finally, as will be apparent throughout this essay, my biggest debt, by far, is to Derek himself.

[2] Derek Parfit, *Reasons and Persons* (Oxford: Oxford University Press, 1984).

Larry Temkin, *To Derek, with Love* In: *Derek Parfit: His Life and Thought*. Edited by: Jeff McMahan, Oxford University Press. © Oxford University Press 2025. DOI: 10.1093/9780191915307.003.0003

discussing our readiness for the next year's job market. Eileen wasn't worried. She was going to France for the year to study at the Sorbonne. What a brilliant idea! Perhaps I could take a year off and study at Oxford with Parfit.[3]

Three days later, I ran into Parfit at the copy machine in Princeton's 1879 Hall. I asked if he was going to be in Oxford the following year. "Why?" he answered. "Were you thinking of coming to study with me?" I said that I was, without, of course, elaborating on my idea's recent origin. Though he hardly knew me, Parfit immediately replied, "I think that would be a *marvelous* idea." Little could Derek or I have anticipated the impact those two sentences would have on our lives—a mere eighteen words, uttered with Derek's characteristic warmth, kindness, and encouragement.

The following summer, my wife Meg and I arrived in Oxford, where, thanks largely to Derek, we experienced one of the greatest years of our lives. Having gained an extra year for research, I decided to treat myself to some pure philosophical fun. Before turning to my dissertation, I would write up some criticisms of Parfit's work regarding future generations. I worked all day, every day, for the next six weeks or so, writing a fifty-page paper on Derek's work. Included within it was a twenty-five-page "aside", entitled "Reflections on Equality."

I dropped the paper off with a porter at All Souls College and returned to our flat on Little Clarendon Street. It took me about fifteen minutes. By the time I had returned, Derek had already called and left a message with Meg. I should come back to All Souls immediately; we needed to talk about my paper! I returned to All Souls, checked in with the porter, and headed towards Derek's stairwell. As I approached, I heard the distinctive clop of Derek's boots as he ran down the stairs at full tilt. Reaching the bottom, he saw me, and, in his clipped British accent, he immediately gushed, "You have written a *most* impressive paper." He then went on to say a lot of other flattering things, some of which I vaguely remember, but most of which I failed to hear, because, frankly, upon hearing his initial sentence, I basically swooned. What I *do* remember is that Derek told me that whatever I was previously thinking about writing my dissertation on, I should forget it. I needed to write my dissertation on equality, because, he claimed, I had something to say about that topic that had never been said before.

Thus began my forty-year relationship with Derek Parfit. Although Derek had already worked with a number of graduate students at both Oxford

[3] This paragraph, and the following five sentences, are taken verbatim from the Preface to my book *Inequality* (New York: Oxford University Press, 1993, p. vii).

and Princeton, I was the first for whom he served as the principal dissertation director. He was my teacher, mentor, inspiration, editor, and colleague. Beyond that, he was my oldest, and dearest, friend in the profession. After that initial seminar with Derek in 1977, and working with him in Oxford in 1978–9, I took another seminar with him in Princeton in the fall of 1979. I then continued working with him in Oxford every summer until my first child was born in 1986. After that, we regularly traveled to work or teach with each other at Oxford, Harvard, Rice, and Rutgers. This continued until his untimely death on January 1, 2017.

Since his death, I have lain awake for *countless* hours on *countless* nights thinking about Derek. My lifetime of memories of Derek could fill up several volumes. However, most of my memories are too deeply personal to be shared or wouldn't be of much interest to those who didn't know him well. Accordingly, I shall restrict myself in this essay to passing along a representative set of first-hand memories that I hope most readers will find interesting.

Before proceeding, I want to emphasize that Derek was, in my judgment, sui generis. He was, quite literally, unlike anyone else I have ever known. In Derek's presence, I always felt like one of the group of blind men in the famous Indian parable—each touching just one part of a great elephant. The one touching the trunk thought the elephant was like a snake; the one touching the tail thought the elephant was like a rope; the one touching the side thought the elephant was like a wall; the one touching the ear thought the elephant was like a fan; the one touching the leg thought the elephant was like a tree; and the one touching the tusk thought the elephant was like a spear. Each, of course, was partly right, but none had a clue as to the full nature of the elephant.

Although there have been times in my life when I felt that I was as close to Derek and knew him as well as anyone else, I don't pretend to have a complete and definitive picture of the remarkable Derek Parfit. Others also knew him well, and in different contexts. And they may have accurate insights into aspects of his life and personality that I lack, some of which, no doubt, may seemingly conflict with the picture that I convey. So, read the following as just one small glimpse into Derek Parfit, filtered through my very particular lens and perspective. I hope that you find it interesting, fun, and perhaps even a bit revealing of my amazing and complex friend.

One last comment. This essay will be divided into a series of first-hand anecdotes. I shall impose some organizational structure on a few of them; however, to a large extent they will be presented as a stream of consciousness. This reflects the way that I like to think about Derek—as I lie awake in the middle of the night, I usually just let my mind wander, basking in the warm glow that my memories evoke.

* * *

I consider myself a perfectionist. I spent five years on my first article, which went through thirteen major drafts. Each draft was subjected to a torrent of detailed criticisms from Derek, accompanied by his persistent mantra that "It can always get better." Similarly, I spent three years on my second article, fifteen years on my first book, and twenty-seven years on my second book. In each case, there was a constant process of ongoing revisions in light of copious penetrating, often devastating, but always constructive, criticisms from Derek.

Derek always had a keen view of what needed to be done to a typescript to get it "just right." And he was relentless in pushing himself, and others, to achieve that end. The first draft of my first article ran to over 120 pages. In that draft, I had a lengthy argument for some claim that ran to around twelve pages. Derek read the draft, told me that he liked the claim, but that I could make that point in about two sentences! The second draft of the article ran to about 100 pages, and the argument in question had been reduced to around eight pages. When he got to that section of the second draft, Derek told me that it was much better, but that it still needed to be shorter. The third draft of the article ran to around sixty pages, and by then I had managed to reduce the offending argument to only three pages. Again, Derek insisted that I could make my point in about two sentences! This continued through each draft. Each draft was, in Derek's view, getting better and better, but it could still be improved. By the penultimate draft, the twelfth, I had managed to reduce the original argument to a mere half a page. It took a lot of work to get to that point, and I was very proud of myself. Derek's response to that version was to scribble a curved line adjacent to that paragraph next to which he wrote "2 s." He was relentless!

In Derek's mind my claim was important, but it called for two carefully constructed sentences, *and no more*. In the thirteenth and final version of that article, "Inequality"[4]—which, thanks to Derek, was ultimately selected as one of the top ten articles published in any philosophy journal that year—the

[4] Larry Temkin, "Inequality," *Philosophy and Public Affairs*, 15 (1986): pp. 99–121.

argument had been reduced to exactly two sentences. At that point, and only at that point, was Derek finally satisfied!

I mention this because, although I know many people who are perfectionists, myself included, I have never known anybody who was even *remotely* as much of a perfectionist as Derek was. Derek's perfectionism as a philosopher was legendary. But, in fact, his perfectionism extended to the very core of who he was. It manifested itself throughout his life, including, most notably, in his devotion to photography.

* * *

There was a significant period of his life, including when I first met him, during which, in addition to his devotion to philosophy, Derek was devoted to photography. Those were the days when one had an old-fashioned camera, with different lenses, that one had to lug everywhere, along with a tripod, if one was serious about one's photography. Moreover, unlike today, you couldn't take as many pictures as you'd like at no cost. You actually had to pay for film, and you had to pay to have your film developed, if you wanted to see how your photographs turned out.

Derek wasn't interested in just any old photographs. He was interested in architectural photographs and, more particularly, in photographs of certain very particular architectural styles, which could be found most notably in his two favorite cities, Venice and Leningrad (renamed St. Petersburg in 1991). Given this, Derek faithfully made pilgrimages to these two cities every year, for many years, to take photographs. These really *were* pilgrimages for Derek, something akin to visiting a holy shrine because of one's faith. He had no interest in going anywhere else simply to get away for a few days on a vacation. No, he went to the same two cities, over and over again, each time for ten or so days.

Why? Because he wanted to take the perfect pictures of the perfect places! Each year, he would go at the same time of year to each city. And each year, he would photograph the very same buildings, or bridges, in an attempt to get the perfect shot.

I remember Derek once telling me that on some mornings he would wake up three hours before dawn, so that he could have his camera, lens, and tripod all set up in order to photograph a particular building just as the sun was coming up and before anyone else was on the streets. However, for Derek, it was all about the lighting and the cloud cover. And if the lighting and cloud cover were not *exactly* right, he wouldn't even bother to take a single shot. He would simply pack up his equipment, go back to bed, and try again the next day! (To fully appreciate this story, one needs to understand that Derek suffered from insomnia that was so severe that he needed heavy doses of prescription drugs, along with vast quantities of vodka, in order to be able to sleep at night. This concoction worked, but made it almost physically impossible for him to even wake up, let alone be alert and functional, much before 11 a.m. So for Derek to be up long before dawn speaks volumes about the level of commitment that he had to his art.)

Derek was extremely selective about everything when it came to his photography. The subject matter. The setting. The time of day. The cloud cover. The presence of extraneous objects, such as people, vehicles, animals, or telephone wires. (Unwanted objects that couldn't be avoided prior to a shot were painstakingly removed later, initially with "touch-ups" during the development process, and later via computer with the advent of digital photography.) However, as selective as Derek was in taking his photographs, he was even more selective in deciding which photographs might be worth keeping.

I remember sitting with Derek in his tiny bedroom at All Souls College after one of his photography expeditions. This was the only time that I was ever in that bedroom. Derek's three rooms in All Souls were, quite literally, the messiest three rooms I have ever seen in my life. His main room and office looked like a tornado had just swept through, with books, papers, photographs, and record albums strewn everywhere, from floor to ceiling. His bedroom had all of that, with Derek's socks, pajamas, and other articles of clothing thrown in for good measure, all scattered across the unmade bed as well as every inch of the floor. Derek didn't seem to mind if visitors saw the mess in his main room and office—one suspected that he even took a bit of pride in having perfected the art of messiness!—but in a rather charming display of modesty he tended to immediately close his bedroom door whenever a visitor entered his quarters.

Anyway, on this particular occasion, Derek was about to comb through a large number of slides from an unusually productive photography trip. He had a *thousand* slides in all, and I sat next to him while he held them up to the light, one by one, with a giant trash bin next to him. He looked at the first, said "no good," and threw it out. He looked at the second, repeated "no good," and threw it out. He looked at the third, again said "no good," and threw it out. This process continued for almost two hours. Bearing in mind that Derek didn't even *take* a shot unless the conditions were "just right," do you know how many pictures he saved out of a thousand? (This is a true story. I remind you that *all* my stories in this essay are true, so far as my memory serves me correctly.) Three. *Three* pictures were deemed worthy of further consideration.[5] So, Derek was very, very particular about his photographs. And when he finally decided to print a photograph from the slide, the result was usually amazing. Derek hung a number of these amazing photographs around his main room in All Souls College. And later, when digital photography enabled him to reprint copies of his favorite photographs, he was extremely generous in sharing them with his friends. I consider myself fortunate to have a good number of his very best photographs in my office at Rutgers, in my wife's home office, and, especially, in my home office.

* * *

The preceding is, I believe, interesting in its own right. However, I include it mainly as useful background to one of my favorite stories about Derek and his passion for photography. The story is deeply revealing about his generosity, the type of perfectionism to which he subscribed, and how very different he was from everyone else I have ever met.

One day, when I was visiting Derek, I found myself moving around his main room admiring his beautiful photographs. One photograph in particular caught my eye, and I paused to stare it at more intently. It was an unusual photograph for many reasons, including the fact that it was not of Venice or Leningrad, but Oxford.

The Radcliffe Camera has been called "the heart and soul of England." It sits in the middle of what is arguably the most famous quad in England, and you could see it directly from Derek's window, towering magnificently above the most beautiful gate of All Souls College. One night, there had been a light dusting of snow—a relative rarity in Oxford—and the Radcliffe Camera was lightly covered in snow, as was the great lawn of All Souls, and the beautiful All Souls gate. Derek had captured this moment perfectly, and the result, in my judgment, was magical.

So, I've stopped in front of this amazing picture, and I'm just staring at it, and Derek asks me, "Do you like it?" "Like it?" I reply. "It's gorgeous. It's unbelievably gorgeous." To this Derek says, and he's like a little kid when he says

[5] This anecdote was previously presented, and mistakenly attributed to Frances Kamm, in Larissa MacFarquhar's *New Yorker* essay "How To Be Good." In fact, MacFarquhar heard it from me, as the transcript of our interview confirms. Frances Kamm has verified (in conversation) that she had no such experience with Derek.

it, "Oh, I'm *so* glad you like it." He then proceeds to tell me, with great pride, exactly how he got that picture.

In those predigital days, Derek wasn't able to modify pictures on his computer and print out whatever he wanted on a high-quality printer. And he wasn't willing to entrust his precious slides to a local printer. Instead, when there was a slide that he thought was worthy of developing into a print, he would personally make the roughly three-hour round trip from his rooms in All Souls College to the office of a professional developer in London to have his slide processed. This particular developer was supposed to be the best in England—also, Derek confided, the most expensive. Hence, Derek claimed, with much pride and just a touch of embarrassment, he, Derek, was the only non-professional photographer to use this person's services.

So, Derek had made the trip to London, dropped off his slide, told the developer what he was looking for, and returned to Oxford. A week or so later, he returned to London to check out the photograph, and to his dismay it wasn't right. The developer needed to reprint it. In particular, he needed to alter the color. It had too much yellow. Derek returned to Oxford. And a week or so later he repeated the process. This time the developer had succeeded in toning down the yellow, but the result was a photograph that was too pink. That, too, was unacceptable. It would have to be redone! The developer was happy to keep at it, but, as already noted, he was the most expensive developer in London, hence it was costing Derek a small fortune each time he did so. Still, to Derek, there were no other options. Derek needed the photograph to be perfect, and he had a very clear idea in his mind of exactly what that meant. Nothing less would be acceptable.

According to Derek, this process went on *seven* times—each requiring a considerable expenditure of time, effort, and money—before the photograph was *just* the way Derek envisioned that it *should* be. (Photography, like ethics, was a normative enterprise for Derek!) And now, after seven times traveling back and forth from London using the most expensive developer in London, there it was, on Derek's wall, unbelievably gorgeous. And I'm standing in front of it, admiring it.

At this point Derek says, "So, you really like it?" I say, "Derek, it's stunning." Derek replies, "I'm so glad you like it. Take it. It's yours!" At this point, the conversation proceeds roughly as follows: "I can't take your picture. I mean, you just told me what you did to get this picture, you went down to London and . . ." "No, no, no, no. None of that matters. I want you to have it. It's yours." "No, I can't take it." "Larry, just take it!" "I can't. I'm sorry. I love it. But I can't take your picture." The conversation ends. I return to my Oxford lodgings, and sometime later I return to my home in Houston, Texas, where I am teaching at Rice University.

A while later, Derek came to visit me at Rice. And, as was usually the case when he visited me for a short while, he stayed with me and my family. Now, in the old days, when Derek traveled, he traveled with only one bag. And it wasn't a suitcase. Rather, it was a medium-size black canvas bag, of the sort that people often take to the beach. It was invariably overflowing, and hence never zippered. This was in the pre-computer days, and everything that he carried with him for a three-week trip to the United States was stuffed into that bag. Everything.

So Derek's at my house, and he's got his bag with him, and his face suddenly brightens: "Oh, Larry! I've got something for you." "OK, right," I reply, wondering what it could possibly be. Derek then takes his bag, puts it up on the kitchen table, and starts rummaging through it. He pulls out three white shirts, some underpants, a couple of pairs of black socks, a red tie, some toiletries, a whole bunch of rumpled papers (because all of his papers are stuffed in there, along with his clothes), several books (because they're all stuffed in there as well), and it's all coming out and being scattered across the table. Finally, he spots what he is looking for. "Ah! Here it is!" he exclaims triumphantly. And he reaches in, and, with great pride, he puts in front of my face a photograph that is, to my mind, nothing short of appalling!

Derek had taken his incredibly gorgeous, magical photograph of the Radcliffe Camera, stuffed it into his overflowing bag, and carried it by bike, train, subway, plane, and car from Oxford to my home in Houston, and he was now proudly presenting it to me as a gift. But it was, of course, totally destroyed! It was wrinkled. It was bent. It was folded. It was creased. It was squished. It didn't look anything like the exquisite picture that had been hanging on his wall in Oxford. And Derek was looking at me with such pleasure and pride: "Here's the photograph!" "Derek. What is this?" "It's the photograph you so admired." "No, it's not! This has no relation to what I was admiring!"

This story reflects how incredibly generous Derek was, in his own way. And also how his way was unlike any other! It also provides insight into the kind of perfectionist that Derek was. For Derek, it was *extraordinarily* important that he get it right. But it was the *creative enterprise* that mattered, not the object itself that resulted from that enterprise. Having gotten it right, the mere physical instantiation of the photograph didn't matter to Derek one bit. Not one lick. Not so for the rest of us, who would have gone to great lengths to protect the incredible beauty of the photograph that Derek had so painstakingly produced.

Before proceeding, I want to add several codas to this story.

First, distraught by the condition of the photograph, I called the Houston Museum of Fine Arts and asked them if they could tell me who their art restorer was. They were kind enough to refer me to him, a man named Danny Clayton. So I took the photograph to Danny Clayton and told him, "I need you to do *something* with this." He replied, "I'll *try*, but I can't make any promises."

Clayton kept the photograph for six months. During this period he employed a host of the tricks of his trade to mitigate the damage: he steamed it, he ironed it, and he kept it in a press for months at a time. It cost me $350 (which in those days was a lot of money) to have the best art restorer in the city do what he could to repair the damage to the photograph that Derek had given me for free. And then I got the photograph professionally framed for another $175 or so. Despite the overall cost, it was well worth it. Besides this story, I now have this incredibly beautiful photograph hanging on my office wall at home, where I look at it, and admire it, almost every single day. However, to this day, and for the rest of my life, there is, and will be, a massive wrinkle right across the bottom half of the photo, and innumerable tiny wrinkles all around the edges, that even the great Danny Clayton couldn't get rid of.

Who does this sort of thing—permanently damaging a beautiful piece of art that they had poured their heart and soul into creating—without giving it a second thought? Only Derek!

This brings me to my second coda. I say only Derek, but perhaps that is too strong. Derek used to tell the story of a sect somewhere in Asia, whose members would throw themselves off the mountaintop on their wedding night, just after their moment of connubial bliss. Apparently, their thinking was that life would never be any better than it was at that moment and, having reached the pinnacle of their lives, it was better to end them then than to live on with the inevitable decline that would follow. I have not, myself, been able to find any information about this sect, but if they did exist, I think they were *crazy* to do what they did, and also *deeply* mistaken. Derek thought that as well, but I think he *understood* their position better than I, as I think he felt it resonated with his own conception of perfectionism.

Similarly, Derek once told me that Jack Rawls (as he was referred to by those who knew him well) once told him that if civilization ever did achieve a society that was perfectly just, it would no longer matter whether civilization continued or came to an end. I find it very hard to believe that Rawls actually held such a view—because I think it's nuts!—though I also have no reason to believe that Derek would make up such a story. Still, if Rawls did hold such a view, it suggests a perfectionist outlook very similar to Derek's.

Finally, I cannot resist one small bit of philosophy in this essay. I can see how someone might be attracted to a perfectionist view like the one that I have attributed to Derek, and which Derek attributed to the eccentric sect and to Rawls. However, if one *were* attracted to such a view of perfectionism, that would, in my mind, provide compelling reason to be a pluralist. That is, I believe there are a multitude of important reasons not to destroy a beautiful artwork, to go on living after the moment of connubial bliss, and to continue civilization far into the future, even if, from the standpoint of *perfection*, there would be nothing to be gained by doing so. Thus, to echo what I have long claimed regarding the ideal of equality, perfection matters. And it matters a lot. But it is *not all* that matters.

* * *

In the fall of 1979, I returned to Princeton from Oxford. One day, I was meeting with the great ancient philosopher Michael Frede. Frede asked me, "What's Derek Parfit like?" I said, "What do you mean?" And Michael, who knew that I'd just spent a year working with Derek and had become pretty close to him, elaborated, "Well, what's he like as a *friend*?"

I was taken aback by the question. I conceded that Derek *was* a little bit odd, and I wondered why Michael had asked me that question. Well, Michael continued, he is *supposed* to be really good friends with Gareth Evans—a philosopher with whom Derek had driven to Andalusia, and the first person acknowledged in *Reasons and Persons*—and Gareth was planning to travel to Venice at the same time that Derek was there. So, Gareth contacted Derek in advance of his arrival and suggested that they might get together for lunch and to talk. When it was determined that Derek was scheduled to leave by train on the same day Gareth was due to arrive, Gareth gently suggested that perhaps he might wait three hours and take a different train, so that they could meet up. But, according to Frede, Derek couldn't understand why he should do that, and he left Venice on his originally scheduled train.

I don't know whether Evans was hurt by this event, but Frede was clearly upset on his behalf. He wanted to know, "What kind of friend does that? What kind of friend isn't willing to delay his departure for a few hours in order to meet up with a good friend?" I didn't have a good answer for Frede, but I confess that his version of events rang true. In many ways, Derek was the kindest, most generous, and most supportive friend that I have ever known. He spent untold hours doing philosophy with me and, other than my wife and parents, Derek did far more to advance my welfare than anyone else. In addition, he went out of his way to host friends and family of mine visiting Oxford, to support students of mine, and to help my son in finding the right school to pursue his music studies. Yet Derek couldn't imagine that it might be worth delaying a return to the crucial work of philosophy—even if only for a few hours—*just* to meet up with a friend and talk. Derek was a great friend. But he wasn't *that* kind of friend.

* * *

Derek had a lot of silos in his life. By that I mean that, while he had a number of important people in his life, with whom he maintained unique one-on-one relationships, with very few exceptions he kept each relationship isolated from the others. So, for example, I was already very close to Derek by the fall of 1979. And he was already partners with Janet Radcliffe Richards by 1982. Yet, despite all the times that I visited Oxford, and that Derek visited me, during the first twenty years of our friendship I only met Janet *once*. And that was orchestrated by Janet, not by Derek, at a small dinner party that she hosted. (It was a particularly memorable evening. First, because I finally met Janet. And second, because it turned into the kind of "salon" event that rarely happens in the U.S. After a lovely meal, we all retired to a piano room, where Derek's mother, Jessie, played whatever tunes people requested, and most people, though decidedly not I, sang along—uncultured as I am, I didn't know either the tunes or the words!)

* * *

Here are a few other examples of the way Derek kept the different aspects of his life compartmentalized. Derek and I both liked art. And we both visited many of the world's great art museums. However, except on one occasion when Derek was visiting me in Houston and I took him to the Museum of Fine Arts, we never toured art museums together. Going to museums was just not something that Derek did with me. Yet it turned out that going to art museums *was* something that Derek did with Frances Kamm, and fairly frequently. But, of course, I only learned this from *her*, not from *him*.

Likewise, one day Derek was at my home, admiring a large onyx chess set that I had bought in Mexico many years previously. I asked Derek if he played chess. And he replied that he did. This was news to me, as I'd never seen a chess set in his lodgings, and he'd never given me any inkling that he might play. I asked if he'd like to have a game. Derek declined. Then, to avoid offending me, Derek offered up that he only played chess with one other person—someone he didn't name, of course! After a brief pause, Derek sheepishly confided that he and this other person occasionally fancied that they might be the two best chess players in the world! However, they would never know, since they never played anyone else.

I mentioned previously that Derek tried to help my son, Daniel, find an appropriate music school. Daniel was a percussionist at the time (he's now a composer), and one of the places at which he auditioned was the New England Conservatory. When Derek learned this, he told me that he had a friend who taught there, and he contacted her to determine whether the New England Conservatory was a good place for percussion (it was not), and where else he should consider. Naturally, he never told me his friend's name or anything about the nature of their relationship.

I learned, many years later, that his friend's name was Patricia Zander, and that she was, in fact, an *extraordinarily* accomplished pianist. Also, more importantly for my present purposes, it turned out that Derek and Patricia had known each other for decades and were extremely close. Of course, none of this information initially came from Derek! More surprisingly, I learned that I had, in fact, been in Patricia Zander's home many times, and that we had often seen each other. However, Derek had never thought, or bothered, to introduce us.

I later discovered that Derek often stayed at Patricia's home when he visited Harvard, and I had often been in her home to talk philosophy with Derek the year I was a Visiting Fellow at Harvard, and on other occasions when I visited Boston. However, I always assumed that Patricia was Derek's landlady, because whenever we crossed paths, Derek gave her a cursory greeting and then rushed me to his room to begin our discussions. Not once did Derek pause to say something like, "Oh, by the way, Larry, this is Patricia; Patricia, this is Larry," let alone tell each of us what the other did, or the roles that we played in his life.

I only discovered all this later, by sheer coincidence, because it turned out that this very famous pianist was the principal teacher of my daughter-in-law, Qing Jiang, when she was doing her doctorate at the New England Conservatory. Qing had often seen Derek going in and out of Patricia's home, when she was doing her lessons, and she later confessed that she occasionally wondered whether perhaps Derek and PZ (as Qing referred to her) were lovers! But they had never been introduced, and she had no idea who Derek was, or why he was staying in PZ's home. Anyway, one day my son, Daniel, accompanied Qing to one of her lessons, and when he walked into PZ's piano room he was immediately taken aback by her collection of photographs. Many of them looked strikingly familiar. So, the following conversation ensued. Daniel: "Who are these photographs by?" PZ: "You wouldn't know him—he's just a friend of mine. A philosopher." Daniel: "Derek Parfit?" PZ, amazed: "How do you know that?" Daniel: "Well, he's one of my dad's closest friends. And we have a lot of photographs just like these at home."

At that point, Patricia Zander explained her own longstanding and deep relationship with Derek, which, of course, Daniel and Qing promptly conveyed to me, along with Qing's observation that she had often seen Derek in Patricia's house, without realizing who he was. It was only then, of course, that I realized that I had crossed paths with Patricia on several occasions, and that Derek had never introduced us to each other, despite—or perhaps because of?—the significant relationships that we each, in our own way, had with him.

* * *

Derek used to call me quite frequently. For many years, the conversation almost always began something like this: "This is Derek." "Derek! Great to hear your voice." "I hope I'm not disturbing you. Is this a good time to talk?" "It's always a good time to talk with *you*." "I read your paper with great interest." And then *boom*, off we'd go. There was *never* any idle chit-chat. We'd start talking philosophy, and then, if I'd sent him a paper or set of comments, he'd invariably spend the next three hours or so destroying whatever I had sent him.

For years, this pattern continued, more or less without exception. Derek was all business. It was all philosophy all the time. This worked well for Derek. But I'm not wired that way. If I can put it this way, I'm kind of a *normal* human being. So, after a while, I would *occasionally* try to squeeze in something that resembled normal human interaction. This led to the following remarkable exchange, which I vividly remember to this day.

Derek had called, and the conversation started off exactly as it always did for him. "This is Derek. I hope I'm not disturbing you. I have read your paper with great interest, and . . . ." At that point, on this particular occasion, I forcefully cut him off before he could proceed: "Wait! Wait. Before we start talking about the paper, how's Janet?" This conversation took place sometime around 2004, so by then Janet had been Derek's significant other for over twenty years.

I could tell that Derek was taken aback. I could almost hear the wheels going around in his head on the other side of the ocean. He paused. He thought about it for a while. Finally, he responded to me with the following words: "She's fine." (Another pause.) "Why do you ask?"

Are you kidding me? I had to explain myself to Derek! So, somewhat exasperated, I said something like the following: "Well, you see Derek, I grew up in Milwaukee, Wisconsin. And you and I have known each other now for about twenty-seven years. And in Milwaukee, Wisconsin, friends ask other friends how the people in their lives are doing. Like, how's your mom doing, or how's your dad doing, or how are your children doing, or how is your wife or significant other doing? Now we have known each other a *long* time, and we're *friends*, and you've been together with Janet for over twenty years. So, asking you how Janet is doing is the *normal thing to do*! That's what normal people do; friends ask other friends how the important people in their lives are doing!"

Derek was quite puzzled by all that. But the story has an interesting and happy ending. From then on, for the remainder of his life, when Derek would call me up, the conversation would start as follows. "This is Derek. I hope I'm not disturbing you. Is this a good time to talk?" "It's always a good time to talk with you, Derek." "How's Meg?"

So Derek was capable of learning. And even if he didn't fully understand it, he was willing to indulge me with a bit of chit-chat about my family before turning to philosophy, because he now knew that it was important to *me*. Even more, as the years passed, he eventually warmed up to the practice. And over the last ten years of his life, we would often share information about what was going on in our lives and those of our loved ones.

* * *

In 1988, Derek Parfit and I agreed to go to a conference in Austin, Texas, on the topic of *Justice between Age Groups and Generations*. I was teaching at Rice at the time, and I believe that Derek was visiting at Harvard that semester. Derek arranged a flight to Austin via Houston so that we could fly to the conference together, and Derek could return with me to Houston to talk philosophy for a few extra days after the conference before he returned to Harvard.

Having arranged adjoining seats, I boarded the plane in Houston and sat down next to Derek. After settling into my seat, I looked over at Derek, and I noticed that he had a ring on his finger. It was a gold ring. A *wedding* ring.

I was so angry. I had known Derek for more than a decade, and I considered myself to be one of his closest friends, and yet here he was, with a wedding band on his finger that he'd told me nothing about! Pointing to his finger, I basically shouted, "Derek! "What the f*** is that?!" He looked at me a bit bashfully and replied, "Oh, you noticed." "Of course I noticed!" I replied angrily. "You're wearing a goddamn wedding ring!" And he said, "Oh. Yes, yes, I am." And then I basically lost it, and I started *yelling* at him. I said, "Derek! I'm your best friend in the profession!" (This may have been a delusion on my part, but it is one that I held for many years, and Derek, in his kindness, never disabused me of it.) "I've known you for more than a decade. You *can't* get married without telling me. I mean, you just can't do that. You have to at least give me a *chance* to go to the wedding, or at least send you a card and a wedding gift!" I continued in this vein for some time, yelling at him for not inviting me to the wedding and, worse yet, not even *telling* me about it. I had to find out, by accident, when I sat down next to him on a plane on the way to a philosophy conference. Derek was completely nonplussed. My tirade provoked no response. Nothing. He didn't see that it was a big deal, and we were soon talking philosophy, as we always did when we were together.

Fast-forward fifteen years. (I remind you that *all* of these stories are true, to the best of my memory, even as some of them, like this one, seem completely unbelievable!) In the intervening years, every time we were together, I referred to Janet as his wife, asked him how his wife was doing, and had told countless people, sometimes in Derek's presence, about his wife, Janet Radcliffe Richards. On this particular occasion, Derek and I were together, with a bunch of other people, and I asked him, "So Derek, how's your wife Janet doing?" And for some reason, on this particular occasion, after *fifteen years*, Derek gently said to me, "You do know, Larry, that Janet and I are not actually married, right?" I was flabbergasted. "Really? You're not actually married?" "No, we are not." "Well then, how come fifteen years ago, when I was sitting on the plane and yelling at you for getting married without telling me, you didn't just set me straight?"

It turned out that Derek was wearing the ring because it was a sign that he and Janet were committed to each other, and when I hastily jumped to the conclusion that they were married and berated him for not telling me, he didn't want to embarrass me for my faulty inference and intemperate response. So Derek just let me continue to think that they were married, and he didn't bother to disabuse me of that notion until this particular occasion.

So, for *fifteen years* I thought that Derek and Janet were married, and lots of other people also thought that, since they had heard about Derek from me.

And it wasn't true. But, for Derek, it was no big deal. Because, in his mind, he and Janet *were* committed to each other, and if others understood that in terms of marriage that was perfectly fine with him. I get that, sort of.

Still, as I so often say about Derek, who does that? Who doesn't just say, in the face of my initial outburst, "Oh Larry, I'm afraid you're mistaken. We're not married to each other. We just decided to wear rings to express our serious commitment to each other. So, you needn't feel bad about not being invited to the wedding!" Only Derek would have responded—or not responded!—as he did.

A short coda to this story as well. Some years later, Derek and Janet did get married. And I wasn't invited to *that* wedding either! I learned about it a few days afterwards, when Derek sent me pictures of him and Janet happily punting down the river following their vows. It was a small affair, at a register office, with only Janet's sister, brother-in-law, niece, and niece's partner in attendance. Derek noted that the wedding was mainly for tax purposes. However, he also confessed to being quite tickled by their new status, much more so than he had expected to be in advance of the ceremony.

* * *

In 1984, I sent Derek a draft of an article called "Intransitivity and the Mere Addition Paradox."[6] It was a 125-page response to Part Four of *Reasons and Persons*, and it was the first major part of a twenty-seven-year project that ultimately resulted in the publication of my book *Rethinking the Good*.[7] My draft arrived in Oxford just as *Reasons and Persons* was going to press. Derek had worked all day, every day, for many months, indeed years, bringing *Reasons and Persons* to press. Thus, at the time my draft arrived, he was utterly exhausted, both physically and psychologically. Derek usually read and responded to anything I sent him within hours of its arriving. Often within minutes. Not so on this occasion.

A year passed without my hearing a word from Derek about my paper. Then he came to visit me at Rice, and he relayed the following story to me. When my paper arrived, he was in no state to read it. More than that, with *Reasons and Persons* already in press, he was afraid of what he might find

[6] Larry Temkin, "Intransitivity and the Mere Addition Paradox," *Philosophy and Public Affairs*, 16 (1987): 138–87.

[7] Larry Temkin, *Rethinking the Good: Moral Ideals and the Nature of Practical Reasoning* (New York: Oxford University Press, 2012).

in it. So he put my paper aside for a while. However, he took it with him on a trip to India, and he carried it with him halfway up a mountain. There, he sat down, cross-legged, and with one of the world's tallest peaks looming in the distance, he finally read it. At that point Derek paused for a moment, before continuing, and he uttered the following words, which remain indelibly imprinted in my brain: "I couldn't remember ever reading a more impressive paper. It destroyed the greatest flower of ten years of my life. But I didn't mind. Because it was so good."[8]

This story is, I believe, deeply revealing about who Derek was. First, of course, it reveals that Derek was a man with a terrible memory! Second, he was unstintingly generous in his praise, and unfailingly encouraging and supportive. And third, he was a philosopher's philosopher. Frankly, if I read a paper that I thought destroyed the greatest flower of ten years of my life, I'd be *extremely* angry, upset, dismayed, disappointed, and probably jealous. Derek displayed none of those emotions. To the contrary, he was genuinely happy for me. However, much more to the point I think, he was happy for philosophy. Derek's first, second, and third priorities as a philosopher, and as a person, were the related aims of discovering the truth and making genuine philosophical progress on important issues. He strove for those aims in everything that he thought and wrote. If he thought that someone else was advancing those aims, that pleased him *almost* as much (though only "almost") as if he, himself, had accomplished those aims. I always admired Derek for that attitude, even though I have always been less committed than he to the impersonal neutralist perspective that would normatively prescribe such a view.

* * *

I want to say something about All Souls College, and Derek's relationship to it, as it was both his physical and intellectual home for most of his life. People outside of England have no clue regarding the almost mythical stature that All Souls College holds in the psyche of those who understand the hierarchies of the British universities. People in the U.S. just assume, for example, that All Souls College is something like Harvard. But to the British, Oxford University is more like Harvard. All Souls College is one of Oxford's many colleges but, like Derek himself, it is sui generis. To get the equivalent of All

[8] A version of this anecdote was previously published in the Preface to *Rethinking the Good*, p. ix.

Souls College in the U.S., one would have to gather up a host of Nobel laureates, and many of the leading academics at universities like Harvard, Yale, Princeton, MIT, Stanford, and Chicago, and then combine them within a single academic institution. From the perspective of the British, only *that* would be the equivalent of All Souls College. Now, I'm not claiming that the British are right about that. Here, I am only trying to convey a sense of where All Souls College stands in the psyche of those "in the know" about the different British colleges.

I remember that before my wife and I first moved to Oxford, in 1978, we looked through two travel guides on England. One listed the ten most prestigious things that one could do in England. Of those, one was to have lunch with the Queen, and another was to eat in the great Hall of All Souls College. The second guide described All Souls College as one of the world's most erudite think tanks. It was a think tank, of sorts, because although it had researchers, it had no graduate or undergraduate students.

Soon after our arrival, we took a tour of Oxford. The tour leader took us to the great quad, with St Mary's Church at one end, the Radcliffe Camera in the middle, and All Souls College along one side. He brought us up to the beautiful side gate of All Souls College, had us peer across the great lawn and the magnificent All Souls sundial, and then directed our gaze to the spectacular twin towers of All Souls that rose sublimely over the Oxford landscape. He then told us the following story: there once was a don (professor) at All Souls College who, in the pre-internet days, bragged that he had no need of an encyclopedia. Why? Because if there were ever any question on any subject to which he didn't know the answer, he merely had to ask his colleagues at dinner that night and one of them was certain to know the answer! The story is probably apocryphal, but it accurately conveyed the prevailing view of what it was like at All Souls College.

One of my son's friends' mother put it succinctly. She was an eminent doctor in her own right, and her husband was a leading figure in the World Health Organization, but when her son asked her about All Souls College, after learning that I was a Visiting Fellow there, her reply was simply: "All Souls College, that's the best of the best!"

***

In Oxford, the very words "All Souls" were magical; like "Open Sesame" in *Ali Baba and the Forty Thieves* from the tales of the Arabian Nights. Here are but two stories illustrating that. Shortly after my arrival in Oxford, I asked

Derek if there were any squash courts that I could use. Derek told me that All Souls didn't have any squash courts of its own, but that it shouldn't be a problem for me to use the university squash courts. I was leery of this, since I had read that the university courts were only open to members of the university—which I was not. I was only visiting Oxford to work with Derek, and I had no official affiliation with Oxford, or All Souls College, of any kind. Still, I thought that I might as well give it a try. Sure enough, when I arrived at the courts, there was a big sign that said, "Admittance to members of Oxford University ONLY." The sign also told me that one had to sign in, that one had to show a university ID card, and that one had to wear official Oxford athletic gear while on the courts.

Of course, I had no ID or Oxford gear, but as there was nobody attending the courts at the time, I put my name on the sign-up sheet, and let myself onto the courts. About ten minutes later, an Oxford porter stormed into my court, gruffly demanding to know what I was doing there, why I wasn't properly attired, and asking to see my ID. As soon as I said that I didn't have university gear, or a university ID card, he blew up at me, telling me that I needed to leave immediately, and demanding to know why I had ignored the clear signage that these were university courts restricted to university members *only*. At that point, I finally managed to explain that I was a visitor who was working with Derek Parfit of All Souls College, and that he had suggested that I might be able to use the courts.

You have never seen someone change his tune as abruptly as the porter did at that moment. He apologized profusely, and as he quickly backed out of the courts, he told me that *of course* I was welcome to use the courts *anytime*. To be clear, I did *not* claim that I was a member of All Souls College, or even a visitor to All Souls College. All I said was that I was a visitor who was working with someone who was at All Souls College. But I had uttered the magic words. And that was enough!

My wife had a similar experience. Derek had arranged a flat for us to move into when we first arrived in Oxford. However, it was only available for a month. So we needed to find housing on our own for the rest of our stay. Of course, being an international university town, Oxford's housing market was incredibly tight, and we found it impossible to find anything within biking distance of Oxford that we could afford. Derek suggested that we might check in with the University Accommodation Office, to see if they might be able to help us. So Meg went to the University Accommodation Office and asked if they knew of any available housing that we might rent. The first question they asked her was if we were members of the university. We were not. At that point, she was politely told that the University Accommodation Office was *only* for members of the university and that, unfortunately, there was nothing that they could do to help us.

Dejected, my wife sighed, and mentioned that her husband was working with Derek Parfit at All Souls College, and that he had suggested that the Housing Office might be able to help us find a flat. The response was immediate: "All Souls College? Let me see what I can do." Two minutes later we were being offered a lovely flat on Little Clarendon Street—one of the most desirable streets in Oxford—a flat that was normally reserved for distinguished visiting professors!

I was a mere graduate student who at that point had not even *started* his dissertation. I had no official Oxford affiliation of any kind. However, it didn't matter. I was working *with* someone at All Souls College. That was enough! Of course, coming from America, we couldn't possibly comprehend at the time *why* the words "All Souls College" had such magical powers. But they clearly did.

* * *

All Souls is a college steeped in tradition. Co-founded by Henry Chichele, the Archbishop of Canterbury, and King Henry VI in 1438, it revels in its stature and its illustrious past. It continues to follow customs that are hundreds of years old, and it is slow to make changes—sometimes glacially so. I remember the first time that I dined at All Souls College, as a Visiting Fellow in 1999. I had been escorted around All Souls earlier in the day by Jerry Cohen, who gave me a brief overview of the lay of the land.

Among other things, Jerry showed me the beautiful Chapel; the spectacular Codrington Library; the Buttery, where Fellows dined for lunch; the Hall, with its magnificent, vaulted, cathedral-like ceiling, where dinner was served most nights during term; the Common Room, where dinner was served on nights when only a few Fellows would be in attendance, and where cheese, fruit, and port were served each night after dinner; and the Fellows' lounge, where one might retire for further drinks, cigars, and snuff after the cheese and port. The Fellows' lounge was also where tea was served twice daily, newspapers and periodicals from around the globe were laid out, a coal-burning fireplace took the chill off the air, and a quill, inkwell, and blotter were available for anyone disposed to pen a letter the old-fashioned way (an opportunity that I couldn't resist when writing to my grandmother from the inner sanctum of All Souls College).

As I was someone whose wardrobe consisted mostly of T-shirts with holes in them and badly frayed shorts, Jerry made sure to warn me that on Fridays, Saturdays, and special occasions a dinner jacket (tuxedo) was required when dining in the Hall, *in addition to a robe of course*! On other days, dinner in the Hall "only" required a suit and tie under one's robe! On those nights when dinner was served in the Common Room, a robe was still required, but not a dinner jacket or suit under it.

That night, I would be dining in college. Since it was before the start of term, and only a few of us would be dining in, I knew that dinner would be served in the Common Room. Being from the U.S., I inferred that "Common Room" implied an informal dress code. Still, as it was my first night dining in college, I decided to dress up for the occasion. I actually wore a dress shirt and a pair of slacks under my robe, along with a tie hastily lent to me by one of the other Fellows, when he saw that I was about to head off to dinner without one. Of course, I assumed that none of this really mattered, since there would only be a few of us at dinner, and nobody would notice, much less care, what I was wearing under my robe.

I could not have been more wrong. As the butler offered me the first dish—yes, *of course* All Souls had a butler, who served at each meal, along with a bevy of assistants—he surreptitiously brought his mouth close to my ear and fiercely whispered, "You may dine with us here tonight, but in the future don't *ever* come to dinner dressed like that again!"

It turns out that proper dinner attire did *not* allow for white socks and tennis shoes, and it *did* require a sports jacket and tie, though not a dinner jacket or suit, under one's robe, *even in the Common Room*. And it was part of the butler's duty to ensure that over 550 years of All Souls traditions and protocols were followed by riffraff like me, from the colonies or elsewhere. Clearly, I was badly mistaken to infer that "Common Room" meant informal; or, more to the point, to think that "informal" at All Souls College was *anything* like "informal" back home in the U.S.

* * *

Mr Spence, the butler, had little to worry about from me, in terms of rule-breaking. I was a guest in "his" home, and once I was apprised of the local norms, I was certainly willing to abide by them. Derek, on the other hand, was another matter. Derek was happy to abide by centuries-old traditions when they suited his fancy. However, he also enjoyed flouting the rules. Sometimes, seemingly, just because he could! But at other times, because he thought the rules were pointless, counterproductive, or warranted exceptions. In addition, there were times when Derek worked assiduously to change the rules, if he knew they were unjust. Let me give an example of each.

All Souls College had a deep-rooted tradition whereby the longest-tenured member of the college who was dining in that night would stand up and say grace, in Latin, before dinner was served. Although Derek was an avowed atheist, he rather fancied that tradition. And so he was quite tickled by the fact that in his later years at college that duty, and honor, inevitably fell to him.

Matters of etiquette were another matter. Some of them were important to him, but others held no sway with him at all. To this day, my children fondly remember Derek taking them to the Fellows' lounge in All Souls, pouring himself a cup of tea, spilling the tea onto his fine china saucer, and then holding his teacup in one hand, while he noisily slurped up the tea on the saucer with his tongue! Nobody else at All Souls would have *dared* act so uncouthly, but Derek *relished* doing so. Indeed, I saw him repeat this activity on numerous occasions over the years.

Here, it is worth bearing in mind that Derek was the product of one of the most privileged upbringings imaginable. Thanks to a series of prestigious academic scholarships and fellowships, he had spent virtually his entire life, as he liked to joke, "institutionalized"—first, at the Dragon School, then at Eton, then at Balliol College, and finally, at All Souls College. These are, respectively, among England's most elite and, if I may say so, snootiest primary schools, secondary schools, undergraduate colleges, and research institutions. This made it all the more incongruous, and hence all the more hilarious, from my children's perspective, for Derek to be slurpy licking tea off his fine china saucer in the hallowed halls of All Souls College.

Grammar rules, by the way, were *not* optional, for Derek. *They* were *sacred*!

* * *

Recall that in 1978–9 I was visiting Oxford to work with Derek. In those days, Derek attended regular meetings of the Oxford Ethics Reading Group. The group met in H. L. A. Hart's All Souls College room, and it included a veritable who's who of British value theorists. Among those who frequently attended the meetings were Ronald Dworkin, Amartya Sen, Philippa Foot, R. M. Hare, John Mackie, John McDowell, and Jim Griffin. Looking out for my interests, as he always did, Derek thought that it would be good for me to attend the meetings. It would give me the opportunity to meet many of Oxford's leading value theorists and, more importantly, an opportunity to benefit from the philosophical discussions.

There was just one problem with the plan. There was a firm rule that the Reading Group was reserved for dons and that graduate students were not permitted to attend. The existence of this rule didn't faze Derek one bit. Seeing it as an unwelcome impediment to my philosophical training, Derek simply ignored it. Or, more accurately, he evaded it by reasoning that, since I was on leave from Princeton that year and wasn't enrolled at Oxford, *technically* I wasn't a graduate student that year, merely a *visitor*. And there was no rule barring *visitors* from attending the Reading Group! Thus, Derek was able to cheerfully bring me along to the Reading Group with a clear conscience. Indeed, he not only brought me along to observe the group; he also arranged for there to be a special session of the group devoted to discussing my earliest work on equality, a session that R. M. Hare was kind enough to host at his home in Ewelme.

* * *

In 1999–2000, I spent a year as a Visiting Fellow at All Souls. During that year, Derek and I would meet for lunch almost every day. As we arrived in the Buttery, Derek would strategically linger near a table, watching as the benches slowly filled from one end towards the other. Then, when there was room for just two more people on one of the benches, Derek would gently push me to take the inner seat, while he took the final, end seat. This practice shielded Derek from having to sit next to anyone but me, and although there would almost always be someone directly across from Derek at the table, he would, with rare exception, simply ignore that person.

Now, All Souls had a number of arcane lunch rules. One was that you couldn't invite your spouse to lunch. Derek was more than happy to help me circumvent that rule, by *his* inviting my wife, Meg, if I wanted her to join us. Another was that you weren't supposed to "talk shop" at lunch. Lunch was supposed to be a time where you actively engaged with the other college members. You could talk about politics, sports, religion, the weather, current events, theater, etc., but you were *not* supposed to talk about your work. So far as I could tell, this was one of the countless unwritten rules that had governed behavior at All Souls for as long as anyone could remember.

Unsurprisingly, Derek regarded this as a terrible rule. He saw absolutely no point in wasting time with idle chit-chat, when he could be making progress on important philosophical issues. As a result, as soon as we sat down, Derek would begin to talk about our work, and that would continue throughout lunch. Then, as soon as Derek was done eating, he would abruptly stand up, curtly bow to the rest of the table, mumble a half-hearted apology that went something like "I'm *so* sorry. That was *terribly* boring of us. We ought not to have done that," and then he would literally run out of the room (more about that anon). But the thing is that Derek would repeat the same behavior and mutter the same apology the next day, and the day after that, and the day after that, for the entire year! So, how sorry was he? He wasn't sorry one bit.

* * *

The previous story is closely related to another.[9] For centuries, All Souls had a standard "ritual" concerning the order of evening events during term. Five minutes prior to dinner, the dinner bell would be rung by one of the porters. Robed Fellows would march into the Hall and line up behind their chairs. The longest-tenured Fellow would say grace, in Latin. Everyone would sit down. Then dinner would be served by the butler and the rest of the waiters and waitresses. Typically, dinner consisted of a soup or salad, a main course, several side dishes, fresh bread, wine, water (still or sparkling), and pudding (dessert). After dinner, everyone would head to the Common Room, where the evening would continue with an assortment of cheeses, fresh fruit, more wine, tea, coffee, water, and port. Following that, everyone would head to the Fellows' lounge, where more wine and port were available, along with an assortment of other drinks, biscuits, cigars, and, for those who were interested, snuff.

As one can imagine, this sequence could stretch on for many hours, beginning promptly at 6.55 p.m. with the ringing of the dinner bell, and extending late into the night. For Derek, this nightly ritual was a massive waste of time. He understood that one had to eat, and he understood the reasons why All Souls might want dinner to be a communal activity, but he couldn't abide by a custom, no matter how longstanding, that effectively ended his productive working day at 6.55 p.m. So, one day, while still a Junior Prize Fellow, Derek decided that he would no longer go to the Common Room following dinner and to the Fellows' lounge after that. Rather, he would finish dinner, and

[9] This is one of only two stories that I include in this essay that I did not witness first-hand. Unfortunately, I don't remember from whom I heard this story. It might have been Jeff McMahan, or Derek himself, but perhaps it was someone else.

when everyone else headed to the Common Room, he would go straight to the Fellows' lounge, gulp down a cup or two of tea, and then run back to his rooms to continue working for the rest of the evening. This practice would enable him to get at least three more hours of philosophy done each day.

Understandably, many of the old-timers were aghast! How *dare* Derek do this? Didn't he understand that he was at *All Souls College*, and that sort of behavior just *wasn't done*? However, before long, a number of other Junior Fellows began to follow Derek's lead, and soon the centuries-old custom had become an optional feature of life at All Souls, in which only a few old-timers continued to participate on a nightly basis.

I first heard this story under the description "How Derek Parfit killed dessert at All Souls College." However, to be strictly accurate, it wasn't *dessert* that Derek put an end to, but the hours-long multi-room procession *following* dessert.

* * *

I have saved until last the most important example of Derek's unwillingness to abide by rules or traditions that he thought were silly, counterproductive, or wrongheaded. In 1967, when Derek became a Prize Fellow at All Souls, Oxford University had five all-female colleges and twenty-nine all-male colleges. However, as the turbulent 1960s turned into the 1970s, the winds of change began to reach even the tradition-bound world of Oxford, and in 1974 five of Oxford's previously all-male colleges began to admit women. Unsurprisingly, All Souls College was not among them. Derek thought that this was wrong, and he fought to have All Souls change its antiquated, and unjust, policy. The fight was a long and hard one. It lasted more than five years. At the time, All Souls was populated by a large number of traditionalists, as well as, unfortunately, a number of Fellows who feared and/or loathed women.

When I first visited Derek, in 1978–9, women were still only allowed to come to lunch or dinner on a few limited occasions each month. There were Fellows at All Souls who chose to dine *outside* of college on those occasions, rather than have to suffer the "indignity" of sharing a table with a woman in their own college! However, that was the year when the issue finally came to a head. I vividly recall Derek describing the debates with a mixture of incredulity, dismay, and scorn. He simply could not understand the views of those who still opposed admitting women. To Derek, it was an obvious *moral* truth that that is what they *should* do.

Derek believed that it was *especially* important for All Souls College to admit women, because of its standing within Oxford and British society more generally. As the knockdown fights continued, he couldn't *believe* what opponents offered as *arguments* against admitting women. One of them, which Derek derisively described as "the potty argument," was that All Souls couldn't admit women because all the Fellows' loos (toilets) were for men!

What would a woman Fellow do when she had to go to the bathroom? Somehow, despite the fact that All Souls already had a loo for the female *staff*, and that all of the loos at All Souls College were single-occupancy rooms, the idea of converting a previously male loo to a female loo was *anathema* to the proponents of this so-called "argument"; and the idea of converting a previously all-male loo to a unisex loo was *unthinkable*. Imagine having to use a toilet that had previously been used by a woman!

Such arguments were easily skewered, and skewer them Derek did. However, as we all know, conclusively refuting an opponent's arguments does not necessarily endear you to your opponent, nor does it guarantee that they will change their position. Still, Derek and his more enlightened colleagues persisted, and eventually the force of reason carried the day, as Derek always believed it should. It was a proud day for Derek when, in 1979, All Souls College finally voted to allow women to apply for their college Fellowships. And it was, I believe, no coincidence that when the first woman was eventually elected a Fellow of All Souls College—Susan Hurley in 1981—she was a not merely a superb candidate but someone who had worked closely with, and had her candidacy strongly championed by, Derek Parfit.

* * *

As the preceding suggests, there was much at All Souls College for which Derek had little use. Nevertheless, he loved his college and his lifelong affiliation with it. He particularly loved its beauty and architecture, and he was delighted to show it off to visitors. On numerous occasions, Derek proudly took me, as well as friends and family of mine, around All Souls College. Tour highlights included the magnificent Hall, with its cathedral ceiling, the beautiful details and powerful quiet of the gothic Chapel, the spectacular North Quadrangle (designed by Nicholas Hawksmoor), the giant sundial (designed, reputedly, by Christopher Wren), and the striking Codrington Library.

Derek was especially keen to take visitors to the Codrington Library after dark, when no one else was there. He would then make his visitors stand outside, while he went in and adjusted the lighting. When his visitor entered the library, his or her eyes would be drawn along the long, central corridor, whose centuries-old leather-bound books were gently bathed with just the lightest splash of illumination. Then, one's gaze would come to rest on the regal marble sculpture of Sir William Blackstone, ethereally glowing under a spotlight. The whole effect was truly breathtaking, exactly as Derek intended it to be. (Blackstone was a Fellow and administrator of All Souls from 1743 to 1762, whose *Commentaries on the Laws of England* has been widely credited with the nearly universal adoption of the common-law system throughout the English-speaking world. However, Derek's interest in spotlighting the sculpture had nothing to do with Blackstone's place in All Souls, or legal history, and everything to do with the aesthetic experience that he wanted his visitor to have immediately upon entering the library.)

The pièce de résistance of a tour of All Souls College with Derek was reserved for the young, the fit, and the adventurous. It was a climb to the top of the southern tower of the famous twin towers of All Souls. The climb began with an ascent along a narrow, centuries-old, spiral stone staircase. This led to a roughly two-story aluminum ladder that shook with every step, despite being bolted to the floor. The top of the ladder disappeared into a landing high above that one stepped onto once one reached the top of the ladder. On that landing there was another aluminum ladder, also bolted to the ground, also roughly two stories high, and also shaky. But this one didn't carry one to a landing onto which one could safely step. It ended against the wall, under the very high ceiling of the space one was in.

As I recall, in the middle of the ceiling there was a roughly 1-meter-square cut-out, with a roughly 4-inch-high stone border and a heavy cover fitting snugly over the outside of the border and the cut-out in the ceiling. Derek had to take his hands off the ladder and, with both hands, push the cover up and off to one side. He then had to reach up over the ledge and pull himself up through the opening onto one of the narrow sides surrounding it. This was very much like pulling oneself up out of a swimming pool—except that one was some 25 feet up in the air, and there was no water to aid one's effort by buoying one's body, or to safely fall back into if one didn't make it up over the side! Derek would then lean over into the opening, grab the arm or waist of anyone following him up the ladder, and help hoist them over the edge onto the top of the South Tower. Once his visitors were all on top, Derek would replace the heavy cover, and everyone could gingerly stand up.

Suffice it to say, the climb was harrowing. But standing on top of one of the twin towers was even more so. The area was cramped, one was completely exposed to the wind, and there was no guard rail. There were spires rising from each corner of the tower, but between each spire was only a very low stone ledge that was not even knee-high, let alone waist-high. And believe me, when one is standing more than eight stories up in the air, the wind is blowing, and the only ledge is below one's knees, the effect can be petrifying.

But it was worth it! Because the unobstructed 360-degree panoramic view that one gets from the top of All Souls College—as one gazes at Oxford's countless towers, spires, medieval walls, courtyards, and cobblestone streets—is truly magnificent. And to do that with Derek made the experience all the more special.

The last time I made the climb of the South Tower with Derek was with two of my children, Daniel and Becky, in 1999 or 2000. Sometime later, the College deemed that climbing to the top of the twin towers was much too dangerous, and they closed them off. They were surely right about that! Still, I am so glad that they didn't make that sensible determination until *after* I, and my two kids, had made that climb with Derek.

* * *

For much of his life, Derek had an extraordinary focus on doing philosophy. And, except for a very brief interlude following the publication of the first two volumes of *On What Matters*, that focus only intensified with each passing year. However, as already implied, Derek had a few other interests in his life outside of philosophy. Let me briefly comment on a few of those, besides the ones I have already mentioned (chess, art museums, architecture, and photography).

First, when he was younger, Derek was an avid moviegoer. He had views—firm views, of course, as almost all of Derek's views were firm!—about the greatest movies, the greatest directors, and so on. Derek could pontificate at great length about the merits, and shortcomings, of Truffaut, Eisenstein, Hawks, Griffith, Huston, Capra, Buñuel, Fellini, Bergman, Kubrick, Kurosawa, Hitchcock, Fassbinder, Welles, and so on. And, if one ever heard Derek talking about cinema with a group of academics, one might have thought that his interest in movies began, and ended, with artsy, high-brow classics. But that wasn't the case at all. Most of the movies that Derek recommended that Meg and I should see, the first year that we lived in Oxford, were not classics per se but ones that Derek thought had great cinematography—for example, *The Duellists*, *Picnic at Hanging Rock*, and, somewhat surprisingly, the 1978 remake of *Heaven Can Wait*. But, more than that, Derek seemingly had an insatiable appetite for almost any cinema, including decidedly low-brow cinema, such as the 1978 trucker movie *Convoy*.

An acquaintance of mine, who was a philosophy graduate student at Oxford, once told me the following story. He had decided to go to a shoot-'em-up martial arts film. He was quite embarrassed to be going to this particular movie, but took some consolation from the fact that since he was going in the middle of the day, and planned to sit at the back, it was highly unlikely that he would run into anybody that he knew. As the movie began, he was slunk down in his seat. Then, partway through the movie, he noticed this tall man with shocking white hair leaning forward intently staring at the screen. It was, of course, Derek, and he was *totally* entranced by what my friend regarded as a completely trashy B-level karate movie. As that point, my friend tells me, he sat straight up in his seat, thinking, "*I* don't have to be embarrassed about watching this movie, since *Derek Parfit* is watching it too!"

Derek was a voracious, and unbelievably fast, reader. I have already conveyed some sense of how fast a reader he was. Here is another example. One day, while he was visiting me at Rice University, he asked me if I had any drafts for him to read. As it happened, I had recently completed a draft of an article of mine called "Harmful Goods, Harmless Bads."[10] I handed him the draft, as we were walking out of my office on the way to my car. It was forty-six pages long. We were heading to my condo for dinner, which was about a ten-minute drive from campus. At the third stop light—about six minutes into the ride—Derek put the paper down and began discussing it with me. Derek had not only completed reading the entire draft; he also had a whole slew of trenchant questions and criticisms to raise concerning it.

Derek hated being without reading material, and he read more or less anytime when he wasn't writing, teaching, or actively involved in philosophical discussions. He often read during meals, while in the bathroom, every night for an hour while on his exercise bike, and before going to bed. He even read while brushing his teeth, which he did, extensively and compulsively, after each meal. For a period, Parfit kept a book open on his dressing table, for the express purpose of reading while putting on his socks!

Derek read virtually everything there was to read in both historical and contemporary value theory, and a great deal of historical and contemporary philosophy outside of value theory. While he tended to focus on works within the analytic tradition, he also read vast amounts of non-analytic philosophy.

[10] Larry Temkin, "Harmful Goods, Harmless Bads," in *Value, Welfare and Morality*, ed. R. G. Frey and Christopher Morris (Cambridge: Cambridge University Press, 1993), pp. 290–324.

In addition, his taste in books included a wide range of literature, general science, music, history books, and novels. He was also a *huge* fan of biographies, and he had an extensive collection of art and architecture books.

Derek was also a fan of comedy, with a special liking for P. G. Wodehouse and Monty Python. And, as was very typical of Derek, since *he* liked Wodehouse and Monty Python, he thought that I should too.

Now, as a young man there were certain kinds of humor that I liked, and other kinds that I just didn't get. For example, many people thought that Charlie Chaplin, W. C. Fields, the Three Stooges, and the Marx Brothers were comedic geniuses. I was willing to believe that they were, but their slapstick humor did nothing for me. On the other hand, I really enjoyed Woody Allen's sense of humor, which I found wry, ironic, sardonic, philosophical, self-deprecating, and neurotic. When Monty Python's Flying Circus first came out, I thought that they were highly creative and original, but I found them to be closer to slapstick than to Woody Allen, and, given that, they didn't do much for me. My wife's family, on the other hand, all *loved* Monty Python. They could recite, word for word, virtually every Monty Python skit, with "Argument" being a particular favorite of theirs.[11] Naturally, I had serious questions about their taste in comedy, and wasn't reticent about openly expressing that view, as they would regale each other with one skit after another, bursting with laughter all the while.

So, you can imagine my chagrin—and my wife's later delight—when one day, while we were sitting in Derek's room, after many hours of philosophizing, he said to me, "Before you go, Larry, you *have* to listen to this. It is *so* good." He then proceeded to play a Monty Python album on his record player, and he was *especially* keen to hear my reaction to one particular skit. It was, of course, "Argument"!

Now, having not attended the Dragon School or Eton, I had no hope of getting all the inside jokes that made Monty Python *so* hilarious to Derek. Thus, I must confess that I *still* didn't really *get* Monty Python, listening to it with Derek that evening in All Souls College. Still, I now felt quite stupid about the way that I had teased my wife's family for their taste in humor, and my opinion of their sense of humor was elevated considerably, thanks to Derek.

The following year, in 1979, *Monty Python's Life of Brian* was released.[12] Derek, who was once again visiting at Princeton, joined Meg and me for

[11] A recording of the "Argument" skit can be found at https://www.youtube.com/watch?v=ohDB5gbtaEQ (accessed February 2, 2021).

[12] Terry Jones (director), Graham Chapman, John Cleese, Terry Gilliam, Eric Idle, Michael Palin, *Monty Python's Life of Brian* (1979).

dinner one evening, and then we all went to see the movie together. Meg and I both enjoyed the movie well enough. But what we especially enjoyed was seeing it with Derek, because he found it hilarious! In our forty-year relationship, that was the first, and last, movie that I ever saw with Derek.

Derek had one other interest that was both deep and abiding. It was his love of music, especially classical music. Here, too, Derek had clear views about who the greatest classical composers were, and here, too, he thought others should share his opinion.

Wagner was a favorite of Derek's. He would tell me of particular recordings of the Ring Cycle that he liked, which conductors were best, which orchestras were best, and so on. He told me, with great pride, how he had once attended a live performance of all fifteen hours of the Ring Cycle (this spanned several days), though mostly he preferred recordings to live performances. One day, in 1978, after another long day of philosophizing, Derek thought that we should top it off with some Wagner. He took out his favorite recordings, and proceeded to play me a number of selections from the Ring Cycle. The whole time he did this, he earnestly searched my face for a look of blissful contentment or at least a glimmer of appreciation for the sublimity to which I was listening. Alas, I failed to live up to Derek's expectations. I did not respond to Wagner *nearly* as positively as Derek thought I should. And, truth be told, in those days I thought that people must love listening to Wagner for the same reason someone might love hitting themselves in the head with a hammer—because it felt so damn good when they stopped!

At first, Derek was quite disappointed with me, and this clearly showed on his face. However, he then recalled that I was only 24 at the time, and his face brightened up considerably. In a cheery voice, Derek noted that there was *still* time for me. He then added, almost triumphantly, that *he* never really appreciated Wagner, either, until he was 30! (Confession. Age 30 came and went long ago, and I have still never found listening to Wagner to be the transcendent experience that Derek did. I am much fonder of Mozart, Beethoven, and Bach, or, for that matter, Bob Dylan and Led Zeppelin! Still, some twenty years after Derek first tried to introduce me to the sublimity of Wagner, I found myself in Oslo with the opportunity to buy a standing-room-only ticket to Wagner's *Tannhäuser*. Thinking of Derek, I jumped at the chance, despite the fact that this would involve standing for some three and a half hours, in the nose-bleed section at the very top of the recently opened Opera House. Jutting out over the water at the head of the Oslofjord, this spectacular opera house proved to be an ideal setting in which to experience the opera. This was especially so after those of us with standing-room tickets were invited to move down into any empty seats after the first act, and I found myself comfortably seated dead center and just a few rows back from the orchestra, with a perfect view of the stage. The production was magnificent, and the whole evening was another one of the special events in my life that I never would have had but for Derek.)

* * *

The first year that I visited Derek, Oxford was filled with an incredible array of leading intellectuals including, among others, Amartya Sen, Ronald Dworkin, Michael Dummett, Peter Strawson, Philippa Foot, John Mackie, John McDowell, R. M. Hare, H. L. A. Hart, David Pears, Jim Griffin, and Simon Blackburn. Feeling like a kid in a candy store, I was drooling at the prospect of taking courses with some of these people, but I wasn't sure to whom I should give priority. So I asked Derek. He promptly splashed water on my plans. He told me, "I'll give you the advice that my advisor once gave me. You can do philosophy, or you can attend classes; but don't pretend that attending classes is the same as doing philosophy."

I saw the wisdom of Derek's advice, but was not entirely convinced. Thus, he consented to listen to a list of all the courses that were being taught at Oxford that term. As I ran down the list, he struck them down one by one. This professor is boring. That class will be uninteresting. This professor is extremely prolific, and you can learn his views more quickly and efficiently by just reading them than by wasting time going to his lectures, and so on. The *only* class that gave Derek pause was a course on Aristotle that was being taught by David Pears. Derek admitted that he had once sat in on a course of Pears's, and that "Pears was jolly good." Then, after a brief pause, Derek continued, "But it meets too early in the morning," and that was that!

Despite Derek's advice, I ended up sitting in on two seminars that year. One was a joint seminar taught by Mackie and McDowell. The other was the famous "Star Wars" seminar taught by Dworkin, Sen, and Parfit in the gorgeous Old Library of All Souls College. In 1978, Dworkin and Sen were already well recognized as academic superstars. Parfit was much more of an up-and-comer. But all the buzz about *that* seminar surrounded Parfit, who was presenting some of the most ingenious, fascinating, and strikingly original arguments that anyone had ever heard—in many ways, the clearest and most powerful versions of the path-breaking arguments that would later appear in *Reasons and Persons*.

The Old Library was normally set up in seminar style, with room for about twenty participants to sit comfortably. For the 1978 Star Wars seminar, people began streaming into the room some thirty minutes early, and by the time the seminar started there were around a hundred people crammed into every nook and cranny of the room. Every chair was filled, each window seat had three or four people crammed into it, and every spot on the floor was taken—including those on the sides of, and *behind*, the speakers. In addition, many people were standing at the back of the room two or three rows deep, and another group took up spots along the stairwell, unable to squeeze into the room but still hoping to hear what was going on inside. It was, as they say, a "happening," the likes of which I had never seen before, and have never seen since, for an ongoing academic seminar.

On one occasion, Daniel Dennett had arrived too late to get a seat. He was young then—we all were—and he ended up sitting cross-legged on the floor, in one of the aisles. I was sitting in one of the window seats, not too far from him. After the seminar Dennett stood up, stretched his legs for a minute, and then walked up to Derek, saying, "It has been an honor to sit at your feet." I am *certain* that he meant it. There was not the slightest touch of irony or facetiousness in his voice. Dennett spoke for many of us when he said that. As Derek presented the earliest versions of *Reasons and Persons*, we all felt that we were in the presence of genius and in at the very beginning of a very special moment in the history of philosophy.

When Derek lectured, he would get extremely thirsty. For this reason, he had a large water bottle that he always intended to bring with him. But Derek was always leaving for the lecture in great haste, and he was extremely forgetful. Fortunately, I was usually with Derek prior to his seminar, talking philosophy, and I usually returned to his rooms with him after the seminar to continue our discussions. So, when Derek forgot his water bottle, as he usually did, it fell to me to get it, fill it with water, and bring it to him, or to pick it up after the lecture and carry it back to his room for him. This was something that I happily did, without giving it a second thought. One day, at the end of the seminar, an acquaintance of mine who had observed this ritual over a period of weeks, came up to me and said, "Larry Temkin, water carrier to the gods!" My mind flashed back to the *Iliad* and the *Odyssey*, and Homer's accounts of the minor characters who were spear, shield, or armor carriers for the great heroes of his epics, and I realized that my acquaintance was right! I *was* the water carrier of a modern-day philosophical hero or "god"—and I was quite honored, and rather tickled, by that thought.

I might add that it was rather ironic that I, of all people, should find myself in such a position, because in many ways I was the most forgetful person that I had ever known, before I met Derek. I was constantly losing items while I was growing up, so much so that my father once told me, in utter exasperation, that if my head wasn't screwed on tight, I would lose that too! And in a reply to a co-worker of hers, who once asked my wife, Meg, if she could have a ride home, Meg said, "Sure, if Larry remembers to pick me up." When her colleague incredulously responded, "You're not serious, are you, that your husband might actually forget to pick you up from work?" Meg matter-of-factly replied, "Sure, he does it all the time." Still, despite my own severe shortcomings in terms of forgetfulness, it fell to me to keep tabs on things whenever the two of us were together, since Derek was even more hopeless than I.

I might also add that my role as water carrier to the gods persisted throughout our lifelong relationship. As I went from graduate student to Assistant Professor, to Associate Professor, to Full Professor, to Distinguished Professor, I was still the one who always made sure that Derek had plenty to drink whenever we taught together, or whenever I was with him when he lectured. And I never tired of that role.

* * *

The fall semester that I first met Derek, way back in 1977, was also the semester that I was preparing for my so-called "comprehensives" at Princeton. This was an oral exam that one had to pass before officially reaching the dissertation stage. Since I was planning to write a dissertation in ethics, I was permitted to prepare for comprehensives by studying the arguments for and against the social convention theory of morality, and for and against various versions of utilitarianism. I had a fairly good set of readings on the social convention theory, but a fairly minimal set of readings on utilitarianism, including Mill, Moore, Ross, Brandt, Hare, Smart, and Williams. I had already begun meeting with Derek, fairly regularly, and thought I should ask him what else I should read in the remaining three weeks before my exam. Derek had a succinct reply: I should read Sidgwick's *The Methods of Ethics*,[13] a book that he regarded as the single greatest philosophical treatise on ethics since Aristotle.

[13] Henry Sidgwick, *The Methods of Ethics*, 7th edn (London: Macmillan, 1907).

This was in the pre-Amazon days. Since I wanted my own copy to mark up, and the Princeton Bookstore didn't have a copy, I had to make the trek into New York City to search the used bookstores for a copy. I was delighted to find one, but my heart sank when I saw that my copy of the *Methods* ran to 547 pages, not including the index. Unlike Derek, I am an excruciatingly slow reader, so, when I returned to Princeton, I rang Derek up and asked him on which parts of the book I should focus. He replied, "All of it."

So, I dutifully slogged through the *Methods*, reading it for hours and hours every day. It took me a full week to get through it. When I had completed reading it, I went back to Derek and asked him what I should read next. He replied, "Reread Sidgwick." He meant it. And once again, he wanted me to reread all of it. I again slogged through the text. It took me another full week. I returned to Derek and said that I had now read and reread Sidgwick, and had only one more week to read anything else that I should read in preparation for my comprehensives. What did he suggest? Derek's answer was firm. I should reread Sidgwick yet again!

Derek's thinking, which I now wholly endorse, was that it was more important to read a genuine masterpiece over and over again than to read some contemporary book or article that would soon be forgotten. Since he was the great Derek Parfit, and I was a lowly and ignorant graduate student, I followed his advice.

The day of the oral arrived, and my examiners were Derek, Tim Scanlon, Gil Harman, and a philosopher named James Ward Smith. The first part of the oral was on the social convention theory, and that went fine. The second part was on utilitarianism, and that one also started out all right. However, like Derek, Gil Harman was an incredibly fast reader, and, like Derek, he had read virtually everything that had ever been written on the topic of utilitarianism. And when it came to his turn to ask me a question, he asked what I thought about the views expressed by a particular author in a particular article of his. I had to sheepishly admit that I couldn't answer his question, because I hadn't read that article. Gil tried again. This time he asked me what I thought about the views expressed by a different author in an article of his. Again, I had to sheepishly reply that I couldn't say, as I had not read that article either. Gil tried one more time. This time he asked me to comment on the views expressed by David Lyons, in his book *Forms and Limits of Utilitarianism*,[14] a book that was highly influential at the time and, I confess,

[14] David Lyons, *Forms and Limits of Utilitarianism* (Oxford: Clarendon Press, 1965).

directly on the topic of this part of my exam. Of course, I had to admit that I hadn't read that book, either.

At this point, Gil said, with a tone of utter exasperation in his voice, "*Larry*, this is supposed to be a *comprehensive* exam—what *have* you read?" At which point Derek, attempting to come to my defense, raised his finger and emphatically interjected, "He has read *Sidgwick*!"

And that is how Derek's admiration of Sidgwick almost caused me to fail my comprehensive exams!

* * *

At the beginning of his Preface for Volume One of *On What Matters* Derek wrote, "Sidgwick remarks that he had 'two masters': Kant and Mill. My two masters are Sidgwick and Kant. Kant is the greatest moral philosopher since the ancient Greeks. Sidgwick's *Methods* is, I believe, the best book on ethics ever written."[15]

As the preceding anecdote reveals, Derek's view about Sidgwick was longstanding. It is impossible to exaggerate the influence that Sidgwick had on Derek's thinking, or the extent to which Derek admired Sidgwick over the course of his life. However, Derek's view of Kant came rather late in the day.

Over the course of our lives, Derek and I had only two really major intellectual disagreements. The first, to which I will return later, concerned the topic of desert. The second concerned the importance of Kant as a moral philosopher. I long contended that Kant was the most important moral philosopher who had ever lived, and that he understood the concept of morality better than anyone who had ever lived, before or since. Derek would have none of it. Derek was willing to concede that Kant was a philosophical genius, but he thought that virtually every substantive claim that Kant made regarding morality was false. This was in stark contrast to his intellectual hero, Sidgwick, whose claims, Derek believed, while mostly boring, were also mostly *true*.

And it was worse than that. For many years, Derek contended that Kant was a greater threat to objectivity, and in fact was a greater anti-rationalist, than Hume! Hume at least believed that there could be substantive moral reasons; he just thought that they all had to be grounded in a person's passions or antecedent desires. But Kant, according to Derek, didn't even

[15] Derek Parfit, *On What Matters*, Volume One, Preface (Oxford: Oxford University Press, 2011), p. xxxiii.

have the *concept* of genuinely normative reasons, despite his insistence that Reason prescribes the moral law.

Derek and I argued about this for years. Every time I insisted on the significance of Kant's moral philosophy, Derek would challenge me to give him a single Kantian claim that was *true*. And no matter what I offered in defense of my view, Derek would proceed to offer a withering criticism, purporting to show that the claim I had offered was meaningless, false, or trivial.

I would argue that one couldn't understand Kant sentence by sentence; that one had to interpret Kant's system holistically. Derek, I claimed, couldn't see the Kantian forest for the Kantian trees. Derek was unmoved. He would insist that if you couldn't show the individual claims of the Kantian view to be both meaningful and true, then there was no hope of the system as a whole being meaningful and true.

We remained at an impasse over the significance of Kant for the first twenty-five years of our relationship. Then, as Derek was working through his drafts of *On What Matters*, he reread the entire Kantian corpus and the work of every major Kantian commentator. And he began to rethink his views of Kant. Parfit *still* thought that, despite Kant's genius, the overwhelming majority of his substantive claims were trivial, meaningless, or false; but he began to think there was something to Kant's views that he had previously overlooked, something that was deeply important and true. And, of course, by the time he completed Volume One of *On What Matters*, Derek had come around to the view that "Kant is the greatest moral philosopher since the ancient Greeks."

I was, of course, delighted to see that our views regarding Kant's significance had converged as much as they did. However, I have to add that that delight was significantly tempered by the fact that our views about what *makes* Kant such a great philosopher remained far apart. Parfit came to value Kant, in the end, because he interpreted him as offering and defending a particularly compelling version of rule-consequentialism. I see the genius of Kant as lying in a very different set of fundamentally important insights.

* * *

Over the years, many people have asked me who Derek looked up to among his contemporary moral philosophers. Delving into this too deeply runs the risk of veering into gossip, which I do not want to do here. However, I will make a few personal observations. From early on, Derek thought very highly of his co-participants in the Star Wars seminar, Ronald Dworkin and Amartya Sen. But the two contemporaries that he most admired were Bernard Williams and Tom Nagel. Tim Scanlon was a philosopher that started out in the group with Dworkin and Sen, but eventually ended up very close, in Derek's judgment, to Williams and Nagel.

Derek told me on many occasions that he thought Nagel's *The View From Nowhere* was flawed, but still the greatest book in moral philosophy of the twentieth century (left unsaid, other than his own *Reasons and Persons*!).[16] However, in one sense, Williams was the philosopher that Derek was most consumed with, because he admired Williams so, and Williams's views were so diametrically opposed to his own.

Although all three were great philosophers, Derek was very different from Williams and Nagel. This was so in terms of the issues that consumed them and their motivations for doing what they did. And it was even more so in terms of their personalities. Williams was worldly, with a sarcastic, and sometimes vicious, wit. Nagel was urbane, with a deeply pessimistic and often cynical worldview. Parfit had a naïve, almost childlike, innocence to him. He was sweet, sensitive, and incredibly kind. Often, it appeared that his life was one long quixotic journey in his single-minded pursuit of philosophy's holy grail—Truth.

I always felt that there was a significant asymmetry in the relationships between Parfit and Williams and Nagel. Although Williams and Nagel both clearly recognized the originality and sheer brilliance of Parfit, it seemed to me that they never accorded him his full due, the way he accorded them theirs. If I'm right about this, I suspect it was mostly because they regarded Parfit's issues as less important and central to ethics than their own. However, it is also possible that they regarded the brilliant, younger Parfit as a rival for the mantle of greatest living moral philosopher. Thus, perhaps their reluctance to acknowledge Parfit's greatness was a bit like an older brother trying to keep a younger brother "in his place."

Derek's admiration for Williams went beyond mere respect for another extremely talented philosopher. I would even go so far as to say that Derek idolized Williams. I remember Derek once showing me a photograph of Williams when he was Provost (Head) of King's College, Cambridge. In this photograph, Williams was standing boldly and erect on the roof of King's College, with his arms crossed in front of his chest. On Williams's face there was a smug expression, which, to me, appeared to be the epitome of a

[16] Thomas Nagel, *The View from Nowhere* (New York: Oxford University Press, 1986).

haughty, British, aristocratic look—one that practically screamed out, "Look at me! Master of the Realm. *I* control this building, and all that lies below and beyond, for as far as the eye can see." Derek clearly viewed that picture differently from the way I did. Gazing at that photo, all he could say, in a reverential tone, was "Isn't he *wonderful*?"

I've only seen that look once before on Derek's face. We were once again sitting in his office, after a long day of philosophizing, and he took out a book of photographs of famous people. He quickly thumbed through the book, looking for a particular photograph that he wanted to share with me. It was a photograph of the ballet dancer extraordinaire Rudolf Nureyev. Nureyev seemed to be suspended in midair, seemingly 5 or 6 feet off the ground. His right leg was extended straight out in front of him, parallel to the ground, and his left leg was similarly extended straight out behind him. He was wearing a skintight leotard, and every muscle in his body was rippling with energy and controlled power. On Nureyev's face was an almost godlike expression. It appeared to me very similar to the expression that Williams wore as he bestrode the summit of King's College. Derek stared at that photograph with a mixture of awe and adulation and said, "Look at him. Isn't he just *amazing*?" And in that case, I had to wholeheartedly agree.

Derek saw something in the photographs of Williams and Nureyev that was worthy of adoration. A human being at the peak of his powers. Even more: someone at the very peak of what a human is capable of.

Towards the end of his life, I heard Derek say, repeatedly, "I loved Bernard." And I saw him break down in tears, on multiple occasions, knowing that he had never been able to get Williams to see what he, Derek, saw regarding the truth about ethics, and realizing that now that Williams had died, he would never be able to do so. For Derek, the problem of disagreement among epistemic peers regarding the most fundamental truths about ethics was *deeply* troubling. And it was exemplified in the unresolved disagreements between him and Williams.

* * *

There was one other disagreement that vexed Derek greatly. It was a disagreement regarding desert. Derek was *convinced* that no one could truly *deserve* anything. More particularly, he was convinced that no one could deserve to be punished or blamed for their character or actions. It troubled him greatly that Tom Nagel, Shelly Kagan, and I were open to the possibility that in some cases, at least, people could be genuinely responsible for their character or actions in a way that would make them deserving of punishment or blame.

This was a position that Derek could not comprehend. And he could not rest comfortably with the thought that this was one issue about which we might just have to agree to disagree. Every single time that we were together, over the last ten years of his life, Derek would reraise the issue of desert. Why did I believe what I did? What arguments could I offer in defense of my view? And Derek would relentlessly try to convince me that I was mistaken, and that there were compelling reasons to abandon my view of the matter and to accept his. I granted that Derek's position was plausible, and that he offered powerful reasons in support of it, but I could never fully accept it.

This troubled Derek *profoundly*. For Derek, the fact that three of the philosophers that he most admired could hold such a radically different view from his own about a topic as fundamentally important for morality as desert raised the specter that *perhaps* Williams was right. Perhaps there *were* no irreducible normative truths of the sort in which he, and we (Nagel, Kagan, and I), so firmly believed. That, of course, was a position that he had spent much of his life trying to refute, and one by which he simply could not abide.

* * *

Derek used to send my work, without even asking me, to major academics. He did this so that they could give me comments on my work, but also, I believe, to bring me and my work to their attention. He also introduced me to many philosophers and recommended many other philosophers and their work to me. It is mainly through Derek's influence, directly or indirectly, that I came to know well Amartya Sen, John Broome, Jerry Cohen, Joseph Raz, Jeff McMahan, Jim Griffin, Roger Crisp, Dennis Thompson, Zeke Emanuel, and Frances Kamm. Many of these people eventually became letter writers for me and, more importantly, many of these people came to be among my closest friends and colleagues.

I shall always be grateful to Derek for this. But, even more, I shall always be grateful for the endless hours of philosophical discussions that Derek had with me from the very beginning of our relationship until the very end. My philosophical interests and abilities were, to a large extent, forged in the philosophical crucible of conversations with Derek, where my views were subjected to the most intense scrutiny and criticisms imaginable, and where I was encouraged, indeed pushed, to return the fire with as much acuity and intensity as I could muster. There were times, early on, when I would meet with Derek starting around noon, and our discussions would continue till around ten at night, including through lunch and dinner. There were other times when I would "only" meet with Derek for two or three hours, because he would be meeting with someone before me for two or three hours that same day, and someone else after me for another two or three hours. I only learned later that, on one of these occasions, the woman who was leaving Derek's room as I entered was Susan Hurley, and the man who was entering as I was leaving was Jeff McMahan!

Derek had the alchemist's ability of turning lead into gold. From the beginning he would treat me, and others, *as if* we were his colleagues and philosophical peers. And then, almost by magic, his treating us so made it so! Or, almost so, since none of us were ever *truly* his peers. Still, thanks to Derek, many of us ended up being far closer to his peer than anyone might have imagined possible when we first began working with him.

Derek also had this way of making each of the students he was working with feel *incredibly* special. One day, Derek suggested to me that I might want to meet another graduate student with whom he was working. He then proceeded to try to convince me of the merits of meeting this other philosopher, by telling me how good he was. However, the *more* that Derek extolled the merits of this other philosopher, the *less* I wanted to meet him! The plain truth is that I was feeling *jealous*. Indeed, as I was listening to Derek, the thought literally ran through my head that it was as if my wife, Meg, whom I had loved since we were 16, suddenly started telling me about this other lover that she had taken, who was really *amazing*, and encouraged me to meet him because she thought that we would really hit it off. I would *not* want to hear that from Meg, and I wasn't particularly interested in hearing its intellectual equivalent from Derek!

I was being silly, of course. And Derek was completely right. However, I didn't learn that until almost twenty-five years later, when that one-time student of his was hired at Rutgers, and Jeff McMahan became one of my closest colleagues and friends.

* * *

By the early 1980s, Derek had told me that I was the best student he had ever worked with, and that he thought the book I was working on was going to be the most important philosophy work on inequality yet written. He also claimed that, ultimately, my book would be more significant than Nozick's famous *Anarchy, State, and Utopia*.[17] (I think Derek believed that Nozick's book, like much of Kant's work, was extremely clever but mostly false, while he thought that my book on inequality was highly original and, though perhaps less clever than Nozick's, mostly true.) It didn't matter to me whether or not Derek was *right* about all this. In fact, I doubted that he was. What mattered to me was that Derek seemed to be *sincere* when he made such claims. It is *impossible* to exaggerate the impact that Derek's boundless encouragement and support had on me.

Still, as much as I loved doing and teaching philosophy, one day I confessed to Derek that being a philosopher was not my dream job. He was surprised, and asked me what else I would rather do. At that point, I revealed that I used to dream that I could slam-dunk a basketball like David Thompson, a basketball player whose 44-inch vertical leap once landed him in the *Guinness Book of World Records*. I then added that, were it possible, I would *happily* trade a career in philosophy for a career in the NBA. Derek was flabbergasted. He could not believe what he was hearing. And, with an air of genuine disappointment, Derek told me, only half in jest, "Oh, Larry, I wish you hadn't told me that. I don't know if I shall ever be able to write a letter of recommendation for you again."

Fortunately for me, Derek *did* continue to write letters of recommendation for me, since, at 5 ft. 7 in. with a 12-inch vertical leap, I was decidedly *not* destined for the NBA. Still, this story reveals a key difference between me and Derek, and between Derek and most other philosophers. Most philosophers that I know do philosophy because they enjoy it and are reasonably good at it. But Derek did philosophy because of his overwhelming commitment to the truth. Derek believed *so* much in the importance of philosophy that he had a hard time comprehending how anyone capable of doing philosophy might even *consider* doing anything else.

* * *

The philosopher Susan Wolf wrote a marvelous paper called "Moral Saints."[18] In it, she argued that she is glad that some people *are* moral saints, but that she would not want to be one, nor would she want anyone that she deeply cared about to be a moral saint. For Wolf, the single-minded focus that it takes to

[17] Robert Nozick, *Anarchy, State, and Utopia* (New York: Basic Books, 1974).
[18] Susan Wolf, "Moral Saints," *Journal of Philosophy*, 79 (1982): pp. 419–39.

truly be a moral *saint*, and to not let *anything else* interfere with being as virtuous as possible, must inevitably come at a cost in terms of personal development and relationships with others that is both unreasonable and undesirable for someone to bear. I have always been sympathetic to Wolf's view, and I have always thought that her view extended beyond the moral realm.

To my mind, Derek has always been the paradigm of a secular version of a moral saint. He has been "saintlike" in his *total* commitment to the pursuit of the truth. But it exacted a toll on him, and on those around him. It was a toll that he readily paid. Furthermore, it is a testimony to his commitment to philosophy and the truth that *he* didn't see himself as carrying a burden or making significant sacrifices to pursue the life he did. However, I did see it that way. Correspondingly, to echo Wolf, while I am glad that there are secular versions of moral saints, and I *deeply* admired Derek, I would not have wanted to live the life that he lived, nor would I wish such a life for any of my children.

* * *

Let me expand on the preceding remarks. In all the years that I knew him, Derek rarely, if ever, took a vacation, just for the sake of a vacation. When he traveled, he traveled with a purpose. So, for example, when he traveled to Venice and Leningrad to take photographs, he often traveled alone. Why? Much as he loved Janet, in his own way, he wouldn't let Janet's availability get in the way of the *purpose* of the trip, which was to take photographs of the outstanding architecture that those cities had to offer.

Likewise, as far as I know, in all the years that he traveled to teach in America, six weeks at a time twice a year, he almost never took Janet along with him. To be sure, Janet had her own career to pursue. She couldn't up and leave every time that Derek took off! Still, surely, there must have been *some* overlap between Derek's college breaks and Janet's. The reality is that Derek came alone so that he could focus on his philosophy while he was in the States, just as he continued to live at All Souls for much of each year, while Janet lived in London, so that both could focus on their work. To be sure, Derek and Janet often spoke by phone, and once the internet came along they spoke at length, without fail, every day, whenever they were apart. But I could never have lived apart from Meg nearly as much as Derek routinely lived apart from Janet, merely for the sake of making more progress in philosophy.

* * *

Derek was visiting Rutgers the year my son Daniel was giving his percussion recital for his undergraduate music degree. Daniel, who had grown up with Derek often being at our dinner table, and who shared with Derek a deep love of music, wanted to invite him to his recital. I suggested that he was more than welcome to invite Derek, but that he shouldn't be too disappointed if, as I expected, Derek declined. Derek called me after receiving the invitation in a state of agitation. He didn't want to disappoint Daniel, but, after all, he had *so* much work to do, he didn't see how he could possibly spare an afternoon to attend Daniel's recital. I told Derek that Daniel would love to have him there, but that he would certainly understand if Derek was too busy. Relieved to hear that response, Derek promptly thanked Daniel for inviting him, indicated that unfortunately he was too busy to attend, and wished Daniel good luck.

Later, I gently reminded Daniel that in all the years that I had lectured at Oxford, Derek had never once been in attendance. He was sure that I would understand! After all, Derek's attending the lecture would be terribly inefficient for both of us. Instead of wasting an hour listening to my talk, he would read it in five minutes. And instead of wasting an hour listening to all the Q & A, he could spend an hour discussing my talk with me, and that was likely to be far more beneficial for both of us. Derek was, of course, completely right about all that. What he didn't understand is that some people might appreciate the show of support that attending someone's lecture conveyed, beyond any philosophical payoff that might arise from his doing so.

* * *

Despite Derek's being my closest friend in the profession, I didn't invite him to any of my children's weddings. My whole family would have *loved* to have Derek at those weddings. However, I knew full well that Derek wouldn't attend. So, all that inviting him might do would be to make *him* feel bad about letting us down, and make *us* feel bad that he wasn't coming. There was no point in doing that.

Derek's sister, Theo, felt differently, and rightly so. She invited Derek to the wedding of her son, and when Derek failed to respond to the invitation, she called him to ask why she hadn't gotten his response. Derek said something to the effect that he was terribly busy, and, besides, his nephew didn't really know him that well anyway, so he didn't see much point in his attending. Theo was, understandably, furious, and unwilling to accept that response. She insisted that if Derek did not want to attend for the sake of his nephew, he should attend for *her* sake. She was, after all, his sister. Properly chastised, Derek did, indeed, attend the wedding, and by all accounts he was his usual charming self the whole time he was there. However, he still didn't really understand why it was so important to his sister that he be there, and why he had to sacrifice several precious days of doing philosophy for a wedding.

* * *

Interestingly, there was a very brief period when Derek allowed himself to relax, just a bit, in terms of his total commitment to advancing philosophy. It came right after he had sent off the final revisions of the second volume of *On What Matters* for publication. It was at this time that Derek had to leave All Souls College due to his having attained mandatory retirement age, and that he married Janet. It was also at this time that two events occurred while he was visiting Rutgers that would have been unthinkable during any other period of our forty-year relationship.

First, Meg and I had decided to drive to the shore for pizza one night. This would likely involve a forty-five-minute drive there, a forty-five-minute wait to be seated, another forty-five-minute wait for the food to arrive, another forty-five minutes to consume the food and talk, and then yet another forty-five minutes to return home. So, the entire outing would take up roughly four hours. However, it was for *really* good pizza, and the drive to the Jersey Shore was relaxing, so Meg and I thought it was worth it. We decided to invite Jeff McMahan and his then wife, Sally, to join us, and they happily agreed to do so. Since Derek was living in Jeff's basement at the time, I suggested that he should probably invite Derek to come along. Jeff and I both agreed that there was *zero* chance that Derek would join us, but we also both thought that it would be nice just to let him know that he was more than *welcome* to join us if he wanted to.

So, Jeff headed down into the basement, knocked on Derek's door, and said something like, "I know you won't want to, but Larry's on the phone, and Sally and I are going to be driving down to the shore with Larry and Meg for pizza, and we all wanted to know if you'd like to come along." Imagine Jeff's reaction, and mine a few minutes later, when Derek jauntily replied, "I'd be delighted to join you!" When Jeff expressed total shock at this response (as I did later), Derek was puzzled. He said "Why wouldn't I want to join you? You must think me some kind of monster!" It wasn't, Jeff noted, simply that Derek had *never* before agreed to an event of this kind in all the years that he or I had known Derek. Derek agreed that that was probably true, but that was *before* his book was completed. Now that *On What Matters* was in press, Derek claimed, it would not be unreasonable for him to join his friends for a lovely outing to the shore! (Yes, it *was* always about *reasons*, for Derek.)

Second, at the time, my son Daniel was studying composing at the Curtis Institute of Music in Philadelphia. One evening, there was to be a concert playing an orchestra piece written by Daniel. Was there *any* chance that Derek would like to join Meg and me for dinner and the concert? The evening would likely run to about five hours, perhaps a bit more. Derek not only accepted but did so eagerly, indeed "with pleasure." You could have knocked me over with a feather on hearing this response. The whole evening was spectacular, and part of what made it so spectacular was that Derek had not only joined us but also thoroughly enjoyed himself and, especially, Daniel's orchestra piece.

As I say, this period in Derek's life was short-lived. Within a few months, Derek was back to being his old self, consumed with the task of making further progress in philosophy. Still, I cannot tell you how gratifying it was for me and Meg to have shared a few very special moments with Derek during the brief period when he was *not* "himself."

* * *

Derek was very much a man of routine. I say routine, rather than habit, because, with the exception of his tooth brushing (which was more of a compulsion), most of his daily routines were governed by reason. Derek tended to do the same thing, over and over again, because he thought that there was good reason to do this. If someone offered him compelling reasons to change his activities, he was prepared to do so. Immediately.

For example, for many years, when Derek was away from All Souls College, he would prepare himself the *very same* breakfast, *every* day. At one point, when he was visiting us in Houston, his breakfast consisted of a combination of foods that included fried sausage links and green peppers, yoghurt, and a banana. Derek would mix this concoction all together in a bowl, and then eat it. He wasn't particularly concerned about the *taste* of this concoction. Rather, he ate it because he had convinced himself that it was a healthy, and efficient, breakfast. The sausage gave him protein, the yogurt more protein and calcium, the banana potassium, and the pepper vitamins A and C.

My wife, who worked as a biochemist and had a degree in Chemistry, Foods, and Nutrition, suggested that Derek's breakfast was okay but perhaps not as healthy as he thought. The fried sausage, in particular, was problematic. Derek wondered what he might have instead. I don't remember exactly what Meg suggested, regarding how he could improve his diet. But what I *do* vividly remember is that *the very next day*, Derek had adopted a new routine for his daily breakfast. *Habits* are not so easily broken!

Derek also had a tendency to *run* from place to place. He would teach a seminar in Firestone Library at Princeton and, as soon as the seminar was over, would run to 1879 Hall, where the Philosophy Department was. He might sit down to read *The New York Times* (it would take but a few minutes for him to read it through!), and then he would *run* to wherever he was heading next. We would meet in my office at Princeton (actually, Richard Rorty's office, but I was using it while he was on leave), and he would *run* to wherever he had parked his bicycle. The same pattern persisted at All Souls College. He would *run* from his office to the Buttery for lunch, *run* from the Buttery to the Fellows' lounge for a cup of tea and a quick read of the daily newspapers, and then *run* back to his office.

Why the constant running? Two *reasons*. First, he was convinced that it was good for his health, and a nice complement to the nightly hour on his exercise bike. And second, and most importantly, there was *philosophy* to be done. And not a moment to waste! Not a moment in each day. And not a moment in his life.

Similarly, Derek was famous for wearing the same thing every day. It wasn't, *literally*, the same thing. But close enough. Basically, there were a lot of tokens of the same type. So, in all my years of knowing Derek, if he were outside of All Souls College, he always wore dark socks, dark suit pants, and a white shirt. If the occasion warranted, the outfit was supplemented with a red tie and/or a dark suit jacket. If Derek were in college, the outfit would be replaced, when necessary, with a dinner jacket and, of course, he always wore a gown at dinner.

Derek's reason for wearing virtually the same thing every day of his life was simple. It was extremely efficient. It saved time shopping, and it saved time every single morning! Derek never had to pause to wonder what he should wear based on his mood or what he would be doing that day. Nor did he ever have to lose time considering what went with what, or if his outfit looked nice. *None* of that mattered to him. Not one iota. Derek wanted to preserve his precious time and mental resources for the important business of doing philosophy. Hence, he had settled on a standard "uniform," once and for all, and he was perfectly content to abide by that decision for the entirety of his life!

* * *

Derek's concern about not wasting time extended to others besides himself. One day, in 1999–2000, the year I was a Visiting Fellow at All Souls College, Jerry Cohen set up a lunch meeting between him, me, and David Miller. Following lunch, we headed over to the Fellows' lounge, where we settled into a side niche to continue our conversation. Derek came rushing into the lounge, as he always did, poured himself a cup of tea, and then ran over to one of the tables, where he proceeded to read several newspapers, while standing up. Having finished the newspapers, Derek began to run out of the lounge, no doubt to return to his rooms and get back to work. As he was running out of the lounge, he spotted us, ran over, and poked his head in on our conversation.

As it happened, we were just chit-chatting, as normal people often do. Disappointed in what he was hearing, a frown crossed Derek's face, and he proceeded to scold us. As he put it, here we were, three of the world's leading egalitarians, all sitting together in one place, and we were *wasting* our time with idle chit-chat. What a shame! With that Derek turned and literally ran out of the room. Properly chastised, by the great Derek Parfit, we immediately, and rather sheepishly, began talking about equality!

* * *

In 1994–5, Derek and I overlapped for a period at Harvard. He was a Visiting Professor in the Philosophy Department, and I was a Visiting Fellow in the Program in Ethics and the Professions (later renamed the Safra Center for Ethics). We would meet regularly to talk, and once a week we would go out to dinner together.

True to his nature, Derek always wanted to go to the same place for dinner, a Thai restaurant in Cambridge. Each week he would order curry. I would always order a half pineapple stuffed with bean sprouts, cashews, and rice. Every week, without exception, Derek would urge that I order his curry. He was *convinced* that his meal was much tastier and less boring. Derek simply could not understand why I didn't order the curry, no matter how many times I explained to him that it was too spicy for me. Suffice it to say—an expression that Derek always used to tease me about for using it so much—Derek was no fan of "*De gustibus non est disputandum*."

Our weekly Thai dinners continued for many years when Derek taught with me at Rutgers. Again, Derek would always order the same meal, though at this restaurant he would start with a spicy soup, before consuming a hot curry. Again, Derek would urge me to order what he ordered, or to at least share his soup and curry. Again, Derek couldn't really understand why

I didn't want to order what he ordered. His meal was "obviously" so much tastier than mine!

Derek would often insist on paying for our meals. After all, as he put it, I had three children to provide for, while he had none. But when the check came, he would push it over to me, and ask me to calculate the tip. For many years, the tip would be 15 percent. However, brilliant as he was, that was beyond Derek. I tried, on many occasions, to tell Derek how easy it was to calculate a 15 percent tip. Take the total bill, move the decimal one point to the left, take that number, and add it to half of itself. Voilà! Derek's eyes would simply glaze over. I may as well have been trying to teach Derek string theory. Funny how a person could be a genius in one area and utterly incompetent in another. Derek could do philosophy at a level that few could approach. But when it came to basic math, most 12-year-olds could do better than he.

Another shortcoming of Derek's frequently surfaced on the nights we went out for dinner. I would guess that on at least 50 percent of the occasions when Derek paid the bill, one or more of the following would occur. He would fish in his pocket or his wallet for his Oxfam credit card and fail to notice that in doing so a bunch of money or other credit cards had fallen to the ground; he would pay the bill but forget to retrieve his credit card; or he would leave his wallet and/or computer bag behind as he exited the restaurant. Hence, whenever I went to dinner with Derek, I had to be hypervigilant whenever he graciously paid the bill, to catch these missteps before it was too late. Thus, I was not only water carrier for the gods but money, credit card, wallet, and computer bag retriever for the gods!

* * *

Our Thai dinners came to an end on a night when Derek almost died. Derek had ordered the spicy soup and hot curry, as usual. We had returned to his rooms in Jeff McMahan's basement to continue talking philosophy, as usual. He had a brief conversation with Janet, as usual. And somewhere around 10.30 p.m., I returned home, as usual. However, later that evening Derek began to have a coughing fit, and, somewhere around midnight, Jeff could hear that Derek was in great distress. Jeff rushed Derek to the emergency room, and somewhere around 1 a.m. Jeff called to tell me that he was at the hospital, that Derek was being tended to by the emergency room doctors, and that it wasn't clear whether or not Derek was going to live.

That night was one of the scariest nights of my life. And in the following days, it was incredibly jarring and sobering to visit Derek in the ICU and see him hooked up to a ventilator. Fortunately, Derek made a complete recovery. However, had he not been staying with Jeff, had Jeff not realized that Derek was in distress and rushed him to the hospital, and had Jeff not lived within ten minutes of the hospital, Derek would almost certainly have died.

The cause of Derek's emergency? As far as we can tell, the spicy soup that Derek had had for dinner that evening. That night, the spicy soup set off a coughing fit that led to a tear in one of Derek's lungs. The lung collapsed, starting a chain of events that undermined Derek's ability to breathe. So the doctors had to reinflate the lung, and then use a ventilator to keep it inflated and help him breathe until the tear healed itself, which it did within a few days. Derek, by the way, was asking for his computer and was back to work as soon as he regained consciousness, even though he was still hooked up to the ventilator and looking unbelievably weak and haggard. For Derek, his brush with death was no reason to slow down. On the contrary, it was reason to redouble his efforts to make progress in philosophy, for as long as he was able.

However, Derek was willing to change his behavior in one respect. Following his trip to the emergency room, Derek and I had our weekly dinners at an Italian restaurant, where he contented himself with rather boring, unspicy fare.

* * *

In 1979, Derek joined Meg and me for dinner one Sunday evening. I was watching a Green Bay Packers football game that afternoon, and Derek had either arrived a bit early or the game was running a bit late. Derek, of course, had zero interest in watching an American football game. However, he graciously suggested that he would be content to read something while I finished watching my game. Since we lived in a tiny one-bedroom apartment, Derek was reading in the same room that I was watching my game. Before long, I noticed that Derek was raptly watching the screen, following every motion.

When the game ended, Derek owned up that he had always heard that American football was violent and brutish, as well as terribly boring with its stoppages after each play and its endless stream of commercials. However, he hadn't found it to be so at all. On the contrary, he found it both beautiful and fascinating. Further, he was struck by how many of the players looked like Greek Adonises, with their bulging muscles, wide shoulders (thanks to the shoulder pads), and narrow waists. I was rather tickled by Derek's response. First, I had inadvertently given Derek a pleasurable experience that he almost certainly would never have otherwise had. Second, perhaps I needn't feel quite so sheepish about my love of American football, if even Derek found it gripping despite having zero interest in who won or lost, no understanding of it, and a predisposition to dislike it.

There was a second experience that Meg and I provided Derek with that evening that was also a first for him. We served Derek his first true ice cream sundae! It had rich creamy ice cream, of the sort that one couldn't get in England in those days, combined with banana, hot fudge, whipped cream, salted peanuts, and a cherry on top. Derek loved it. He was particularly struck by the combination of the sweet and the salty, and he suggested that he thought that his father, Norman, would really like that. This was odd, since he almost never mentioned his father, with whom he had a difficult relationship. And I have no clue why, in particular, he thought that his father would like that combination, rather than, say, his mother, Jessie, or the two of them, or anyone else for that matter! Still, I like to think that Derek's long-term love affair with rich, creamy ice cream began that evening, in our ninth-floor home in Princeton's Lawrence Apartments.

A coda to the preceding. When my children were young, Derek would always ask me to stop at a grocery store if I were driving him over to our home for dinner. He would then pick up four or five pints of expensive ice cream, for everyone to share after dinner. Derek would always have a large scoop of each pint, and then leave the rest with us to enjoy later. This is but one of the many reasons that Derek always had, and still has, a special place in the hearts of all of my children.

Also, one day my son Daniel and his wife, Qing, were visiting Patricia Zander's home in Boston. Derek had been staying with her earlier in the year, for one of his visiting semesters at Harvard. Patricia offered Dan and Qing some ice cream that Derek had left in her freezer. Dan reports that there were no fewer than 30 pints of different-flavored ice creams to choose from, bought at the local specialty ice cream shop.[19] Apparently, Derek had decided that he had to have a taste of *every* flavor that they offered and bought a pint of each! Seriously, who does that? Nobody I know, other than Derek.

* * *

The monastic life of All Souls College suited Derek in many ways. One way is that it enabled him to focus on his research. Another is that it protected

[19] This is the other anecdote that I include in this essay that I heard secondhand.

him from having to interact with others. At 6 feet tall, with shocking white locks that spilled in all directions and good looks that lasted well into middle age, Parfit cut a dashing figure. Coupled with his upper-crust British accent, boyish charm, stature as a philosopher, ability to converse intelligently about a vast array of topics, and the fact that he was almost always the smartest person in the room, Parfit had a way of leaving a lasting impression on those who met him. But what most people who met Derek didn't realize is that he was terribly shy. He almost always found interactions with others uncomfortable and would go to great lengths to avoid them.

Derek rarely went to conferences. And when he did, he kept his socializing to a bare minimum. When he gave a series of lectures that I hosted, he only attended the party in his honor under great pressure from me—because I knew how much it would mean to my students to be able to meet the great Derek Parfit, about whom they had read and heard so much. When I wanted to host a conference for Derek in honor of his sixtieth birthday, he had absolutely no interest in an event that would make him the center of attention, until I agreed to turn it into a workshop that would provide him with valuable feedback on an early typescript of *On What Matters*. And, as already mentioned, whenever I ate lunch with him at All Souls College, he would sit at the last space on the bench, strategically placing me between him and the next person on the bench, so that he wouldn't have to talk to anyone other than me during lunch. It wasn't only strangers with whom Derek felt uncomfortable; it was even his longtime colleagues at All Souls College!

I remember one year when Derek was visiting at Rutgers, he called me in a bit of a panic. My son Daniel had reached out to him and asked Derek to meet him for lunch. Derek didn't know what to say. Why did Daniel want to meet with him? And, more importantly, what would they talk about for an entire lunch? I told Derek that Daniel probably just wanted to see Derek because he liked him! That he should remember that Daniel had grown up with Derek joining us for dinner on countless occasions. That Derek had shown Daniel around All Souls College, and had taken him up to the top of the twin towers, and so on. I also pointed out that Derek could talk about virtually any subject for hours on end! Derek was still hesitant. Finally, I reminded Derek that Daniel was a music major, training to be a classical percussionist, and that they shared a love of music. Derek let out a great sigh of relief. He had forgotten that Daniel was a musician. In that case, they *would* have something to talk about, and he could "safely" meet Daniel for lunch!

* * *

One evening, when Derek and I were dining in the All Souls Common Room, Derek made sure that I sat next to a particular Fellow. There were only ten or so people dining that night, and as the evening progressed, there was a spirited discussion concerning events that were unfolding in apartheid South Africa. Around the table were highly intelligent legal scholars, historians, philosophers, and economists. All offered their two cents on the subjects under discussion. However, I began to notice that whenever the person to my left spoke, the rest of the group seemed to be giving special credence to whatever he had to say. It was as if, among all of them, *he* were the expert on what was going on inside of South Africa at the time.

When the dinner came to an end, Derek and I headed towards 10 Merton Street, to listen to a lecture by an up-and-coming young philosopher by the name of Peter Singer. On the way, Derek casually asked me if I'd ever seen the James Bond movies. When I replied that I had, Derek continued, "Well, the man sitting next to you at dinner tonight has led a rather more interesting life than the rest of us boring old Fellows at All Souls College." Derek then paused, for dramatic effect, before continuing. "That was M." Like an idiot, I replied, "Oh, I *thought* he looked familiar." To which Derek responded, "No, Larry, I don't think you quite understand. That wasn't the actor who *played* M in the movies—that was the *real* M."

Suddenly, I realized why Derek had made sure that I sat next to the person I did, and why everyone else at the table was giving so much weight to whatever he had to say. In England, unlike the United States, the head of MI6 is not just a political appointment. He is the one who oversees the intelligence agency, who has to know what is going on, on the ground, in the world's hotspots, and who, when necessary, licenses agents to kill for the sake of King and country. M was in retirement at the time we dined together, but shortly afterwards I read in *The New York Times* that my dinner companion, Maurice Oldfield, had been brought out of retirement and put in charge of overseeing British Intelligence operations in Northern Ireland.

* * *

Notwithstanding this essay's many detailed anecdotes—Derek was also sui generis in his ability to leave a lasting impression on me—I have always had an unbelievably terrible memory. For example, I once found myself in the embarrassing position of being unable to remember the name of a girl, even though I had been dating her for *two years* and I loved her very much. Similarly, on multiple occasions, I have been face to face with people that

I have been close to for more than fifteen years and yet been unable to recall their names. Likewise, I have been at conferences where people have warmly embraced me, and I have had absolutely *no* recognition of them *at all*—only to learn, in one case, that my embracer had recently spent an entire semester at Rutgers auditing a seminar of mine; and, in another case, that my embracer had recently lectured at Rutgers and *stayed at my home* during his visit! On another occasion, I thought that I should glance at Charles Fried's book, *Right and Wrong*,[20] in advance of meeting him. When I took his book off my shelf, I found it *filled* with notations, in my handwriting, from cover to cover; yet I didn't remember having even read it, much less anything about it.

As bad as *my* memory is, Derek always claimed that *his* was even worse. Indeed, after almost every phone discussion that we had, Derek would tell me that he hoped that I had taken really good notes that I could share with him later, because his memory was so poor that he almost certainly wouldn't remember any of our conversation.

I have always suspected that Derek's and my extremely poor memories were somehow related to our having full-blown versions of *aphantasia*. People with this condition are unable to picture something in their minds, at will. So, for example, I cannot picture—in the sense of producing or calling to mind an *image* in my head—a horse, an apple, my home, my favorite childhood event, or even my parents, wife, or children. I know many facts about such people, objects, or events, and can describe them propositionally—as I am doing throughout this essay—but there are no inner mental images accompanying those descriptions that I am consciously "seeing in my head" when I talk about them.

Bearing in mind that Derek was a voracious reader who also had countless philosophical discussions with a multitude of students and colleagues each year, the preceding helps explain, I believe, one of Derek's biggest failings: namely, that Derek would sometimes glean an important idea from his endless readings or conversations with others, develop and defend that idea using his own original terminology and arguments, and then discuss that idea as if it were his own, having totally forgotten its initial source.

This happened to me, regarding the prioritarianism/egalitarianism distinction,[21] and I know that I am not alone in this respect. Still, given Derek's

[20] Charles Fried, *Right and Wrong* (Cambridge, MA: Harvard University Press, 1978).

[21] To be clear, it was Derek who first introduced me to the substantive view now referred to as prioritarianism. He did this by calling my attention to Tom Nagel's article "Equality," in which Nagel refers to "a very strong egalitarian principle . . . [which] is constructed by adding to the general value of improvement a condition of priority to the worst off" (see Chapter 8 of Nagel's *Mortal Questions* [Cambridge: Cambridge University Press, 1979], p. 110). Importantly,

unfailing generosity to me and others as a mentor, I cannot help but believe that the best explanation for any harm that Derek may have caused by failing to properly credit someone for his or her ideas is his self-acknowledged terrible memory, which may well have been linked to his aphantasia. I do not believe, for a second, that Derek would ever *intentionally* take someone else's ideas and pass them off as his own.

However, having said that, I would be lying if I said that my conviction in this matter lessens the sting of seeing my prioritarianism/egalitarianism distinction constantly credited to Derek—who hardly needed any more recognition than he had already rightly been accorded. And I imagine that any others whose ideas Derek may have inadvertently presented as his own feel similarly, even if, as in my case, they benefited far more from their exchanges with Derek than he did.

* * *

I have long thought that much of Derek's work and character was spurred by his fear of death. I cannot point to particular exchanges that we had that led me to this view, but I held it, firmly, for many years. I never thought that Derek was *terrified* by the thought of death, but I did think that, were it not for his fear of death, Derek might never have produced *Reasons and Persons* and many of the particular substantive views within it. Accordingly, I have long placed *Reasons and Persons* among the other great works of human civilization that would never have been produced but for our mortality, such as the Pyramids, the Sistine Chapel, the Taj Mahal, Mozart's *Requiem*,[22] and Keats's "Ode on a Grecian Urn".[23]

however, Parfit originally *endorsed* Nagel's view, commending Nagel's principle to me as a particularly plausible version of egalitarianism that I should consider, rather than the version I advocated. I later convinced Derek that while the position in question *might* be regarded, by some, as the closest thing to an egalitarian position that was *plausible*, it was a deep *mistake* to conflate this kind of a position with egalitarianism. (I originally dubbed the position in question *extended humanitarianism*; Derek later renamed it *the Priority View*; and still later I gave it its current name, *prioritarianism*). Thus, the *distinction* between prioritarianism and egalitarianism that Derek is widely credited with making in his famous article "Equality or Priority?" is, in fact, my idea. (See Derek Parfit, "Equality or Priority," *The Lindley Lecture*, University of Kansas, 1991; repr. in *The Ideal of Equality*, ed. Matthew Clayton and Andrew Williams [London: Macmillan; New York: St. Martin's Press, 2000], pp. 81–125. I first made the distinction in my 1983 Princeton PhD thesis, *Inequality*; I first defended it in print in my article "Equality, Priority, and the Levelling Down Objection," which also appeared in *The Ideal of Equality*, pp. 126–61.)

[22] Wolfgang Amadeus Mozart, *Requiem in D Minor*, K 626.

[23] John Keats, "Ode on a Grecian Urn," in *The Eve of St. Agnes, And Other Poems, with Biographical Sketch, Introduction and Notes* (Boston: Houghton Mifflin Co., 1915).

Derek and I would occasionally debate this matter. He would try to convince me that his philosophical views were not spurred by his fear of death, merely by his pursuit of truth. However, he never fully convinced me, in part because some of the very philosophical issues that he chose to focus on were ones for which the topic of death was particularly pressing, such as personal identity and future generations.

Still, I am open to the view that some of Derek's characteristics, which I associated with a fear of death, may instead have been associated with a closely related, yet distinct, concern—the fear of running out of time. It is arguable that it wasn't so much death, *per se*, that strongly motivated Derek, but the fear that death might arrive *too soon*: that is, before Derek had accomplished what he wanted, and needed, to accomplish in the short time span that humans are allotted.

Derek wanted to make significant progress in philosophy. He wanted to discover great truths. And he wanted to be remembered for the contributions that he made long after he was gone. Yet he was acutely aware of the frailty of human existence and that he could be gone at any moment. Hence, for Derek, there was always a frantic race against time: a race to complete the great work of his life, before it was too late.

This, I believe, is why he literally ran from his rooms in All Souls to the lunchroom, and from the lunchroom to the Fellows' lounge, but a few feet away; why he had no time for idle chit-chat; why he read while exercising or brushing his teeth; why he wore the same basic outfit throughout his life; and why, for most of his life, he prioritized philosophy over everything else. It is also why, with each passing year, Derek allowed fewer and fewer distractions in his life, even to the point of ending his longstanding attachment to photography.

Derek rightly thought that he was capable of accomplishing much of lasting significance. However, he also thought that time was a scarce, and incredibly precious, resource. It was not to be squandered on trivialities or anything less than the weightiest of human endeavors.

* * *

Consistent with Derek's impersonal approach, his eye toward the future extended to others as well as himself. In an early draft of *Inequality*, I had an example that referred to the American oil tycoon J. Paul Getty. Derek asked me why I was referring to Getty. I thought the context made it obvious. It was because Getty was, at the time, the world's richest person, and I wanted an example that illustrated the inequality between the best-off person (in this case in terms of wealth) and everyone else.

Derek immediately insisted that I should drop the reference to Getty and just put my example in terms of the world's richest person. Why, you might ask? Because, Derek said, in 500 years' time, when future scholars are reading my work, no one will know who J. Paul Getty is, and the editor will have to include a note to explain the reference to my future readers, and hence the point of my example!

Who thinks this way? Certainly not I, who was a graduate student at the time, and who had absolutely *no* thought that my work might be read even ten years later, let alone 500 years later. But Derek not only wrote *about* future generations, he constantly wrote *for* future generations. Derek thought in terms of the lasting significance of the truth. Correspondingly, he wrote with the hope, and thought, that his work would still be read for many centuries after he was gone.

Derek was, of course, right that I should change my example, even if he was overly optimistic about the shelf life of my work. The truth is that most students today have no idea who J. Paul Getty was. Moreover, since my *Inequality* was published, a host of different people have occupied the position of world's richest person. Indeed, in the past ten years alone, that mantle has been worn by three different people (Bill Gates, Jeff Bezos, and Elon Musk), and there is every reason to believe that the title will continue to change hands on an ongoing basis.

* * *

Sometime around 2010, I was trying to recruit a prospective graduate student in value theory to Rutgers. One of my big selling points was that if he came to Rutgers, he would have the opportunity to work with, and learn from, Derek Parfit. Much to my shock, the student was unimpressed. Apparently, his advisor at his home institution had told him that "Derek was slowing down." I was furious! Derek had accomplished vastly more than his advisor ever had or ever would. How *dare* his advisor talk Derek down in that way? Besides, even a "slow" Derek was a much better philosopher than the vast majority of living philosophers.

Still, after my anger subsided, I had to admit, in my heart of hearts, that what the student's advisor had said was true. The Derek Parfit of 2010 was still a brilliant man, with incredible powers of concentration, an unwavering commitment to truth, and a wealth of knowledge that was astounding.

However, he was nothing like the supernova that I knew in the late 1970s and 1980s. The torrent of astounding and remarkably original insights that gushed from the youthful Derek whom I first met—and which left so many of us bowled over and awestruck—had slowed considerably in his later years.

When I first met Derek, questions from the world's leading philosophers left him completely unfazed. I never heard a single question posed to Derek, in his early years, that he had not already anticipated, and to which he had not already formulated multiple carefully thought-out responses, as well as responses to the responses, and responses to the responses to the responses! In his final years, I heard naïve undergraduates ask Derek questions that he failed to understand, or that stymied him at first. On many occasions, Derek would begin a class we were teaching together with an apology for being so dense in the last class, and the answer that he now thought he should have given to some question that he had failed to fully appreciate in the previous class.

Derek's extraordinary mind began to develop ruts that he would fall into with increasing frequency. So, for example, he would repeat the same story, over and over. Or he would give a lengthy standard answer to a question that he had frequently heard in the past, but which was not, in fact, the question that he was being asked on that occasion.

In addition, in his later years, Derek confided in me that his memory—which was always poor to begin with—was failing. This bothered him greatly. Derek was worried about his current state. He was worried that he would not be able to provide his partner, Janet, with the support that she needed and deserved. Furthermore, he was worried about what the future held in store for him, and what impact, if any, that would ultimately have on his philosophical legacy. This was, of course, exceedingly difficult for me to watch. Moreover, I was helpless to do anything about it. All I could do was offer Derek my ongoing love and support; and assure him that his place in philosophy was secure. Whatever the future held, he needn't worry on *that* score.

I mention this, here, for two reasons. First, I have heard some philosophers disparage Derek, having only met him in the final few years of his life. They don't understand what all the fuss about Derek is, or why some of us revere him as much as we do. I can only say that the Derek that they experienced was very different from the Derek that we experienced, when he was younger.

Second, when I first learned that Derek had died, I was overwhelmed with grief. From a personal standpoint, I had lost my oldest and dearest friend in the profession. And I continue to miss him on a daily basis. However, I confess that I was also relieved. I was relieved for Derek's sake. An intensely proud man, he would no longer have to face the slings and arrows with which fate unceremoniously bombards the aging.

I was deeply saddened when I learned that Derek had died, but I was not surprised. The surprise, for me, was that he had lived as long as he had. Derek's intensity and unremitting commitment to philosophy led him to burn the candle not only at both ends but in the middle as well! In fact, I genuinely used to worry that Derek would work himself to death before I finished my dissertation. This scared the heck out of me for selfish reasons, of course, but also for unselfish ones. I will always be grateful that those worries were never realized; and that Derek made it to 74, and managed to complete three volumes of *On What Matters* in addition to *Reasons and Persons.*

* * *

Interestingly, but perhaps not surprisingly, it was during his final years, when Derek had "slowed down," that his personal relationships with others took on their greatest significance for him. It was also during this time that Derek could be easily overwhelmed by emotion. In addition to his breaking down in tears, on many occasions, when thinking about Bernard Williams, I saw Derek break down in tears when thinking about his wife, Janet; when talking about my wife, Meg; when considering the plight of the world's needy; and when reflecting on the case of Nancy Cruzan. (Cruzan was the woman at the center of one of the U.S.'s most high-profile "right to die" cases. Parfit discussed Cruzan's case in his paper "We Are Not Human Beings," where he observed that "On Cruzan's gravestone her parents had inscribed: Departed January 11 1983; At Peace December 26 1990.")[24]

My admiration for Derek knew no bounds, from the very first seminar of his that I sat in on. However, my love for Derek continued to deepen throughout his life, and it was only enhanced by the more emotional stage of his later life.

* * *

Many years ago, I was having dinner with Jon Elster, the eminent social scientist who has published more than a dozen books with Cambridge University Press, and who is equally at home in the fields of philosophy, political

[24] Derek Parfit, "We Are Not Human Beings," *Philosophy*, 87 (2012), p. 18.

science, economics, and sociology. Elster, who himself has a prodigious intellect, noted that for many years the person that he had put on a pedestal as the most brilliant person he knew, personally, was the All Souls philosopher G. A. Cohen. Elster then added that Cohen himself regarded Parfit in the way that he, Elster, regarded Cohen—as up on a pedestal, and more brilliant than anyone else. I thought Elster's anecdote was both revealing and accurate. People like Elster are incredibly smart, accomplished, and rare. People like Cohen are even smarter and rarer still. And people like Parfit, the sort that even the Cohens of the world look up to, are in a league of their own.

Over the course of my career I have been fortunate to spend significant time at Princeton, Harvard, Oxford, the Australian National University, Rice University, Rutgers, and the National Humanities Center. Thanks to that, I have had the good fortune to get to know, fairly well, many people who were among the world's leaders in their respective fields. I have known someone who at one time was widely regarded as the "Dean of English Literature;" the former head of the President's Council on Bioethics; a former president of the American Historical Association; several former presidents of the American Philosophical Association; the former head of the National Endowment for the Arts; the former head of the National Science Foundation; several MacArthur Award winners; several presidents of distinguished universities; one of the world's leading cancer researchers; one of the principal architects of Obamacare (the Affordable Care Act); and several Nobel laureates. All of these people are, or were, genuinely brilliant. Each has made extraordinary contributions to their field. Still, while I can't pretend that I knew each of them as well as I knew Parfit, I can say that, in my judgment, none of them rivaled Derek at the peak of his powers, in terms of his incredibly rare combination of insight, originality, intensity, single-minded focus, argumentative abilities, and sheer brilliance.

* * *

In the last years of his life, Derek's hugs were longer and warmer, and he peppered our conversations and email correspondences with expressions of affection. My favorite is when he would refer to me as his "great life enhancer." I cannot imagine anyone other than Derek ever invoking such an expression, but that made it all the more special.

I'd like to think that Derek was referring to my introducing him to ice cream sundaes and American football! But I know better. He was mainly referring to my role in three events that meant a great deal to him.

First, in the spring of 2003, I organized a workshop on an early draft of Derek's *On What Matters*, in honor of Derek's sixtieth birthday. Besides Derek and myself, the conference participants included John Broome (Oxford), Ruth Chang (Rutgers), Stephen Darwall (Michigan), Allan Gibbard (Michigan), Tom Hurka (Toronto), Shelly Kagan (Yale), Frances Kamm (NYU), Chris Korsgaard (Harvard), Jeff McMahan (Rutgers), Tom Nagel (NYU), Thomas Pogge (Columbia), Peter Railton (Michigan), Tim Scanlon (Harvard), and David Sussman (Princeton).[25] The overall quality of the papers, and Derek's responses to them, were the best I have ever seen at any conference, and numerous participants commented on the historic nature of the conference. One participant noted, only half-jokingly, that the conference was perhaps the greatest collection of moral philosophers since Plato was teaching Aristotle at his Academy. Derek was deeply moved by the proceedings, and he was always grateful to me for organizing it.

Second, in 2004, Ruth Chang came up with the brilliant idea that Rutgers should try to entice Derek to start visiting Rutgers regularly, in addition to NYU and Harvard. Jeff McMahan and I were enthusiastic about this idea, and the three of us persuaded the Department to pursue it. It was, of course, an easy sell. A slightly harder sell was convincing Derek, and convincing the Administration to go along with the idea since, as a rule, they opposed what they regarded as so-called "letterhead" appointments. Because of my position in the Department, and my relationship with Derek, I ended up serving as the main intermediary between Derek, our Department, and the Administration, in the effort to turn Ruth's dream into a reality.

I was aided in this task by Peter Klein, the main architect of Rutgers's rise to prominence as a philosophical powerhouse. He thought that we should not only try to come up with an offer that Parfit "couldn't refuse"; we should try to come up with an offer that would entice Derek to make Rutgers his *sole* destination for U.S. visits, and to eventually move to Rutgers full-time when mandatory retirement forced him to leave All Souls College. If successful, this would simultaneously strengthen Rutgers, while also weaking our main rival, NYU!

Derek had been visiting NYU and Harvard for six weeks each semester, in alternating years. We offered Derek twice the amount of money that he was getting from NYU or Harvard, but he only had to teach six weeks a year for us. So, for the same amount of money, he could teach one quarter as much,

[25] Here, I indicate in parentheses the primary academic homes of the participants at the time of the conference. Many are no longer at the institutions they were at then.

which would enable him to spend more time on his research. Derek was thrilled by our offer, but NYU and Harvard quickly matched it. And Derek was reluctant to give up the opportunity of continuing to work with Nagel at NYU and Scanlon at Harvard, as well as the excellent graduate students that those programs attracted. Thus, ultimately, Derek ended up splitting his visits between all three universities. However, the upshot of our offer was that Derek ended up making four times as much as he was previously making, for the same amount of work.

Other than books and ice cream, Derek had very few material wants and needs. He didn't drive a car, own a lavish home, take vacations, dine out extravagantly, have a TV, or have any expensive habits. So, in fact, Derek's change in fortune had no visible impact on his daily life. Still, it meant that he and Janet could look forward to being financially secure for the rest of their lives. It also meant that he and Janet would be able to leave a much larger estate to various charities. This was much more important to Derek than any increase in his own wellbeing. For my role in helping to make that happen (for which Derek gave me far too much credit), Derek was deeply grateful.

Third, in 2013 I was invited to submit a nomination for the 2014 Rolf Schock Prize in Logic and Philosophy, to be awarded by the Swedish Royal Academy. Along with my nomination, I was asked to provide a "short motivation" of one or two sentences in support of my nominee. I provided the nomination requested, and then added another eight single-spaced pages detailing why I thought that Derek Parfit merited the Prize! In addition to sending my nomination to the selection committee, I sent a copy of it to Derek. Derek called me, obviously touched by what I had written, and asked me if he could share my recommendation with his wife, Janet, and his sister, Theo. I was, of course, very pleased by this reaction.

In the end, Derek was awarded the Prize. He received it from Princess Christina, sister to the King of Sweden, and the ceremony was held in the House of Nobility, in a room in which all of the coats of arms of the Swedish heraldry, dating back to the twelfth century, hung on the walls. The ceremony was followed by a posh dinner in the same room where the Swedish Nobel laureates were feted. The celebration spanned several days, and it was one of the highlights of Derek's life. Later, Derek and I learned that my letter had played a key role in persuading some of the committee members that Derek should be awarded the Prize. After everything that Derek had done for me over the years to help advance my career, this was *enormously* gratifying news to receive.

Much less consequentially—since they were mere formalities at that stage—it was my great pleasure to supply recommendations, at Derek's request, in support of his final reappointments at All Souls, NYU, and Harvard. I cannot overstate how proud I was, and deeply honored, to be writing letters of recommendation on behalf of Derek.

***

Before concluding this essay, I want to include a segment from my Rolf Schock letter, commenting on the testimonials that were made about Derek in the celebratory dinner at the conference. To wit: Six people spoke about Parfit that evening, and when they were done, there was literally not a dry eye in the room. Never have I seen such an outpouring of gratitude, affection, love, and respect in an academic setting. It was clear that G. A. Cohen was not the only one who put Parfit up on a pedestal. The entire assembly did. Moreover, what they admired most about Parfit was not his magnificent intellect and contributions to philosophy but his incredible spirit and generosity, and the role that he had played in their lives as teacher, mentor, and inspiration.

Most of the speakers pointed out the profound influence that Derek had exerted on the profession, not only through his own writings but through the extraordinary support and penetrating criticisms that he generously gave to countless others. It was observed that Derek was notorious for giving feedback on papers and book manuscripts that was often equal in length—and far superior in quality!—to the original material he was commenting on. In support of this, one speaker read acknowledgements from a number of books that he happened to have on his bookshelf at home. They included the following:

> It [my book] got longer . . . thanks to the extraordinary and painstaking attention showered on it by Derek Parfit. Derek commented on the whole, not once, but three times, and I have incorporated his suggestions in well over a hundred passages. My thanks go beyond this, however, for his general encouragement and enthusiasm have themselves been equally important to me. (Shelly Kagan, *The Limits of Philosophy*)[26]

[26] Shelly Kagan, *The Limits of Morality* (Oxford: Oxford University Press, 1989), p. xiii.

> My greatest debt is to Derek Parfit. From his early enthusiastic encouragement, without which I probably would not have written this book, to his more recent voluminous comments on my manuscript, which corrected several important errors and led to improvements on almost every page, his generosity to me has been literally astonishing. (Liam Murphy, *Moral Demands in Nonideal Theory*)[27]

> My biggest debt over the years is to Derek Parfit, for encouragement, discussion, and wonderfully detailed comments" (Frances Kamm, *Morality, Mortality, Vol. I*)[28]

> My debt to Derek Parfit is, quite simply, extraordinary . . . his written comments on the penultimate draft were almost as long as the draft itself, and I blush to think of the errors the book would have contained but for his detailed and sensitive criticisms . . . I suspect that only those who have received comparable assistance from him, and they are by no means few in number, will be able to fully appreciate the real extent of my debt. (Samuel Scheffler, *The Rejection of Consequentialism*)[29]

These are but a smattering of the many such acknowledgements that have been written to Parfit. My own acknowledgement, in *Inequality*, went as follows:

> It would be impossible to exaggerate his influence on this work. Morally and politically, I had been concerned about equality as long as I could remember. But it was not until I read Parfit that I was first stimulated to examine inequality seriously. Moreover, it was Parfit who encouraged me to develop my views on this topic—no small point, since, looking back, my initial "Reflections on Equality" was unbelievably crude and ill-formed. Parfit has been an extraordinary source of rich ideas and penetrating criticisms, and he has had a profound influence on this book's development and

[27] Liam Murphy, *Moral Demands in Nonideal Theory* (New York: Oxford University Press, 2000), pp. vii–viii.

[28] Frances Kamm, *Morality, Mortality, Volume I: Death and Whom to Save From It* (New York: Oxford University Press, 1993), p. vi.

[29] Samuel Scheffler, *The Rejection of Consequentialism: A Philosophical Investigation of the Considerations Underlying Rival Moral Conceptions* (Oxford: Oxford University Press, 1982), pp. v–vi.

content. In addition, he has been an inexhaustible source of inspiration and encouragement, for which I am deeply grateful.[30]

The above acknowledgements are high praise, indeed. However, in fact, they *understate* the importance and extent of Parfit's influence and support. I remember talking with Sam Scheffler about his acknowledgement shortly after his book came out, and he told me that he had originally written a much *more* effusive acknowledgement, that Derek had vetoed. At that point, Scheffler told me, he couldn't help thinking that it was bad enough that Parfit had written much of the book, but now he was writing his own acknowledgement and insisting that he *not* get proper recognition for his contributions! What they *should* have done, Scheffler said—only half in jest—is simply change the attribution of authorship. It should have been *The Rejection of Consequentialism* by Derek Parfit, with help from Samuel Scheffler. I know from my own case, as well as discussions with many others, how close to the truth Scheffler's story is.

The authors listed above are all major figures in contemporary moral theory. However, I know that Parfit spent comparable amounts of time helping countless philosophers, graduate students, and undergraduates of whom most people have never heard. His inexhaustible support for philosophers worldwide, famous or not, was nothing short of astounding. So, too, was his ongoing dedication to the generations of students that he taught at Oxford, Harvard, NYU, and, before that, Princeton.

As I listened to the many testimonials that were given to Parfit, I was struck by the tone and terms in which he was praised. Again and again, Parfit was spoken of in spiritual terminology, and in reverential terms usually reserved for religious figures. He was literally described by one person as a saint; by another as a gift to man from God; by yet another as someone who was different from everyone else, as if he were from another planet, with special powers, who came to earth with the aim of trying to help our world, filled with so many lesser mortals, to become a better place; and by yet another as like the Buddha himself, whose views he so admired. In addition, each speaker touted Parfit as a shining inspiration of what a philosopher should be. As I listened to the testimonials, I was dumbfounded by what I was hearing. I had long thought that I took a backseat to no one in my gratitude towards, and admiration of, Parfit. But it was apparent that he had touched

[30] Temkin, *Inequality*, p. ix.

countless people in the way that he had touched me, and that there were literally dozens of people who owed their entire philosophical careers to him.

After the dinner, Holly Smith, the then Dean of the Graduate Program and Faculty of Arts and Sciences, came up to me and exclaimed that she wished that we had videotaped the proceedings. She said that she would have liked to show it to each of her faculty members as an inspiration of what a mentor should be. I shared her sentiments, but I realize full well that there was only one Derek Parfit. While the rest of us can be inspired to *emulate* him, we cannot realistically hope to actually *be* like him.

* * *

These are but a smattering of my memories of Derek. I have *so* many others—memories of Sunday-night dinners with Derek at his parents' home in Oxford; memories of Derek urging Meg and me to travel to Russia before the breakup of the Soviet Union; memories of a small dinner party honoring Derek at the President of Harvard's house, with A. K. Sen, Hilary Putnam, Tim Scanlon, Theo and Van Ooms (Derek's sister and her husband, a former Chief Economist of the Senate Budget Committee, the Office of Management and Budget, and the House Budget Committee, and also a former Chair of the President's Council of Economic Advisers), and, of course, the President and his wife, Neil and Angelica Rudenstine (whose friendship with the Oomses dated back to when Ooms and Rudenstine were both Rhodes Scholars at Oxford in the early 1960s); memories of Derek wanting, and expecting, to stay at our home when he regularly visited Rutgers—and my wife putting the kibosh on that because she knew how much Derek and I always talked philosophy whenever we were together, and she wasn't willing to have me lost to her and our three children for six weeks at a time on a yearly basis; and so on. The memories are seemingly endless. And, strikingly, they are overwhelmingly fond ones.

Still, this essay has to end at some point. So, let me end it with the following final thoughts.

Over the course of my life, I sent countless pages of comments to Derek on countless drafts of his work. In addition, I sent countless letters and emails expressing my admiration for Derek, and my deep gratitude and affection for him. These correspondences were, in their own way, love letters from me to Derek. And Derek, in his own way, responded in kind.

I was so lucky, and privileged, to have had the relationship with Derek that I did. He improved my life immeasurably, and for that I will always be profoundly grateful. This essay is, in essence, my final love letter to Derek. Although he knew full well how I felt about him, it saddens me to know that he will never read this, and that I will not hear back from him. Ever again. I wish that I shared Derek's attitude towards death. But I don't. If I did, I might not miss him so.

4
My Brother Derek

Theodora Ooms

I am the only person now alive who knew Derek for his whole life. It remains a puzzle for me to understand how he changed from the ordinary British schoolboy I knew into the brilliant, highly regarded, and somewhat eccentric moral philosopher that he became.

There are several factors that I believe helped shape Derek's character, interests, achievements, and passions: namely, the series of educational and academic institutions he lived in, the way he chose to spend his time, the influence of his immediate family, and his family history.

Derek and I were born three years apart in Chengdu, China, where our British parents, Jessie and Norman—both qualified doctors—lived and worked for nearly ten years, under the auspices of the British Church Missionary Society (CMS), teaching public health at the university. Our family left China in 1944 and traveled back to England via America, by plane and by ship. The whole journey took eighteen months. Derek took his first steps when we traveled through the Panama Canal. We lived in New York City for a year, and it was here that our sister Joanna was born. Then we finally got berths on the Queen Mary's first postwar voyage and landed in London in 1945, where we were greeted by our extended family. Derek, who was 3 at the time, was so overwhelmed by the excited greetings of all these family members that he developed a temporary stutter.

Jessie, our mother, described Derek in a letter at this time as a "curly-headed blond . . . a mischievous, active little rascal with a very wicked glint in his eye." She commented that he was a very late talker and that Norman worried they might have to put Derek in a private school for backward children!

After two years living in South London, in 1949 my parents moved to Oxford, where they bought a house, and I was sent off to boarding school. After that, Derek and I spent time together only during the school holidays.

We went to very different boarding schools—my sister Joanna and I attended Dartington Hall, a very progressive boarding school in South Devon,

Theodora Ooms, *My Brother Derek* In: *Derek Parfit: His Life and Thought*. Edited by: Jeff McMahan, Oxford University Press. © Oxford University Press 2025. DOI: 10.1093/9780191915307.003.0004

while Derek went to Eton, just outside London. I then attended Oxford University, and after graduating went to America to follow my American boyfriend Van Ooms (whom I married a year later) and to attend Columbia University's School of Social Work.

At Eton, Derek did very well academically and socially, but he left Eton early and managed to get a job as a summer intern at *The New Yorker* in New York. We learned later that it was Derek's mention, in his letter asking for a job, of his great love of classical jazz, and specifically Charlie Parker, that led *The New Yorker* editor William Shawn to hire him for a year.

I got to know Derek best when he came to New York in the spring of 1961. He lived in the West End Avenue apartment I shared with Van's friends—three American Rhodes Scholars who were alternately entranced and exasperated by this cocky, argumentative 18-year-old British kid.

Derek fell in love with New York City—the tall buildings, open blue skies, and vistas of long avenues—as well as with the openness, diversity, and general brashness of Americans—a love that lasted for the rest of his life.

Van and I took Derek to jazz clubs, to museums, and on many walks around Central Park. Derek was the only witness at our first "secret" wedding in City Hall. He was not able to come to our "real" wedding in Oxford two months later, but gave us as a wedding gift James Thurber's classic book *Is Sex Necessary?* After our wedding and a summer spent in Europe, Van and I moved to New Haven, Connecticut.

Three years later, after studying at Oxford, Derek won a two-year Harkness Fellowship, which required him to spend three months of the year traveling across the USA and spending time at various universities. Before he headed off on his travels, he visited us in New Haven several times at weekends so that Van could teach him to drive. Derek behind the wheel of a car was then, and always remained, a rather alarming phenomenon. So we were nervous when he went off to take his driving test, but he returned triumphant and declared, "I ran through a red light, hit a curb, and drove on the wrong side of the road, but I passed the test!"

At the memorial for Derek held in All Souls in June 2017, several of those who knew Derek well at the Dragon School, Eton, and Oxford—including two of his former girlfriends—took me aside and said they didn't recognize the Derek everyone was talking about. They described the Derek they knew as a perfectly normal, clever, gregarious, and happy young man with a wide range of interests and activities, admired and liked by all, enthusiastic about life, and with many friends. They agreed that at school Derek had been highly competitive and unusual in that he excelled at everything that he did—but he was never viewed as eccentric, odd, or reclusive.

Edward Mortimer, who knew Derek well at Eton and at Oxford, described the images that came to mind when he thought about the Derek he remembered: Derek the Intellect, the Actor, the Debater; Derek the Jazz Trumpeter, the Journalist, and the Romantic. Edward added that Derek was also a social climber who, on the eve of his hoped-for election to join Eton's Pop Society (the most exclusive social club at Eton), bought a large box of marrons glacés—a favorite candy—to hand around to all the voters.

Later in life, Derek admitted that he realized his behavior was different from that of most of his colleagues and friends, and that he sometimes wondered why. Derek himself would often attribute this to his spending so much of his life living and working in educational and academic institutions, albeit unusual ones. And I think there is some truth in that.

Derek attended the famous Dragon School, a preparatory school in North Oxford (a few blocks from our home), first as a day boy and then as a boarder. At the Dragon from the age of 6 onwards, he was exposed daily to heavy doses of Latin and Greek and romped straight through all of English history three times before he was 13. (He studied very little mathematics or science.)

Derek then won a scholarship to attend Eton College. Here he had his own room, living alongside other scholars in an intellectual hothouse, quite separate from the building where the ordinary scions of English aristocracy lived. The scholars all wore top hats and tails every day and learned to play often quite brutal games such as rugger (rugby football) and the arcane Eton wall game.

After leaving Eton, Derek spent three years at Balliol College, Oxford, studying for his BA in history and living in college. Derek's one traumatic adventure at Balliol was tearing a 12-inch gash in his left arm on a metal spike when he slipped while attempting to clamber up a drainpipe to get back into college after hours, having spent the evening at Somerville (one of the five women-only colleges at Oxford). I was aware that, while at Oxford, Derek developed strong romantic relationships with at least two clever and beautiful women students, both of whom I came to know and like a lot.

After graduation, Derek was awarded a Harkness Fellowship to the USA. This entailed a two-year odyssey to several universities, during which time he switched his field from history to philosophy. He then landed a fellowship at All Souls College, where he lived and worked until he retired in 2010.

Derek told me that he was acutely aware that by being at All Souls, where he had no teaching or family responsibilities, he could focus entirely on his own work. He admitted that he had very little experience of "normal" family life and responsibilities. He marveled at his academic friends interacting with and caring for their children and simply couldn't imagine himself doing the same. He didn't think he would be a competent parent.

He was frequently away teaching in America. He told me that this was partly because American universities paid better (and his photography hobby was very expensive!); and also because he enjoyed teaching American students more than English students, saying that they were more outgoing and argumentative. He had also developed close friendships with several American philosophers.

Over the next several decades, Derek and I saw each other occasionally when he was invited to give talks to philosophy departments all over the US. He spent Christmas with us a couple of times and got to know our three children—Katrina, Alex, and Tamara—when we lived in Swarthmore and then in Washington, DC. We had brief visits with Derek and his then partner and later wife, Janet Radcliffe Richards, after they bought their stunningly beautiful Georgian home in West Kennett near Avebury. Because they talked about planning to explore the lovely countryside and get to know and entertain their interesting neighbors—Janet, we already knew, was an excellent cook—we expected that this purchase might significantly change their lifestyle, but it didn't (as Janet explains in her contribution to this volume).

After the publication of *Reasons and Persons* in 1984, we saw Derek less and less frequently, as his own teaching and writing absorbed him more and more. I realized early on that although Derek loved his family, he would not give priority to spending time with us.

On August 30, 2010, I was at our summer home in Maine when I received an unexpected phone call from Derek. "I just want you to know that Janet and I are getting married in Oxford tomorrow." "That's wonderful," I shrieked, "but I'm in Maine and won't be able to get there in time!" Derek replied, "I wasn't *inviting* you—I just wanted you to know." A couple of weeks later he confessed that they had decided, after some twenty-six years together, to get married, which Derek said was largely for tax reasons. He added he was surprised to find that it felt "very sweet."

To our delight, Derek and Janet did finally take us up on our longstanding invitation to visit us in Maine for a week's vacation. We were thrilled, and though Derek escaped to our guest cottage to work much of the time, he did also relax. We went on a long boat excursion in the Penobscot Bay, kayaked around our cove, and went to a lovely chamber music concert in Blue Hill. We lazed in the sun, admired the glorious views, and talked and talked.

I learned that there were a few occasions when Derek would shift from his focus on his own work and would be so moved by a family member's, friend's, or colleague's problems or suffering that he got very involved in trying to help them. For example, Derek and my sister Joanna loved each other but had little in common. Joanna would call Derek when she was depressed or in trouble (she was often short of money), and he would listen and try to console her and often sent her money. A major, very poignant, example of his capacity for empathy was when in 1986 Joanna was tragically killed in a car accident. She was a single parent and thus her 6-year-old son, Tom, became an orphan. A major battle then ensued between the Parfits and the child welfare authorities about Tom's future. Derek threw himself into this battle, determined that justice, rationality, and good sense should prevail. He spent hours with my mother and Janet writing and rewriting our court affidavit, making sure all the arguments were perfectly expressed. At the court hearing, Derek yelled out angrily "Rubbish!" when the judge misunderstood or misstated an argument. (The outcome of this battle was a very happy one: the Grant family—Frances, Adrian, and their daughter Zanna—adopted Tom, and they became part of our family and vice versa.)

Another major factor influencing Derek was his attitude towards, and use of, his time. After the publication of *Reasons and Persons,* Derek gradually developed a monomaniacal focus on his work. This intense focus provided him with the rationale for his much-commented-on eccentric habits—what he ate, what he wore, and various behaviors which were all rationally designed to preserve his time for thinking and writing.

I recently found a letter that Derek wrote to us in 1996, which enclosed a long memo titled *Plans for Future Books.* After giving a detailed outline of his plans for the next four books, he added, "I would then turn, if alive, to my fifth book, for which my ideas are much more vague—and it will address Truth, Evil, Time, and the Sublime."

Since his first book had taken him twenty years to write, it is no wonder that Derek became acutely aware of the diminishing amount of time he had left to fulfill his daunting agenda.

As several people have pointed out, this monomaniacal focus on his work was at the cost of some of his non-philosopher friendships and interests, including spending time with his wife, Janet, and with other family members. He stopped traveling for pleasure and gave up his beloved photography. He became more and more hermit-like. Yet, as my husband, Van, has always noted, Derek remained able to converse brilliantly on almost any topic—somehow keeping up with world news, environmental issues, and the latest scientific discoveries.

Our parents were clearly a major influence on Derek's personality, interests, and activities. Whenever he was in Oxford, he visited our parents faithfully every Sunday to share a meal and to catch up on conversation, which they hugely enjoyed. Derek said he had nothing in common with our father, who wanted him to be a scientist and who was quite mystified by Derek's choice of philosophy as his vocation and profession. Though very proud of his brilliant son, Norman was clearly quite baffled by him. And indeed they did have very little in common. But I was very happy that Norman lived just long enough to admire Blackwell's two-window spread of books and photos of Derek that celebrated the publication of *Reasons and Persons* in 1984.

Derek was much more directly influenced by our brilliant mother, Jessie. She was a lifelong learner. She taught at the Open University, and she herself took an overview course on philosophy so that she could talk more knowledgeably with Derek about his work. Awarded major prizes in her medical school career, in midlife she obtained a second degree from Oxford in child psychiatry and soon obtained a very high-level job at the Inner London Education Authority, in charge of all the mental health services for emotionally disturbed children in the Inner London area.

Jessie also shared with us her love of books and reading. She encouraged us to read widely throughout our childhood. During our school holidays, we would cycle each week to the public library in Oxford to return the dozens of books we had borrowed and read the previous week and to choose new ones. Jessie took us on long walks in the countryside and encouraged Derek's interest in the architecture of Oxford buildings, and they visited all the Hawksmoor churches in London. Jessie was very musical, played the piano well, and sang in choirs all her life. Derek and I shared this interest in music, and for several years Derek played the trumpet.

Norman, on the other hand, was unable successfully to encourage in Derek, Joanna, or me his own passions for playing tennis, collecting stamps, and going to the movies. (However, Derek did enjoy playing various games including chess, mah-jong, and ping-pong, and was good at them.)

Norman was the second oldest of five children. Of the other four—Cyril, Eric, Marion, and Ruth—the two brothers, who were fond but distant uncles, were both interested in photography and in making films. It was Cyril who gave Derek his first camera as a teenager, and it was this which started Derek on his love of taking photographs.

Derek was interested in politics, but it was Norman who held strong and very passionate views about politics, war, and peace, and especially health (he spent much time advocating more and better cancer prevention and promoting dental health through fluoridation). He was a socialist and lifelong, ardent pacifist and teetotaler. Both our parents were active supporters of the Labour Party. After he retired, Norman continued to attend political meetings and listen to politicians' speeches.

Although they were, indeed, very different in personality, Norman and Derek shared some characteristics: Norman always believed that others would in time come to agree with his views—and I think that Derek similarly thought this about his own work.

Norman used to remind us that our name, "Parfit," derived from the Middle English word "parfit" (or "parfyt"), meaning "perfect" (the "verray, parfit gentil knyght" was a key character in Chaucer's *The Canterbury Tales*). Each year, Norman would spend days writing and revising his short Annual Medical Officer of Health Report to make sure it was all correct and perfect. In many ways I think that, both in his work and his photography, Derek also tried hard to live up to our Parfit surname.

I always knew that spending time with family was simply not a priority for Derek—but he occasionally made exceptions. When I realized that Derek would be teaching at New York University, I called him to invite him to the wedding of our son, Alex, to Heather Lamm, which was to take place in Aspen, Colorado, in September 2001. Derek sweetly declined the invitation, using his work as an excuse, and adding, "Besides I don't go to weddings, only funerals." I decided to be assertive and replied, firmly, "I don't care, Derek, whether you come to my funeral or not, but I do want you to come to Heather and Alex's wedding." He then agreed and came bearing a sheaf of his astonishingly beautiful photographs to give to all my family as treasured gifts. Derek, of course, charmed our newly expanded family and friends and seemed to have a thoroughly good time at the wedding. I learned from this that when I told Derek firmly that something mattered a great deal to me, he would be more likely to say yes. Using this strategy, I succeeded in getting him to come to the first and only reunion of our five Parfit cousins—who all happened to be in North America at the same time—which we held in our summer home in September 2006.

Our family has strong missionary genes. In addition to both of our parents and an uncle, all four grandparents were religious missionaries, in the Middle East and India. I thus like to think of Derek as a modern *secular* missionary. He had such a passionate zeal to set the world right, to increase human happiness, and to do good through the vehicles of his philosophy and his involvement in the effective altruism movement.

My journey to try to understand and truly appreciate this extraordinary, complex person, my brother Derek, will continue for the rest of my life. But I have learned so many interesting and wonderful things about Derek at commemorative events, through the outpourings on the internet, and through the many conversations I have had with Janet, Larry, Jeff, Frances, and Ruth. I much appreciate their vibrant circle of friendship—one that had nourished and supported Derek for decades. By talking to those who knew him in different ways, I have also learned what a good, kind, and caring human being Derek could be, and how as a teacher he gave so much of himself to his students, colleagues, and friends.

5
Derek Parfit as I Knew Him

Jeff McMahan

1 Introduction

My first sighting of Derek Parfit was in the autumn of 1978, at the beginning of my first term as a graduate student at Oxford. It was in 10 Merton Street, the building that at the time housed Oxford's Sub-faculty of Philosophy. I recall following Parfit from the library there into the small lecture theater for the first meeting of the seminar he taught that term. I distinctly remember thinking that he was rather peculiar in appearance: gangling and bent forward from the waist, with his trousers pulled too high and a slightly pompadoured hairdo. I would later recognize the same angle at the waist in his mother, in whose house I would be living a year later.

I am chagrined to be unable to remember even what the topic of the seminar was. Apart from that initial impression of his slightly unprepossessing appearance, only two memories linger. One is of Parfit writhing almost convulsively in his chair, taking occasional swigs from a vodka bottle, as he wrestled with the ideas and arguments that vied for his assent. The clear liquid in the bottle was, I soon learned, water. The reason it was in a vodka bottle, I later learned, is that he always had an abundant stock of those bottles, as he drank vodka copiously, and directly from the bottle, just before going to bed, as a means of treating his insomnia. The vodka, together with a fistful of tablets of amitriptyline, one of the old tricyclic antidepressants, was the only way that his doctors could find to subdue the ideas and arguments that raged in his mind long enough to enable him to go to sleep and stay asleep for a time. I recall his once telling me, with envy, about a classmate at Eton who thought that going to sleep was entirely voluntary and who could *will* himself to sleep. All this student had to do, he claimed, was tell himself, "Cripps, go to sleep," and he would immediately fall asleep.

My second memory from that seminar is that there was one student who raised his hand once after every lecture to ask a question that was barely

Jeff McMahan, *Derek Parfit as I Knew Him* In: *Derek Parfit: His Life and Thought*. Edited by: Jeff McMahan, Oxford University Press. © Oxford University Press 2025. DOI: 10.1093/9780191915307.003.0005

comprehensible but, to the extent that one could make any sense of it, was invariably stupid. Soon, when this student hoisted his arm, there was an audible collective sigh, and every eye in the room other than Parfit's rolled. I have no recollection of whether the collective exhalations and rotating eyeballs subsided later in the term, but I, for one, came actually to relish these questions—for they provided the audience with a rare intellectual treat. Parfit would listen courteously while this rather pompous student spouted nonsense and would then say, "Thank you; that's very interesting. As I understand what you are saying . . .," and would immediately go on to introduce some novel and fascinating idea that had been suggested to him by a cluster of words the student had uttered. He would set this idea forth lucidly, confect an ingenious objection to it, offer a reply to the objection, then reply to the reply, and so on. These were captivating displays of spontaneous intellectual and philosophical brilliance. But Parfit was not showing off; nor were his impromptu intellectual gymnastics only an effort to prevent the student from being humiliated. He also took every suggestion, however daft, sufficiently seriously to consider whether there might be some more reasonable idea lurking nearby. The student, I assume, always left the seminar in a glow of pride at having posed such a probing question.

Kindness and charity came entirely naturally to Parfit. Throughout the thirty-eight years in which I knew him well, I never heard him utter an unkind word about anyone, even those who had been unkind or unjust to him. His behavior in seminars, lectures, and other discussions was in this respect unusual at the time. Lectures by visiting speakers in Oxford and Cambridge seemed to be regarded by many members of the faculty as occasions for competitions to determine who could most cleverly and wittily not only refute but eviscerate the speaker. Even students were not always spared. I recall attending another graduate seminar a few years later in Cambridge that was co-taught by two distinguished philosophers. There was an American student whose questions were earnest but rather ploddingly and laboriously expressed. On one occasion while this student was speaking, one of the professors tore off a little scrap of paper, scrawled something on it, and passed it with a knowing look to the other. The other professor read it and they shared a chuckle, obviously at the expense of the student who was speaking. On another occasion the more senior philosopher asked the class, "Are there any further questions before we move on?" The American raised his hand in a way that was visible to all, but the professor swept his gaze across the room and announced, "In that case we'll move on to the next topic." It is unimaginable that Parfit would ever have been flagrantly cruel in that way to anyone.

During the autumn term in 1978 when I attended Parfit's seminar, my DPhil thesis was being supervised by Jonathan Glover. Although being able to work with Glover was a consummation of my hopes, he soon recognized that the issues in which I was most interested—abortion, when we begin to exist, the difference between killing an embryo or fetus and preventing a person from coming into existence, whether there are reasons to cause well-off people to exist, and so on—were more closely related to what Parfit was working on at the time. He therefore asked Parfit if he would be willing to become my supervisor, and Parfit agreed.

An abbreviated history of my subsequent relations with Parfit can be stated in a few brief paragraphs—though because I am now describing a period in which we had become friends, I will henceforth refer to him as "Derek" (a name, he once told me, he had always hated). He became my official supervisor for the next two terms, until the summer of 1979. At that point the funding I had had from the Rhodes Trust ended. I had been offered a couple of what were called research studentships at different Oxford colleges, but the stipends were insufficient for me to live on. St John's College, Cambridge, however, offered me a research studentship with a stipend on which I could live and free housing as well. Derek's advice, almost verbatim, was: "Take Cambridge's money, go there on occasion to satisfy whatever requirements there may be, but live in Oxford and continue to work with me. I will arrange for you and Sally [my wife at the time] to have the top-floor flat in my parents' house in North Oxford." So, for the academic year 1979–80 we alternated between Oxford and Cambridge, living for a short period in one place and then the other, driving back and forth in a second-hand car I was able to buy for £500. But the small house that St John's gave me was a block and a half from the college and half a block from Jesus Green, a large park on one side of the Cam. So coveted were the properties on our little road that, when he was not in London, Clive James (the celebrated writer and broadcaster) lived in a house across the street. Furthermore, I requested and was assigned Bernard Williams as the supervisor of my PhD thesis. These two circumstances, together with the fact that Cambridge offered a more bucolic environment than Oxford, persuaded me after the end of the year to leave Norman and Jessie Parfit's house—the house in which Derek would have grown up had he not been almost continuously resident in boarding schools—to live full-time in Cambridge.

Yet I continued, at his invitation, indeed insistence, to meet with Derek regularly in Oxford to discuss both my work and, to a lesser degree, his, as the issues I was addressing overlapped substantially with those on which he was writing in his increasingly obsessive work on *Reasons and Persons*. I therefore had an almost uniquely privileged career as a doctoral student. I had not only frequent supervisions with Bernard Williams but also almost equally frequent supervisions with Derek. (I recall insisting that I should pay Derek whatever he would have been paid by Oxford for the supervision of a DPhil student; but that turned out to be around £20 per term, and I think my punctiliousness about not exploiting his generosity soon lapsed.) It was also a slightly befuddling graduate career, as I was writing what I think may have been the first doctoral thesis wholly within the area of systematic ethical theory that later came to be known as population ethics—and I was writing it under the simultaneous supervision of both the progenitor of that entire area of philosophy and the most eminent living moral philosopher, who, as it happened, was then writing a book (*Ethics and the Limits of Philosophy*) devoted to explaining why systematic ethical theory was misguided and a waste of time.

As I had generous funding from St John's for seven years, I stayed there until the funding ended. After that, in 1986, I returned to the US. This was before there was widely accessible email, but Derek and I continued to exchange letters, mostly commenting on each other's work; and we occasionally spoke on the phone, sometimes for several hours, particularly during the last couple of years of the twentieth century, when we had long discussions of arguments I was developing in completing the writing of a book, *The Ethics of Killing*. But apart from these discussions and my occasional visits to Oxford, my contact with Derek was less extensive between 1986 and 2007, when he began to teach at Rutgers, where I was teaching at the time. Between 2007 and 2014, when I left Rutgers for Oxford, Derek taught at Rutgers five times, each time for seven weeks. During those periods, he lived in my house. And when I moved to Oxford in early November of 2014, I lived in his house there until he died in London shortly after midnight on January 2, 2017. During his final decade, therefore, I probably had more personal contact with him than anyone other than his wife, Janet—though he also had extensive contact with Larry Temkin, whose work (on the issues addressed in his *Rethinking the Good*) was closer to what Derek was working on in those years than mine was (as I was working primarily on the ethics of self-defense and war).

2 Elements of Character: Genius and Generosity

The two most striking of Derek's attributes as a supervisor were his extraordinary generosity and kindness and his formidable and involuntarily intimidating intelligence. He would often begin our supervisions by saying of the material that I had submitted in advance, "This is all excellent and can go straight into the thesis with little alteration. I have only a few minor comments . . ."—whereupon he would produce, in the gentlest possible way, as if they really were only minor points, a series of objections to my arguments that seemed to me both devastating and decisive. I had, however, only a moment's dejected contemplation of the ruins, for his objections would be immediately followed by a range of constructive suggestions about how the argument could be rebuilt or the conclusions modified in response to the objections. As Frances Kamm observed in the brief remarks she sent to me to read out at the memorial event I organized at All Souls College about five months after Derek's death, "One never had to fear Derek because he presented his comments in the kindest and most constructive way." I think everyone who discussed philosophy with him over the decades would confirm this.

Although it was exhilarating to participate in these discussions, it was also deflating, as the gulf between his analytical abilities and mine seemed almost unbridgeable. I was just intelligent enough to be intensely aware of how much more intelligent he was. He was by far the most brilliant thinker I have ever known. Over the years while he was alive and I was engaged in thinking about his ideas and arguments, I often thought that I had found a mistake in his work. But almost invariably when I discussed the matter with him, I discovered that I was the one who had been mistaken. He had simply seen deeper than I had. He was by far the deepest, most rigorous, and most imaginative thinker I have ever known.

In his responses to my objections, there was never the slightest trace of defensiveness or dogmatism. If one of my objections had been correct, he would almost certainly have recognized that, acknowledged his mistake, and altered his views accordingly. I have known a number of philosophers, some of whom have been highly distinguished, who have been profoundly averse to admitting that they have advanced an unsound argument or defended an erroneous view. This has always struck me as odd, even in egoistic terms. Errors are eventually exposed. Why would someone want to become known as the tenacious and unyielding defender of an exploded view? Derek was less egoistic about his work than any other philosopher I have known. His was a largely disinterested concern with discovering and making known the truth, particularly about morality. He therefore always invited and welcomed criticism of his arguments. Philosophers now routinely send their work in progress to colleagues, and sometimes even to philosophers they do not know, with a request for comments. My sense is that these practices were largely unknown when Derek entered the field in the late 1960s. But very early in his career he sent photocopies of long manuscripts both to philosophers he knew and to philosophers he did not know. A number of the returned manuscripts were among his papers when he died and on some of them he had written in hand that he had made the left margin unusually wide so that the recipient could write comments by hand and then return the manuscript to him. I think, though I cannot confirm, that Derek's practice was the source of the freedom that contemporary philosophers feel in sending their work out to others they do not know in the hope of receiving comments.

I had always assumed that Derek's praise of my work at the beginning of a supervision, before the demolition work began, was uncalculated, just the natural expression of his kindly and generous character. But during the last year of his life, when I was living in his house, we met by chance in the hallway outside his study. He took the opportunity to thank me for some written comments that I had recently sent him on some of the material on which he was working for *On What Matters: Volume Three*. After expressing his gratitude, he observed that my comments had not included anything complimentary about the work I had read and encouraged me never to neglect to find something in a person's work to praise, even if I thought the person did not need any reassurance. That last phrase was intended to indicate that he was aware that I had simply assumed that he knew how highly I thought of his work. But his remark prompted me subsequently to wonder whether his earlier praise of my student work was after all calculated to support my morale—and also, indeed, whether even at that late point in his life he really did still need reassurance about the quality of his work.

I will insert here one endearing piece of evidence for the view that, at least earlier, he did need such reassurance. Shortly before the manuscript of *Reasons and Persons* had to be delivered to Oxford University Press for there to be any prospect that his fellowship at All Souls would be renewed, he asked me if my wife and I could come from Cambridge to help him. We accordingly went to live in All Souls for the final week before his deadline to do whatever he asked of us. One of my tasks was to sort through the chaotic piles of paper in his study to determine whether there were, for example, papers that he needed to cite or that should be included in the bibliography. (Although Derek was one of the first philosophers to use a computer for writing, he seems never to have learned about a couple of other items of advanced technology: the stapler and the paper clip.) On one piece of paper I found, he had typed comments that various highly distinguished philosophers had written about his work. As I subsequently discovered, the quotations were mainly drawn from letters of reference or letters of evaluation that All Souls had solicited when the fellows had deliberated about the extension of his fellowship. There were passages praising his work by such luminaries as John Rawls, Bernard Williams, R. M. Hare, and Thomas Nagel. Indeed, all the passages were written by eminent and famous philosophers—or, rather, all but one. At the very bottom there were a couple of lines taken from a letter he had received at some point, which were attributed to "Jeff McMahan, a graduate student." I was, of course, delighted but also incredulous: it was simply unimaginable that the genius who had just written *Reasons and Persons* could have bothered to record a bit of praise from someone as utterly insignificant as I was, a beginning doctoral student who was still years from completing his PhD thesis, and whose status as a graduate student had to be recorded, I assume, so that I could be identified later after I had vanished from memory.

Although Derek may well have consciously adhered to the principle that one ought always to find something nice to say about every philosopher's work, he also had an entirely spontaneous sensitivity and gentleness in his way of expressing criticism. I am confident that it was not calculated when, in a much later email thanking me for sending him the comments I would be presenting on some of his work at a conference devoted to discussing manuscript material that eventually developed into *On What Matters*, he wrote that "I'm glad to say that we don't disagree as much as you think we may." This was his way of saying that I had completely misunderstood his view. He then went on to say that "it's my fault that you thought we disagreed more," on the ground that he had omitted some material in the draft that he had sent me that would have enabled me to understand his view better. (I was not the only one at the subsequent conference who disagreed with Derek less than he or she supposed. Shelly Kagan gave what I thought was a brilliant critique of one of Derek's arguments, only to learn when Derek responded that if he had read a certain passage a bit more carefully, he would have perceived that Derek's actual view was not the one he had criticized. I vividly recall Shelly flinging up his hands with a beaming smile and saying, in his characteristically resonant voice, "Well, Derek, I gave it my best shot!")

In his relations with me when I was his student, Derek was extraordinarily generous, not only in the encouragement he gave me but in various other ways as well. He was, for example, generous with his time. In the early 1980s, after I had ceased officially to be his student, I had some draft material for my thesis that I wanted to discuss with him. I was in North Carolina, preparing to return soon to Cambridge for the start of term. He was already in Princeton, where he was to teach that semester. He invited me to visit him in Princeton so that we could discuss my work, if I were willing to make the trip. Because I had to leave the country very soon, I was able to be in Princeton for only one day. Since he never got up in the morning before 11:00, he told me to come to the house where he was staying just after 11:00, which I did. As was always the case when I met with Derek, we immediately began to discuss philosophy. The discussion continued without any substantial intermission (he had a pizza delivered for dinner, which we ate while we talked) until 11 p.m. I have never known anyone else who has received or given a twelve-hour graduate supervision (and this, recall, occurred when Derek was no longer my supervisor).[1]

Derek was generous with other people's time and resources as well as with his own. Not long after he had become my supervisor, and thus before I had got to know him well, I told him that I would be unable to meet during a certain short period because both my mother and mother-in-law would be visiting from the US. In a rare instance of willingness to engage in small talk, he inquired what we planned to do while they were in the UK. I replied that, among other things, we planned to visit Cambridge, where at that point I had never been. He remarked that the bus ride to Cambridge was lengthy and tedious and that he regretted that he did not own a car that I could borrow. But inspiration descended and he immediately picked up the phone to call the distinguished philosopher Christopher Peacocke, who at the time was also at All Souls. He knew that Peacocke owned a car and asked him if I could borrow it for a few days. To my amazement, Peacocke consented without demurral, and a few days later I showed up at his residence, met him for the first (and, I think, last) time, and drove away in his car. What neither Derek nor Peacocke knew was that, although I had, of course, driven in the US (as every American does), I had never before driven on the left in the UK, so that Peacocke was quite fortunate to receive his car in unmauled condition a few days later.

Derek was legendary for his generosity in commenting on other people's work. Many important books in moral philosophy contain effusive

[1] David Edmonds notes in his biography that I once had a fourteen-hour supervision with Derek (*Parfit: A Philosopher and His Mission to Save Morality* (Princeton: Princeton University Press, 2023), p. 244). He is there referring to the meeting in Princeton. The mistake was mine. I thought when I spoke to Edmonds that my meeting with Derek had continued until 1 a.m., but I have subsequently found notes I took at the time that indicate that we adjourned at about 11 p.m.

expressions of gratitude to him. In *The Rejection of Consequentialism*, for example, Samuel Scheffler writes that

> My debt to Derek Parfit is, quite simply, extraordinary. His written comments on several drafts were extremely helpful and led to major improvements at points far too numerous to acknowledge individually. Indeed, his written comments on the penultimate draft were almost as long as that draft itself, and I blush to think of the errors the book would have contained but for his detailed and sensitive criticism. For all of this, and also for his support and encouragement, I am very deeply grateful. In fact, I suspect that only those who have received comparable assistance from him, and they are by no means few in number, will be able to fully appreciate the real extent of my debt.[2]

This book developed from Scheffler's doctoral dissertation at Princeton, where Derek taught as a visiting professor. Very few among even the best teachers ever receive, or deserve, a tribute such as this.

There are countless other testimonies to Derek's generosity in helping others with their work, both in the "Acknowledgements" sections of books and in footnotes in articles crediting those to whom the author is indebted. I will here reproduce one that is not in print but was sent to me by a former student of Derek's, Paul Linton, when he learned that I was planning to write this memoir. Linton reports that, when he had written a draft of his term essay for Derek's postgraduate seminar at NYU, he thought that this draft was rather disappointing.

> This was the first proper philosophy paper I'd ever written, and I went to his office hours to check how I might improve it. He could have given me a few pointers and sent me on my way. But he took 2+ hours to really teach me how to write a philosophical essay, and absolutely transformed my approach (and indeed my grades). I often think, if he hadn't spent those two hours I could have simply continued at roughly the same level for the next two years, thinking I was unavoidably bad at philosophy.[3]

[2] Samuel Scheffler, *The Rejection of Consequentialism: A Philosophical Investigation of the Considerations Underlying Rival Moral Conceptions* (Oxford: Clarendon Press, 1982), pp. vii–viii.

[3] Paul Linton, personal communication, email of August 24, 2018.

Derek's response to Linton's request for guidance was entirely characteristic.

In my experience, Derek had little proprietary concern about his ideas and was magnanimous in his acknowledgement of others in his work. What mattered to him was to find the truth, not to be known as the producer of original and important ideas. In a couple of places in his published work, for example, he credits me with ideas that probably emerged in discussions we had and that I cannot confidently say were mine rather than the product of our collaborative thinking. On one occasion, I was surprised to find a footnote in an article by Ronald Dworkin that says, "I owe this last suggestion to Derek Parfit, and through him, I understand, to J. P. Griffin and J. McMahon."[4] So even in discussions with others, Derek was careful to ensure that people got credit for ideas that may have emerged in discussions with him, even if he could not ensure that their names would be correctly spelled in subsequent citations.

Since, in his contribution to this volume, Larry Temkin reports a conflicting experience with Derek's citation practices, I should perhaps note that Derek had very little sense of the distinction between *meum et tuum*. During the periods when he lived in my house in New Jersey, he would occasionally borrow CDs that would somehow find their way into his luggage on his departure and disappear forever into his vast collection in Oxford—though happily on one occasion one of my box sets of the complete symphonies of Sibelius fell out of his carry-on bag onto the floor of the car when I was taking him to the airport. Characteristically, he did not notice when this happened, so I was able to preserve that set without having to embarrass him by identifying it as mine. On many other occasions, he would borrow books of mine that I would later find somewhere or other with the margins littered with the hieroglyphics—in black ballpoint pen—that he used for marking his own books. It simply never occurred to him to wonder whether a book or CD in his possession happened to belong to him or to someone else.

I have claimed that what mattered to Derek was to find the truth. Bertrand Russell was similarly driven. He once wrote, "I suppose that people who are not philosophers don't mind so much when things are puzzling—to me it is intolerable until I understand."[5] My sense is that, for Derek, it was not so much that he could not rest until *he* understood certain matters of importance as that he cared deeply that the truth about these matters *should be*

[4] Ronald Dworkin, "What is Equality? Part 1: Equality of Welfare," *Philosophy & Public Affairs*, 10 (1981): pp. 185–246, p. 214.

[5] Caroline Moorehead, *Bertrand Russell: A Life* (London: Sinclair-Stevenson, 1992), p. 195.

known. There is, nonetheless, an element of egoism in everyone, and I know that Derek sometimes worried whether his compulsion to find the truth about matters of morality was entirely disinterested. He once told me that, at both of his schools (the Dragon School in Oxford and Eton College), each student was evaluated every two weeks in the various different subjects and that, except in mathematics, he nearly always came first. And he *loved* it. He then said that while he hoped that he worked at his philosophy because it was worth doing for its own sake, he occasionally worried that he was "still the little boy who wants to be at the top."

He did not need to worry. It was very clear in the way he lived that he did not seek recognition or fame. Although he cared very much that his arguments should affect the way people live and act, he sought in the first instance to influence the thinking of other philosophers, presumably in the hope that his ideas would ultimately find their way into the public culture and influence the formation of public policy in the way that Rawls's ideas have done. That his ideas should appear in public discussions under his name did not matter to him. He never sought to be a "public intellectual." For decades he declined invitations to speak and almost never wrote for the popular media, as these activities would have taken time away from his philosophical work. He had no interest in social media and never had a personal website.

It is a depressing reflection on contemporary culture, and an even more depressing reflection on contemporary academic culture, that Derek received very little recognition during his lifetime. While many British philosophers have been elevated to the peerage, knighted, or awarded other honors conferred by the government, Derek never appeared on any "Honours List." He did not receive prizes that various other contemporary moral philosophers have received (Templeton Prize, Kyoto Prize, Berggruen Prize, Holberg Prize, John W. Kluge Prize . . .). And, while some of his philosophical contemporaries have received well over fifty honorary degrees from universities around the world, Derek was never offered a single one. (It is, it seems, better public relations, and thus better for fundraising, to confer honorary degrees on people who are already admired by the public, preferably celebrities of some sort.) To the best of my knowledge, the sole "honor" he was awarded other than by Oxford was the Rolf Schock Prize, which he received at a ceremony in Stockholm in 2014.

I find this note in my diary from February 13, 2014, while I was living in his house:

> I was in my bedroom last night when Derek knocked to tell me that he had been awarded a Swedish prize. He had just received an email. Initially he misread the letter and thought that the prize was for work on personal identity, future generations, and the structure of moral theories. He commented that the prize seemed designed just for him. But when I read the email I saw that those topics were only what his work was specially cited for. His first reaction had apparently been to calculate the amount of the prize money by converting Kronor to pounds on the internet. He told me the amount and then commented, with delight, that the prize money is tax free. [He was not delighted because he intended to spend the money on himself. He never spent money on anything other than food, books, and CDs. His intention was that all his wealth, including any continuing royalties from his books, should go to charity after he and Janet had died.] Rather than celebrating, he went right on with his routine, going up for his daily hour-long stationary biking. This morning he hadn't looked for the announcement, to which Gustaf [Arrhenius] had sent me a link. I had to find it for him.

Towards the end of his life, and after his death, he made a few appearances in the popular media—most importantly in a profile published in *The New Yorker*.[6] That there has been some public awareness of his status as an arcane philosopher is presupposed by this passage from a review in *The Guardian*, published some months after he died, of a book about Gershom Scholem:

> Yet Scholem also became a source of pride to the new Israel, symbol not of its martial valour or economic chutzpah but its intellectual excellence. Prime minister David Ben-Gurion reportedly shut his office for five days in 1957 and went to bed to read Scholem's magnum opus on the false Jewish messiah, Sabbatai Sevi. Imagine, by way of parallel, Theresa May suspending Brexit negotiations to curl up with volume three of philosopher Derek Parfit's *On What Matters*.[7]

He is also recognizable in an autobiographical passage in a recent novel:

> I audited a few meetings of an ethics seminar taught by a famous philosophy professor from Oxford. He had wire-rimmed glasses and wild

[6] Larissa MacFarquhar, "How to be Good," *The New Yorker*, September 5, 2011.

[7] Stuart Jeffries, "Stranger in a Strange Land by George Prochnik review—Gershom Scholem and Zionism," *The Guardian*, July 14, 2017.

> white hair, and used a lot of overhead transparencies, usually putting them on upside-down or backward. The transparencies were charts and graphs, about the quality of life for different populations. . . . The ethics professor was smart. When anyone made a suggestion or asked a question, he half smiled and immediately rattled off all kinds of implications that a normal person wouldn't have thought of if they had sat there for years. He was kind, too, never saying anything to make anyone feel dumb.[8]

David Edmonds's splendid recent biography, *Parfit: A Philosopher and His Mission to Save Morality*, is now having a substantial effect in remedying the neglect that Parfit suffered—but did not suffer *from*—during his life.[9]

In this section, I have discussed and given examples of Derek's generosity to students and others. It does not, I believe, detract from Derek's generosity that he was able to provide such extensive help to so many philosophers in part because he was able both to read and to think at speeds almost incomprehensible to others—particularly to those, like me, who are pathetically slow. (This is not affected modesty. When I first applied for teaching jobs, Derek wrote in his letters of reference for me that "I should add that McMahan is not a fast thinker, and may therefore not do himself justice in an interview.") On one occasion when I showed up at his rooms in All Souls for a supervision, he was profusely apologetic for having failed to read the material that I had sent him in advance. I said that I could easily come back another day, but he replied, "No, no, have a seat. I'll read it now." The paper was around forty double-spaced pages and consisted of densely argued material in the difficult area of moral philosophy known as population ethics; but Derek read it in perhaps ten minutes or less and then immediately began to present the usual detailed and penetrating comments that demonstrated that he had mastered every detail of the argument, spotted the inconsistencies and other mistakes, and had already thought of many ways in which the piece could be improved.

I recall another occasion much later when he was living at my house in New Jersey and came up to my study just to see how I was doing. I was at the time an associate editor of *Ethics* and had received five or six manuscripts that had been submitted to the journal that I had to read to determine whether they should be rejected or sent out for review. I pointed at the stack

[8] Elif Batuman, *Either/Or* (New York: Penguin, 2022), pp. 60–1.

[9] David Edmonds, *Parfit: A Philosopher and His Mission to Save Morality* (Princeton, NJ: Princeton University Press, 2023).

of manuscripts at the foot of my chair and said despairingly that I would not be able to do any of my own work for a while because I had to read all of those papers for *Ethics*. He cheerfully snatched them all up and said, "Let me read them and give you my opinion of them," and strode off without even waiting for a reply. Had it been anyone else, I would have protested that this was a task I could not delegate to anyone. But because it was Derek, I submitted without protest, for no one could legitimately complain about having their paper assessed by Derek Parfit rather than by Jeff McMahan. Reading those papers carefully would have taken me at least a couple of days of nearly full-time work. But Derek returned in what I think was less than two hours to give me careful explanations of precisely what was good and bad about each paper, together with characteristically generous recommendations about which should be rejected and which should be sent to reviewers.

I will conclude this section by observing that, over the many years in which I knew him, I never heard Derek speak ill of anyone (except, of course, certain people in public life, such as Donald Trump). This was true even in the case of philosophers who had written dismissively, in sneering tones, about his work. He would instead say, "I wonder why so-and-so believes this, and writes so bitterly about my arguments to the contrary." I never observed him become angry with anyone, though he could become furious with inanimate objects, particularly computers, in which respect he said he was like his father. (We were always in agreement that every software update to every application on our MacBook Pros was a disastrous change for the worse in virtually every respect.)

Derek simply had no retributive emotions. Although he accepted arguments I gave for the claim that people can make themselves morally *liable* to be caused to suffer when the only alternative is that they will wrongly cause others to suffer, he found it incomprehensible that any decent person could think it good in itself that another person should suffer—for example, that a person could *deserve* to suffer. Once, in September 2005, when we were standing in the hallway of my house in New Jersey discussing the notion of desert, he exclaimed, "I could die happy if I could convince the five of you not to believe in desert!" According to the note I made at the time, the five were Thomas Hurka, Shelly Kagan, Thomas Nagel, Larry Temkin, and me. I also recall seeing an advance copy of Kagan's book *The Geometry of Desert* in Derek's study in Oxford. When I expressed surprise that the book was available, he replied rather gloomily, "I just can't bring myself to read it. It's too depressing."

Derek once told me that he lacked some of the other "reactive attitudes," such as jealousy, as well. Although I did think that his immunity to certain emotions was a deficiency, I did not have the same view of his inability to experience the retributive emotions. Although I myself experience these emotions to a high degree, I have been convinced by his arguments, and by his example, to try to suppress them and to deny retribution any role in my thinking about the morality of defensive and punitive harming. I have come to think that, in lacking any impulse to seek vengeance, revenge, or retribution, and failing to take any satisfaction when some public villain "gets what he deserves," Derek was not less than fully human in his range of emotions and dispositions but was, rather, a higher form of being.

3 Elements of Character: Monomania

Derek's compulsion to know the truth about matters of moral and prudential importance (matters that he believed to be within the scope of "what matters") amounted to a virtual monomania. As he grew older, his obsession with the areas of philosophy that he thought matter most became all-consuming, and he had little interest in discussing anything else. Shortly before I accepted my current position at Oxford, I was on leave from Rutgers and decided to go to Oxford for January and February of 2014. Derek invited me to stay at his house. As I was scheduled to arrive in Oxford very late at night, I had arranged to stay at Julian Savulescu's empty house in Headington that night and to borrow one of his bicycles to cycle to Derek's house in Oxford the following morning. When I arrived at Derek's with a knapsack on my back and a briefcase dangling from my neck in front, he urged me to leave the bags just inside the front door and accompany him into the sitting room. Within minutes of my arrival and without any preliminary conversation, he began to explain to me his recent views about the relevance of intention to permissibility, which we continued to discuss for the next two hours. We then walked out to buy food at the local supermarket, continuing the discussion all the while. Only after that was I finally able to put my bags in my room and get a cup of tea. Later, we resumed the discussion over dinner, which, according to my diary, consisted for him of brown bread, a carrot, some leaves that looked like celery leaves, and a couple of clementines.

I find in the diary I kept at the time that the next day I wrote in an email to my son that

> I went down to the kitchen this morning to get breakfast and Derek was just finishing his, while listening to opera. Another 90-minute philosophy discussion. It's all vastly interesting and challenging. But just imagine staggering, groggy and jet-lagged, out of bed to go get something to eat and a cup of tea and being waylaid by the world's greatest philosopher to discuss deep issues in philosophy while in that state.

The diary also records that we had another discussion at dinnertime that day, this time on how the number of aggressors can affect the assessment of proportionality in the morality of self-defense and on the moral difference between killing people and allowing them to die. As we left the table, I noticed that we had been talking for fully two hours and remarked—partly just to bring the discussion to an end—that we had better get back to our work, to which he replied, "But we *are* working."

During those two months when I was living in his house, he left the house only once other than to walk to the supermarket. This was when we were having a philosophical discussion that I attempted to conclude, as I had to walk to one of the colleges to discuss with the chair of the faculty board the terms of the offer that I had received to teach at Oxford. Derek immediately rose and said that he would walk with me so that we could continue the discussion, which we did. The college was about a mile from his house, but he happily walked with me there and then walked home alone while I had my meeting.

Another instance of his single-mindedness about his work occurred about seven months later when he was living at my house in New Jersey. Around midnight on September 3, 2014, he had a spell of violent coughing that resulted in severe respiratory distress. I looked up "collapsed lung" on the internet and judged that his condition fitted the description of the symptoms, so I helped him to get downstairs and into my car and took him to the emergency room. I was in the room in which he was placed along with a substantial team of doctors and nurses. One of the doctors asked him for his consent to be sedated and placed on a ventilator. He was conscious but unresponsive. I put my hand on his shoulder and said I knew it was difficult for him to speak but could he just nod his head to give the doctors permission to intubate him. But again there was no response. I was immediately told in urgent terms to leave the room, whereupon his shirt was literally ripped off so that he could be instantly anesthetized and connected to the ventilator. When he was finally allowed to re-emerge into consciousness, I was the only one present in his area of the intensive care unit. His first act was to gesture for pen and paper, as the tube down his throat prevented him from being able to speak.

I still have the seven pages of scrawled, barely legible words he wrote as he began to recover from the sedation and became increasingly clear-headed. Although most of what he wrote remains indecipherable to me, I am fairly confident that the first sentence he wrote is "I don't know what's going to happen with my teaching." The second is "I'm going to go to Cambridge talk to 5". On another sheet there is what seems to be "after trip to talk to 5 students," which is followed by one or two words that are underscored but indecipherable. On the same page there is also "I fly to Boston to coteach with." As I tried to understand what he was writing, I asked him questions to which he could respond by nodding or shaking his head. My recollection is that what emerged most clearly was that he was determined to travel to Cambridge, Massachusetts, in just a few days to participate in Johann Frick's doctoral examination. And he was also concerned about satisfying his teaching commitments at Rutgers.

After our brief, initial "discussion," he was no doubt already exhausted, and what he wanted was to close his eyes and listen to classical music. After two unsuccessful attempts on one sheet, he managed to write on a third, "Put my I-pod in my ear." Shortly afterwards, however, he wanted to try to work. One shaky note says "computer power supply." There are a great many more phrases strewn about the pages I have preserved, but only a single word, though written twice, indicates any curiosity about his own condition on finding himself in the intensive care unit: "diagnosis."

When the ventilator tube was finally removed and Derek could speak again, he immediately began to discuss with me the ideas and arguments on which he had been working when I had had to rush him to the emergency room. We discussed not only various arguments he was developing for inclusion in *On What Matters: Volume Three* but also another set of problems with which he was much obsessed: his various disagreements with Bernard Williams, who had died more than a decade earlier.

In my reading over the years, I have found two passages that either amusingly or seriously characterize the intensity of the commitment to and absorption in ideas that everyone who knew Derek recognized in him. One is from *Gulliver's Travels*:

> The Minds of these People [the Laputans] are so taken up with intense Speculations, that they neither can speak, or attend to the Discourses of others, without being rouzed by some external Taction upon the Organs

> of Speech and Hearing; for which Reasons, those Persons who are able to afford it, always keep a *Flapper*... This *Flapper* is... employed diligently to attend his Master in his Walks, and upon Occasion to give him a soft Flap on his Eyes; because he is always so wrapped up in Cogitation, that he is in manifest Danger of falling down every Precipice, and bounding his Head against every Post; and in the Streets, of jostling others, or being jostled himself into the Kennel.... The Husband is always so wrapped in Speculation, that the Mistress and Lover may proceed to the greatest Familiarities before his Face, if he be but provided with Paper and Implements, and without his *Flapper* at his Side.[10]

The second passage is from Schopenhauer, who well understood the type of person of which Derek was an exemplar (as Schopenhauer seems to have been a person of this type as well). The ordinary person, he wrote,

> cannot entirely identify himself with [intellectual] pursuits, or have his whole existence so completely filled and permeated with them that he loses all interest in everything else. It is only the highest intellectual power, what we call *genius*, that attains to this degree of intensity . . . This is the only type of man of whom it can be said that his centre of gravity is entirely in himself; which explains why it is that people of this sort—and they are very rare—no matter how excellent their character may be, do not show that warm and unlimited interest in friends, family, and the community in general, of which others are so often capable . . . If he is destined to impress the character of his mind upon a whole race, he has only one measure of happiness or unhappiness—to succeed or fail in perfecting his powers and completing his work.[11]

Many of Derek's friends wondered at and deprecated his practice of working all day in his study, very seldom leaving his house, very seldom spending time with others, and discussing nothing but philosophy on the rare occasions when he did. Some thought that this could not be a good life for a person and told me that they would never want a child of theirs to have a life like Derek's.

[10] *The Prose Works of Jonathan Swift, Edited by Herbert Davis, Volume the Eleventh: Gulliver's Travels, 1726* (Oxford: Basil Blackwell, 1941), pp. 143–4 and 149.

[11] Arthur Schopenhauer, *Essays from the Parerga and Paralipomena*, trans. T. Bailey Saunders (London: George Allen & Unwin, 1951), pp. 38–9.

I, by contrast, share Schopenhauer's view. For almost anyone, myself included, a life like Derek's would be unfulfilling. But he was happy—by which I do not mean that he was subjectively contented, though he was certainly that. I mean, rather, that although there are various dimensions of well-being in which his life was relatively impoverished, there are others in which his life was richly fulfilled. Derek believed, and I agree with him, that there can be various elements in a life that are objectively good for the person in whose life they occur. He referred to this belief as the Objective List Theory of self-interest. He cited as examples "moral goodness, rational activity, the development of one's abilities, having children and being a good parent, knowledge, and the awareness of true beauty."[12] (He also mentions, on the preceding page, loving and being loved by many people.)

Derek also suggested, as perhaps the most plausible understanding of well-being, that for these objectively good features of a life to be genuinely good for a person, the person must desire and take pleasure in them.[13] I think this was a mistake. If one must take pleasure in the objectively good elements in one's life for them to be good for one, then it seems that one must also be averse to the objectively bad elements for them to be genuinely bad for one. But this is not true of various of the evils Derek lists: "being betrayed, manipulated, slandered, deceived, being deprived of liberty or dignity [particularly if one is unaware of being treated in these ways], and enjoying either sadistic pleasure, or aesthetic pleasure in what is in fact ugly."[14]

Of the objectively good elements that a life might contain that Derek lists, his own life contained in abundance all but having children and being a good parent. He greatly desired and enjoyed rational activity, high aesthetic experience, the cultivation of his abilities, and the possession and discovery of knowledge. Another item that would appear on the lists of most Objective List theorists is achievement, which Derek's life contained to a preeminent degree. His achievements were *prodigious.*

In short, by Schopenhauer's "measure of happiness or unhappiness," Derek's life was an eminently happy one—except that he did not complete his work. I recall that around the time he turned 60, he told me that he had begun to feel the pressure of mortality and was making a concerted effort to clear almost everything out of his life—including his photography—except

[12] Derek Parfit, *Reasons and Persons* (Oxford: Oxford University Press, 1987 repr.), p. 499.
[13] Ibid., p. 502.
[14] Ibid., p. 499.

his philosophical work. He nevertheless had a great many ambitious projects remaining to be completed when he died.

It is true that, at least through the decades during which I knew him, Derek never had what is called a "social life." And his social contacts progressively contracted as he became older and increasingly concerned about having insufficient time to develop and defend the ideas he had about the many philosophical issues in which he was profoundly interested. Even when his friends would arrive from other continents to give lectures in Oxford, he would generally not attend the lectures. I recall being told (though I cannot recall by whom) that on one occasion he did decide to walk with his wife, Janet, to the venue where a friend was going to give a lecture, though his intention was only to walk her there and then walk back home to continue his work. But as they were approaching the venue, they saw the speaker in the distance. To avoid being seen, so that he could avoid the lecture without embarrassment, he spun around to dash away, tripped over the curb, and was flung sprawling onto the pavement. I do not remember whether he was able to continue his escape or was compelled to surrender the next hour or two to attending the lecture.

His being largely asocial did not, however, prevent him from caring deeply about those to whom he was close. I recall, for example, that when he learned that my then wife suffered from chronic depression, he immediately bought and read Peter Kramer's then-new book, *Against Depression*, in order to be able to offer help and advice.

I mention this case in particular because he was in general unusually empathetic with people afflicted with depression, perhaps because, as he once told me, he had been especially close to four women during his adult life, all of whom had been prone to depression. Among the few non-philosophical articles I found among his papers after he died was a photocopy of an article about depression from a 1998 issue of *The Economist.* (He also once told me of a bizarre experience he had of suddenly, for no apparent reason, feeling suicidally depressed for about ninety minutes, after which he felt entirely normal again. He speculated that this was the result of his having taken a proton pump inhibitor, which listed dissociation or something of that sort as a possible side effect.)

I also remember speaking with Derek on Skype four months before he died. He was in London with Janet, who was experiencing serious medical problems. As he was trying to explain the problems to me, he broke down repeatedly, with convulsive sobs, unable to continue until he had composed himself. He was far from being the stolid, impassive, impersonal intellectual who, according to one of his former colleagues at All Souls, "didn't see what is obvious to many others: that there are persons, non-fungible and non-interchangeable, whose immense particularity matters."[15]

My own sense was always that, on the contrary, Derek struggled with intense emotions, none of which were egocentric or impersonal but were instead elicited by sympathy, or empathy, for other people, or animals. Indeed, in his later years especially, he became notorious for his lachrymosity. I witnessed many occasions on which he wept when moved by compassion, two while he was delivering public lectures.[16] The first was during a lecture at Rutgers on issues in metaethics and normative ethics. He referred to his belief, by which he was obsessively troubled, that the late Bernard Williams, whom he had admired enormously, lacked the concept of a normative reason. He then paused and, departing from his notes, said slowly and quietly, almost to himself, "I wonder why. I wish he were still here so I could ask him." He then fought back tears, wiping them away with ferocious strokes of his hands in an effort to recover himself.

The second such occasion was when he was giving a public lecture on personal identity, again at Rutgers. To illustrate one point he was making, he cited the words on the tombstone of a young woman, Nancy Cruzan, who had been in a persistent vegetative state for almost eight years before her parents received legal permission to have her life support withdrawn. The tombstone read: "Departed Jan 11, 1983 / At Peace Dec 26, 1990." Again Derek was unable to prevent himself from weeping. A prospective graduate student visiting from the UK who was in the front row, just in front of the desk at which Derek was sitting, kindly handed him a pocket-sized packet of tissues.

Derek would sometimes watch videos on his computer to wind down before going to sleep. One day when we were discussing music, he wanted to show me a passage in a documentary video he had watched about the Russian-Soviet pianist Sviatoslav Richter. At one point during the segment he showed me, Richter commented to the interviewer (as I recall), "I don't like myself very much." Again Derek began to cry, saying that he found those words very moving (perhaps because they were suggestive of depression).

A final instance: at one point late in his life, I was somehow able to persuade Derek to abandon his work briefly to have dinner at Al-Shami, a Lebanese restaurant in Oxford, with the philosopher Victor Tadros and me.

[15] Amia Srinivasan, "Remembering Derek Parfit," *London Review of Books*, January 6, 2017.

[16] Other instances are recounted in Edmonds, *Parfit*—for example, on p. 322.

Somehow the First World War, about which Derek was vastly knowledgeable, came up in the conversation. As he poignantly expressed his sorrow at the vast number of young men who had been pointlessly killed in that war, he was again unable to restrain his tears. Once he had recovered his composure, he apologetically described himself as a softie and then, to turn the conversation in a humorous direction, playfully accused Frances Kamm and me of defending a "kill-them-all" view about the morality of defense when the number of culpable attackers greatly exceeds the number of innocent potential victims.

One reason that some people—especially academic philosophers—perceived Derek as uninterested in other people may be that he had no interest in or capacity for small talk. When he met with someone, he wanted to discuss ideas. And when he concerned himself with ideas, which he did more or less continuously, his ability to concentrate his attention on them was greater than that of anyone else I have ever known. Hence, in conversation, Derek may well have seemed insensitive to his interlocutor—to that person's facial expressions, body language, vocal intonations, and so on. His mind would be wholly occupied with the ideas under discussion. And because he continued to ruminate during the brief breaks he took from work for mundane chores, he may often have seemed remote. This may be the explanation behind his former colleague's observation that "Sometimes I would pass by him in college and he would smile at me in a way that didn't entirely convince me that I was recognized."[17] It is possible that he did recognize her but was in such an abstracted state that his mind was unable to break its concentration on whatever he was thinking about. But it is also possible that he in fact did not recognize her. He also once told me that, because he had no visual images and no visual memory, he could not recall faces. He said that if he were asked to describe a student with whom he had just had a supervision, he would be unable to do so.

I believe that, somewhere in his autobiography, Bertrand Russell commented that, in periods of great stress such as when one of his children was dangerously ill, he could find at least momentary peace by becoming wholly absorbed in his work. Although I read that passage many decades ago, before I had children, I found it appalling. How could one lose oneself in philosophy when one's child's life was threatened? I think, however, that I now understand Russell's statement somewhat better. He has written elsewhere

[17] Srinivasan, "Remembering Derek Parfit."

that "Most men and women are very deficient in control over their thoughts. . . . The wise man thinks about his troubles only when there is some purpose in doing so; at other times he thinks about other things."[18]

A similar view is found in the commentaries on meditation by various Hindu and Buddhist thinkers. Meditation is an exercise in training the mind in concentration, and accomplished meditators are able to be intensely compassionate one moment, yet entirely detached a moment later when that is necessary for effective action. Derek may well have simply been born with the ability, sought by meditators through long practice, to concentrate his mind at will, blocking all distractions from the object of his attention. His readers will know that he was keenly aware of the parallels between his theory of personal identity and Buddhist views of the self. His capacity for concentration, for "being wholly in the moment," may be yet another affinity he had with Buddhism. (That his concentration *could* be disrupted by trivial distractions, and that he found this highly disturbing, is revealed in Ingmar Persson's amusing anecdote, in his chapter in this volume, about Derek's reaction to houseflies.)

4 Elements of Character: Asceticism

Of the great American journalist and essayist Henry Mencken, one biographer writes that,

> Now in his late twenties, he gravitated toward settled habits . . . He never had to make the minor choices of life—where to eat, what to wear, how to spend his Saturday evenings, and with whom—and thus he was free to devote his energies to the major decisions—the merit of a given novel, the soundness of a given philosophy, the turn of phrase best suited to a given idea.[19]

Yet, compared to Derek, Mencken was wildly profligate in his use of time. I do not know when Derek began to simplify his life in order to have more time for his work, but when he began to live at my house while teaching at Rutgers, he had already reached considerable heights of asceticism. He used

[18] Bertrand Russell, *The Conquest of Happiness* (London: George Allen & Unwin, 1930), p. 73.
[19] William Manchester, *Disturber of the Peace: The Life of H. L. Mencken* (New York: Harper Brothers, 1951), p. 50.

to make a cup of instant coffee every morning, not because he enjoyed it but because the caffeine helped to propel him into his work. He made it with hot water from the tap. I actually had a water dispenser that produced hot and cold distilled water. I showed him how to put a spoonful of ground coffee into a filter, perch the filter on top of his mug, and hold it under the hot tap from the dispenser. He told me, however, that he liked to get things done quickly and that this process took too long. My estimate is that making his instant coffee took about thirty seconds, whereas the other method took about two minutes. But that was clearly a minute and a half wasted. My wife at the time felt so sorry for him that she began to make him a full thermos of filtered coffee each morning before he awoke and leave it for him at the top of the stairs to his basement rooms. The empty thermos would reappear on the kitchen counter late each evening.

One more coffee anecdote. One morning at his house I went down to the basement to get something to eat for breakfast. He had just arrived and was about to prepare his breakfast. But when I arrived he deferred that and immediately launched into a discussion of some philosophical problem. I prepared and ate my breakfast standing up while we talked. Finally he decided to begin making his. While explaining some characteristically dense and complicated argument, he got out his cereal bowl and poured his instant coffee granules into it. Realizing his mistake, he muttered "I'm being stupid," put the powder into his coffee mug, and poured water over it from the kettle. I pointed out to him that he had not turned the kettle on. He sampled the liquid in the mug, found it to be cold, poured it out, and began the complicated process over again, succeeding on the second try.

He was equally indifferent about what he ate, provided that it was healthy, vegetarian, and required minimal time for preparation. To save time, he ate more or less the same foods every day. For breakfast, which he always had shortly after waking at around 11 a.m., he invariably had a bowl of plain yogurt, into which he would mix three types of cereal—Grape-Nuts, muesli, and bran flakes—and cover with berries, usually blackberries but sometimes blueberries.

He ate his second meal of the day between around 5 and 5:30 p.m. It consisted, with very little variation, of romaine lettuce leaves, occasionally dipped in hummus; celery, often with a little peanut butter applied with a knife; a raw, unpeeled carrot; and Pink Lady apples and a couple of tangerines or clementines for dessert—though on rare occasions he indulged in a bit of Ben & Jerry's ice cream.

I rarely saw him drink anything after his one morning cup of coffee, though occasionally he would drink prepared soup straight from the carton at dinner. He very seldom ate cooked food at home and certainly never cooked anything himself. When he lived in my house in New Jersey, we had a spare microwave oven that we offered him, but he declined it. When I lived in his house, I once wanted to cook a pot of beans and asked him if he had a cooking pot, to which he replied that he had no idea but that if he did, I would be better able to find it than he would.

Five p.m. is a very early dinner time in the UK, especially for someone who went to sleep well past midnight. Although this does not explain why he did not eat later, he did say to me once that he ate only two meals a day because, if he ate three, he would have to clean his teeth again, "and that's rather a bore."

On reflection, however, this explanation never satisfied me; for Derek seemed to take great satisfaction in cleaning his teeth, at length and with fanatical thoroughness. Of all the anecdotes I have stored up about Derek over the years, the one that delights me most concerns his teeth-cleaning rituals. During the five times he lived for seven or eight weeks in my house in New Jersey, it never occurred to me to ask him to pay rent, or for utilities, or anything else—it was such a privilege just to have him there. He nevertheless felt that he should offer me something in return, and what he sometimes offered was something that would have been greatly coveted by any moral philosopher: comments on my work. Until his last visit in 2014, when I had moved to a quite tiny house, his rooms were in the basement and my study was in the attic. One night around 10:00, he came up the stairs into my room and said, "Surely you've got some new work on which I can give you comments." I realized that I did indeed have two papers in rough draft that I needed to revise for publication. I printed them and handed him the pages. Each was about forty to fifty pages double-spaced. When he took them, he remarked rather apologetically that "I won't read them tonight because I've already cleaned my teeth; but I'll read them in the morning and we can discuss them tomorrow." Thinking that I had misheard him, I said, "I'm sorry, I thought you said that you had already cleaned your teeth." He replied with what seemed considerable pride: "That's right! I spend more time each day cleaning my teeth than I do eating. And that's when I do much of my reading." Given the superhuman speed at which Derek read with full comprehension, it would not have been in the least surprising that he could have read both of those papers during a single, twenty-minute teeth-cleaning session.

Derek's wife, Janet, once told me that he even kept a book open on top of the chest of drawers in their bedroom to read while he put on his socks in the morning. When I reported these two anecdotes to my friend the philosopher Gopal Sreenivasan, he offered the acute observation that I ought to have been highly flattered that when Derek took away the two papers I gave him that night in my study, he did not say, "I won't read them now because I've already put my socks on."

I have no idea why he was so obsessed with dental hygiene. But both around his chair in his study in Oxford and around the lounge-chair he bought to keep in my house in New Jersey, the tables and floors were littered with toothbrushes, most with the bristles splayed almost flat, glasses half-filled with cloudy water, mangled tubes of toothpaste, chewing gum stuck to various surfaces, and chewing-gum wrappers and lengths of dental floss strewn everywhere. Derek would often emerge from his study draped and festooned with strands of dental floss. There were even strands of dental floss interspersed among his papers when I collected them after his death.

It is probably by now common knowledge among readers of this memoir that, at least during the last few decades of his life, Derek always appeared to be wearing the same clothes he had worn the last time one had seen him—and indeed the time before that. And readers probably already know that at least one part of the explanation for this is that he bought a number of items of clothing of the same sort—dark trousers, white shirts, and red ties—so that he would never have to waste time deciding what to wear. I discovered at his death, however, that there was actually quite considerable subtle variation among at least his shirts and ties, though none significant enough to raise any question about what might "go" with what. He left a stack of perhaps eight or ten shirts in unopened packages. They were made by different clothiers and were of slightly different shades of white or off-white; some had buttoned cuffs, while others required cufflinks. Janet, his widow, brought his collection of red ties to a memorial event I organized at All Souls College some months later, for distribution among any of his friends and students who might want one as a keepsake. I was again surprised to discover that few, if any, were actually qualitatively identical. I have no idea whether the differences were accidental or whether Derek actually fancied a limited amount of variation in his wardrobe.

There is, however, another part to the explanation of Derek's appearing always to be wearing the same clothes—namely, that he did wear the same clothes for days on end. I remember that when I first came to Oxford—for a summer school program in 1975 and then to attend the university in 1976—I was surprised and mildly unsettled to learn that Brits often wore the same clothes for several days. I was, after all, from the US, where of course every right-minded and hygienic person showers several times a day and would never wear the same clothes for more than one day, if that. But Derek may have been committed to wearing the same clothes for longer even than the average Brit would consider acceptable. And I suspect that this tendency arose not only from his determination not to waste time plucking clothes off hangers or time and resources doing laundry but also from his familial inheritance. Derek's father, Norman, worked as an official in various areas of public health, including public hygiene, both as a missionary in China and later in the UK. He thought, however, that people were excessively concerned about trivial aspects of cleanliness, and his views were once cited in the newspapers under the headline "Germs Find a Friend." Derek once told me that after Norman had been haranguing him about how unnecessarily often people changed clothes, he told Derek to close his eyes, which Derek did. Norman then waved something underneath Derek's nostrils and said, "Tell me what you smell." Derek replied, "I'm not sure; something rather lemony. . . ." Norman then told him to open his eyes, and what he beheld was a pair of socks that Norman had been wearing every day for several weeks.

Before leaving sartorial matters behind, it may be worth noting three further facts. One is that, because of our concern about climate change, Derek and I kept our houses quite cold. In his house in Oxford, he compensated for this by wearing what the British call a greatcoat—in this case a rather dressy, thick wool coat that extended well below his knees. It was amusing, on the rare occasions when he left his study, to see his tall, slouching figure stumping through the house in this rather military-looking garment with his long, disheveled white hair dangling around the collar.

I owe to Harvey Shoolman, a philosopher who attended some of Derek's earliest lectures in Oxford, the revelation that there was an earlier Parfitian self who had not yet become addicted to his later uniform. "What I specifically remember," Shoolman reports, "is Parfit turning up with unzipped cowboy boots sticking out of his trouser bottoms. He wore an open-necked white shirt, [and] an unzipped leather biker jacket," surmounted by "that cascade of blond hair."[20] It is a tragic loss to the pictorial history of philosophy that there is apparently no photographic record of this astonishing phenomenon.

[20] Personal communication, email of October 6, 2020.

The final fact was related to me by Derek's cousin, Gavin Parfit:

> Derek's uncle Cyril, a very elegant businessman, took Derek to Savile Row to have a suit made by a tailor when Derek turned 21. Cyril was surprised to find out that Derek was still wearing the suit well into his 40s and my guess is even beyond that.

My sense here is that Uncle Cyril had over-exacting standards of dress. What might be surprising to someone who did not know of Derek's dietary habits is that he could still fit comfortably into the suit in his forties and beyond. But that he would continue to wear a fine suit indefinitely seems to me nothing more than vestiary good sense and sound domestic economy. What we will never know is whether Derek was also motivated by the fact that suits made in 1963 tended to have attractively narrow lapels and proper trouser cuffs.

I earlier described Derek's habits of eating and drinking as ascetic. I should emphasize, to avoid giving a misleading impression, that his asceticism was entirely pragmatic—a means of preserving time for his work—rather than principled or ideological. I once said to him in passing that I admired T. E. Lawrence. Perhaps a bit baffled that I would admire a military man, he challenged me to explain why. Among the virtues I attributed to Lawrence, I included a highly disciplined asceticism. Derek's response was playfully scornful—something along the lines of "What good can it possibly do to stand for great lengths of time on a pillar in the desert?"

Derek was highly sensitive to architecture, art, and music. But, unless he had raised his antennae to be attentive to some aesthetic phenomenon, he was generally, as I noted earlier, absorbed in thought and thus oblivious to his immediate environment. He would, for example, often sit down in a chair without checking to see whether there was anything in it. His glasses usually looked rather mangled, and I suspect the best explanation of that is that he would sit on them and then bend them back into shape as well as he was able. And he had a V-neck sweater that he seemed to wear back to front as often as not.

But sometimes I think his absorption in his thoughts passed beyond mere inattentiveness. Early during his first extended stay in my house in New Jersey, in the autumn of 2005, I noticed that he had what seemed to be an open sore at the top of his forehead. I thought nothing of it for a while but, after a couple of weeks, it had still not healed at all. Because I had read that one of the signs of cancer is an open sore that does not heal, I asked him about it. The explanation was simple and benign. The ceilings in the basement were comparatively low, and there were ducts covered in paneling that were fixed to the ceiling and extended from wall to wall in a couple of places. The tops of the doorways in the basements were also at the height of the ductwork. Derek had simply been failing to notice these obstructions and was thus repeatedly banging his head against them as he walked around. Since it was unrealistic to hire a Flapper to stay with him in the basement rooms, I had to tape vast lengths of thick bubble wrap over the lower edges of the encased ductwork and on both sides of the tops of the doorframes. His head thereafter simply gently rebounded whenever he collided with one of his erstwhile nemeses, and his wound soon healed.

In other instances, Derek was not so much inattentive as incurious. At the beginning of that first extended visit, he arrived late in the evening. We showed him only a little of the house before taking him to his basement rooms where he could go to sleep. As we went through the kitchen, he could not avoid noticing a large, well-appointed cage at the top of the stairway down to his rooms. This was the cage in which my daughter's pet lop-eared rabbit spent the nights. Derek made a cursory inspection and then passed on without comment. The next morning I took him on a more comprehensive tour of the house. When we got to the master bedroom, I told him that our three dogs would be there and asked him whether he would like to meet them. He agreed, noting that he had already seen one of them "in the box" the night before. I cannot remember whether he ever realized that what was regularly in the cage at night and hopped and frolicked about in an enclosed area in the backyard during the day was actually not a dog with exceptionally long ears. But, as for the actual dogs, who were all lying on the bed on that first night, he was at a complete loss to know what to do or say in their presence. They were all, of course, eager to befriend him, but he neither touched nor spoke to them—though nor did he recoil from them. He simply had no idea what to make of them. Although he was a vegetarian on principle, animals were *in person* a mystery to him. I stress, however, the qualifier "in person," as he greatly delighted in watching nature shows on television and once even dragged me off to watch with him what I believe was the last film I saw in a cinema: a documentary about penguins in Antarctica that I recall having beautiful cinematography that was somewhat spoiled by inane, sentimental commentary.

I wrote earlier about Derek's immediate and almost panicked concern, on emerging from total anesthesia, about being sufficiently well to travel to Harvard to participate in Johann Frick's dissertation defense. But when the matter did not involve philosophy, he could be considerably more absent-minded and forgetful. When Derek's sister, Theo, married Van Doorn Ooms, they had two weddings: an initial, largely clandestine one at which Derek was their only witness, and a later, large, ceremonial one. When the second event took place, Derek not only failed to appear but seems to have forgotten about it altogether. Theo has shown me the relevant part of the letter their mother, Jessie, who did not know about the earlier wedding, sent to her on her honeymoon. It reads as follows:

> What your wretched brother is doing in NY not sending a cable on the right day is more than I can say and if I were able to tell him straight now what I think, he would, I hope, be quite chastened. I even wrote and reminded him to send one. He clearly still needs an organizer—doubtless he will produce some super excuse which just will not bear examination—by me at any rate, who was getting progressively crosser (hope you didn't notice) as each wire arrived and still nothing from him. Perhaps he mistook the day—the date—the month or the address—or is he so busy inventing a cablegram/poem the shape of a wedding bell that he is still in the throes of composing? Or perhaps he is quite frankly so immersed in his dates that he forgot your most important one. You wait till I see him!

By "organizer," she presumably had in mind some combination of Personal Assistant and Flapper.

As my earlier observations about Derek's obsession with dental hygiene indicate, he did not keep his work area well organized. To me this was surprising because he was more of a perfectionist about his work than anyone I have ever known. Every argument—indeed every sentence and every word—had to be exactly right, and in its appropriate place. One might suppose that such a meticulous concern about every detail of his work, which reflected the surpassing orderliness of his mind and thinking, would also be manifest, at least to some degree, in a desire that the environment in which he worked be orderly as well. But Derek was always so absorbed in his thinking, and his power of concentration was so great, that he could simply screen out any awareness of the vast clutter that surrounded him in the tiny space in which he worked day after day. While he worked—which was more or less all the time—his otherwise acute aesthetic faculties took a holiday.

In his house in Oxford, his study was sometimes tidied by a woman Janet paid to clean the house. But at my house in New Jersey we had no cleaner and we left Derek to take care of himself in his rooms there. What that meant was that no cleaning was done for the seven or eight weeks in his area of the house. He would gather up all the rubbish just before he left and dump it all in large plastic garbage bags. But after he had been in the house for a week or two, when I went down to discuss some matter with him, I would find him ensconced in his La-Z-Boy armchair with his computer on his lap, surrounded by a rising level of detritus that he had cast aside as he pursued his labors. In addition to the toothbrushes, rolls of dental floss, packages of chewing gum, chewing-gum wrappers, strands of dental floss, and pieces of chewed gum stuck to various surfaces that I mentioned earlier, the following items, among many others, completely covered both the tabletop and floor around his chair: books, papers, CD cases, pieces of mail and miscellaneous shreds of paper, empty paper packages from which a variety of products had been extracted, numerous blister packs of pills—mainly full, partly full, or empty packs of amitriptyline, which he took for insomnia—empty or partly empty water bottles, empty or partly empty vodka bottles (which he took with the pills for insomnia), one or more bottles of cough syrup, one or two red neckties, several pairs of glasses, numerous ballpoint pens, several power cords, one or more rolls of toilet paper, which he used as tissues, with much of the landscape blanketed by a layer of crumpled, discarded ersatz tissues.

Derek told me a number of times about his system of "gold-star rules." These were rules he formulated and imposed on himself that required exceptionless obedience. He found these rules invaluable as a source of willpower. Once he had made some form of behavior or action the subject of a gold-star rule, the motivation not to violate it was exceedingly strong. This is because the sanction for a single violation was that the entire set of rules could no longer be regarded as requiring exceptionless adherence. So the penalty for lapsing, even on a single occasion, was the loss of a powerful tool of self-discipline.[21]

In 2016, I adopted a gold-star rule—not to add salt to food at the table—and have adhered to it rigidly ever since. I can confirm Derek's claim about the psychological effect of making such a resolution. I, however, would lose only one benefit if I were to violate my rule. Derek, by contrast, apparently had many such rules, so the consequences of a single violation would have been much worse for him. And that, of course, was the point. It had to be the case, however, that gold-star rules would be beneficial on balance and that one could be confident that one could always obey them. Surprisingly, Derek never told me, at least to the best of my recollection, what any of his gold-star rules were. But he did tell me, more than once, one candidate gold-star rule

[21] I am grateful to Edmund Tweedy Flanigan for sharing with me a short recording he has from a class at Harvard in which Derek describes his system of gold-star rules. (Email of January 28, 2017.)

that he could not impose on himself because he knew he could not always obey it: namely, a rule requiring tidiness.

This was true even though he recognized that such a rule would be highly beneficial, as he frequently had to waste enormous amounts of time trying to find things he needed amid the chaos in which he lived. His CDs, for example, of which he had a vast number, were almost all in the wrong cases, as he usually had many cases open and would, in his haste, put a CD he needed to get out of the way into the nearest open case rather than look for the one in which it belonged.

5 Morality and Politics

Many of Derek's philosophical views are esoteric and might seem to most people—if they were to become familiar with them and to understand them—quite irrelevant to ordinary life. But Derek worked on philosophical problems that he thought really matter. He devoted his adult life to trying to understand how we ought to live and what we have reason to do. And he took the conclusions at which he arrived with the utmost seriousness. His philosophical views informed his life in various ways. One instance of this that is well known among philosophers is described in a passage in *Reasons and Persons*. There he recounts the way in which the view he developed of personal identity—that our continued existence is not a deep "further fact" independent of continuities of psychology—radically altered his attitudes to the prospect of his own death and to his relations with others:

> When I believed that my existence was a such a further fact, I seemed imprisoned in myself. My life seemed like a glass tunnel, through which I was moving faster every year, and at the end of which there was darkness. When I changed my view, the walls of my glass tunnel disappeared. I now live in the open air. There is still a difference between my life and the lives of other people. But the difference is less. Other people are closer. I am less concerned about the rest of my own life, and more concerned about the lives of others.[22]

He was entirely sincere in this. In the email from which I quoted earlier, Paul Linton offers confirmation in an episode that occurred more than a quarter of a century after the publication of *Reasons and Persons*:

[22] Parfit, *Reasons and Persons*, p. 281.

> A few of us were back in his little office in Harvard in 2010, and *Reasons and Persons* came up, and Derek mentioned out the blue, and completely unrelated to the discussion: "You know, it still helps me feel better about death." (Or words to that effect.) And I smiled, perhaps a bit dismissively, as I thought he was making a joke, as he said it with a smile. And he suddenly became more serious (but not grave), but in the hope of converting us (again, remembering as best I can): "I find it very comforting to think that all it means is that there will be no future person who is related to me in a certain way." And seemed cheery about it as he reflected on it, and the conversation continued.

Sometimes, however, philosophical views that affected his own attitudes and emotions, occasionally quite profoundly, seemed utterly bizarre to others. One instance of this is in an email that he sent to the novelist Joyce Carol Oates after the death of her first husband, Ray Smith. I had come to know Oates through my decade-long affiliation with the Princeton University Center for Human Values, with which she too was officially connected in some way. Earlier, because of her strong interest in philosophy and her awareness of Derek's reputation, she had wanted to meet him. I therefore invited her and Ray to dinner when Derek was in residence in my house so that they could get to know one another. After that, whenever he lectured at Princeton, she was always in attendance. Later, in 2008, Ray died unexpectedly of pneumonia. I wrote to Derek to let him know and he wrote immediately to Joyce by email, as follows:

> Dear Joyce,
>
> I am very sorry to learn from Jeff McMahan that Ray died a couple of weeks ago.
>
> When someone I loved died I found it helpful to remind myself that this person was not less real because she wasn't real now, just as people in New Zealand aren't less real because they aren't real here.
>
> Don't trouble to reply to this.
>
> With warm good wishes, Derek

Derek had come to believe, through philosophical argument, that the past is real in the same way that the present is, and that time and space are analogous in many ways. So I am confident that he genuinely found some consolation in the thought he expressed to Joyce. But she, understandably, did not. She forwarded his email to me with this apt comment:

> This strange note of "consolation"—it seems to have come from outer space—someone who has never "lost" anyone—or felt any actual "pain." It's like reassuring a quadriplegic that his missing limbs are not really missing but might be drifting about in New Zealand, so don't fret. . . .[23]

Although Derek devoted his adult life almost single-mindedly to trying to discover and convey to others the truth about how we ought to live and what we ought morally to do, his efforts left him no time for political activism. Although he was desperately concerned about the most urgent practical moral and political problems, such as climate change, he understood that there has to be a division of labor and that his unique abilities were most effectively deployed in the search for moral understanding.

During the period between 1978 and 1986, when I was a graduate student working first with Jonathan Glover and then with both Derek and Bernard Williams, I was heavily engaged in political activism, primarily with the Campaign for Nuclear Disarmament (CND) and European Nuclear Disarmament (END), but also with other organizations, such as a group of Chilean exiles in the UK who organized campaigns in opposition to the Pinochet dictatorship. During those years, I wrote two political books intended for both academic and non-academic readers, one on British nuclear weapons policy and one on the Reagan administration's nuclear weapons policies and its violent interventions in what were then called Third World countries.[24] Jonathan Glover joined me on some CND marches (during which we heard fiery speeches by Michael Foot and E. P. Thompson in Trafalgar Square, reminiscent of the one Bertrand Russell gave there at the end of a CND march a couple of decades earlier). And Bernard Williams, when asked at my publisher's urging to write a blurb for

[23] In his biography, David Edmonds quotes an almost identical note of consolation that Derek sent to Bill Ruddick following the death of Bill's wife, Sally, three years later, in 2011 (Edmonds, *Parfit*, p. 322).

[24] Jeff McMahan, *British Nuclear Weapons: For and Against* (London: Junction Books, 1981); Jeff McMahan, *Reagan and the World: Imperial Policy in the New Cold War* (London: Pluto Press, 1983; rev. and expanded US ed., New York: Monthly Review Press, 1985).

my book on British nuclear weapons, volunteered instead to write a preface (which sometimes received more hostile commentary in the reviews than the book itself, as he was a major public figure who had to be reckoned with). But Derek, though he provided moral support, never became involved in any activist work.

When I lived part-time in his parents' house in North Oxford in 1979–80, Derek's mother had made photocopies for me of the pieces he wrote for the Oxford student magazine *Isis*, both before and during his tenure as its editor. Another student who wrote for *Isis* at the same time was Terry Jones, later to become a member of Monty Python. I have a vague recollection of Derek's telling me that Jones was his deputy editor but have no idea whether this was true. Clearly, however, they did work together on the magazine. In any case, because I had read these articles that he had written as an undergraduate, I was aware that Derek had written critically about nuclear weapons and nuclear deterrence in the early 1960s in ways that were in agreement with the views promulgated by CND during that period. And when I was writing my book on nuclear weapons, he read drafts sympathetically and give me detailed comments on them. I recall asking him around 1981 why he was no longer politically active. As I recall, though admittedly vaguely, his rather apologetic reply was that he had become so absorbed by the intellectual challenges of the philosophical puzzles and paradoxes that he had discovered (which in a few years would constitute much of the subject matter in *Reasons and Persons*) that he had to some extent lost interest in other matters.

This leads me to suspect that there may have been a period in his life when his philosophical work had, at least to some extent, the character of an intellectual game to him. In support of this conjecture, I remember another occasion around the same time when, as I was having a supervision with him in his rooms at All Souls, the phone in his little study rang (a rare occurrence). He answered, but, rather than telling the caller that he would call back after the supervision, as he normally would have done, he asked me whether I minded if he took the call. I of course replied that he should certainly take the call, and I then waited five or ten minutes while he had an intense philosophical discussion. When he had finished, he told me that the caller had been T. M. (Tim) Scanlon and that the subject of discussion was a proposed solution to Derek's Mere Addition Paradox that Ronald Dworkin had suggested earlier that day during a seminar at which they had all been present. Derek had been terribly *worried* that Dworkin had actually solved the paradox; but he was now relieved that the thinking he had done during the conversation with Scanlon had been sufficient to reassure him that he could refute Dworkin's argument.

This behavior would have been highly uncharacteristic—indeed, almost unthinkable—later in Derek's life, when he had become obsessed with trying to *solve* the problems and paradoxes he had earlier discovered. He desperately sought the solutions—the truth—and was profoundly disturbed by moral disagreement, especially between or among the best moral philosophers, as it seemed to challenge equally the view of each disputant and thus, even more distressingly, suggested that there might not be a truth of the matter to be known.

The pieces that Derek wrote as an undergraduate for *Isis* are in general better argued and better written than the majority of editorial writing for the major newspapers now. His contributions were diverse and included commentaries on debates at the Oxford Union as well as arguments about the major political issues of the period. The pieces that I was given by his mother that are concerned with politics were written in 1962 and 1963. This was well before university students were radicalized by the Vietnam War, the civil rights movement, and other phenomena that led to the development of the left-wing counterculture of the later 1960s. But Derek's short articles contain powerful indictments of nuclear "first strike" capacities, the deployment of nuclear weapons in Europe, the US's war in Vietnam, right-wing politics in the US, apartheid in South Africa, the appointment of formerly powerful ex-Nazis to high offices in West Germany, and the failure of wealthy countries to eliminate or even ameliorate extreme poverty in the rest of the world.

Some of the most striking passages in these pieces have already been quoted in Edmonds's biography, so I will not repeat the quotations here. But I will quote a few other samples just to convey a sense of what Derek's views were and how he expressed them.

In "The Warfare State," he wrote:

> Mental Health, the Jews, Fluoridation, Income Tax, the Negroes, Federal Grants, the Supreme Court, the Liberals, Foreign Aid, the United Nations—what have these in common? Answer: HATE. They are all detested by a small but steadily growing group of Americans. (November 21, 1962)

Since Derek was alive when Trump was elected President in 2016, he had some idea of how large that group had in fact grown at that point. I am confident that his dismay would equal my own if he could know how virulent, well-armed, and utterly deluded and deceived that 35 to 40 percent of the American population are now.

On South African apartheid, he wrote, with bitter sarcasm:

> Yes, Apartheid is a policy of sacrifice. The staggering sum of 15/- per head is thrown away each year on Bantu education. And 120,000 young White civilians now spend their free time training with the latest weapons in order to give the native the security he so badly needs. (October 17, 1962)

On the war in Vietnam:

> Like Vietnam, Germany is an artificially divided country. Most people in the West would agree in their estimate of the two German régimes. The 'Free' half has a popular, efficient government; the Communist half is a repressive dictatorship, ruled by the puppet of a foreign power against the wishes of the great mass of its population. Yet what is the situation in Vietnam? It is the Communist half of Vietnam which has a popular, efficient government; it is the 'Free' half which is a repressive dictatorship, ruled by the puppet of a foreign power against the wishes of the great mass of its population. (May 8, 1963)

On global poverty:

> We, the rich countries, must step in and help them [the poor countries] build. We can do this, firstly, by giving *many* times more aid. And the aid must be *real.* Far too much of it has been sheer good business—"export credits for six weeks at 5 percent interest". When the gap between rich and poor is growing wider every year, it is absurd that the developed countries have not submitted to such systems as . . . an "International Income Tax", organised by the UN, which would automatically take away a certain proportion of their annual growth. . . . We may have to halt our living standards, or even depress them for a while, while they catch up. (March 6, 1963)

Derek's views remained consistently left-wing, egalitarian, internationalist, and cosmopolitan. And by the beginning of the twenty-first century, he had reverted to a more active, though never activist, engagement with morality and politics. He had become, as I mentioned earlier, almost entirely vegetarian for moral reasons (I say "almost entirely" because he would, on very rare occasions, eat fish). He had been deeply concerned about the possibility of human extinction even while writing *Reasons and Persons*, and his anxiety increased as the predictions about climate change became ever more dire. He followed political developments closely by reading online newspapers while having breakfast. Given the speed at which he read, he could get through many articles in a short time. He donated copiously to charities, including some with left-wing activist agendas, such as Avaaz, to which he introduced me and which I continue to support. In his later years, he became an enthusiastic supporter of Effective Altruism, giving lectures in defense of its aims. He arranged for Toby Ord, co-founder with Will MacAskill of the organization Giving What We Can, to ensure that his estate, including any continuing profits from his writings, will eventually be donated to the most effective charities.

Although his actual view was more subtle and complicated, it is not inaccurate to say that he believed that we should all do our part in refraining from contributing even in small ways to potential bad effects of collective action. For example, as I noted earlier, he kept the house quite cold. He also thought that academics ought not to fly to give only one lecture or attend only one conference. (This belief suited him well, as he always declined to travel to give lectures, preferring to stay home and make progress with his work.) He never owned a car and, when staying at my house in New Jersey, got where he needed to go on an extra bike I had in the shed. (After once cycling in to campus with him and observing how incautious he was, I insisted that he never cycle without a helmet and I enforced this injunction rigorously. On one occasion he returned with various small injuries, having crashed while moving from the road onto the sidewalk. The helmet was completely shattered.) He had read somewhere about the amount of energy that is routinely wasted by unnecessary electric lighting, and so, as Frances Kamm recollected in her remarks for the memorial I mentioned earlier, "when we would leave the office he would always make sure lights that weren't needed were turned off. I turn off such lights a lot now because it reminds me of Derek." In all of this he may have been influenced by his father, who, Derek once told me, used to try to save petrol by turning off the car's engine to coast downhill.

Sometimes his little acts of environmental concern were amusingly but endearingly eccentric.[25] I am again indebted to Paul Linton for one example.

[25] Two comments on these passages from Ruth Chang: (1) "When he stayed with Kit and me, he would regularly unplug our appliances without our permission, including vacuum cleaners that were in need of recharging . . . but he made me more aware of wasted energy consumption to be sure." (2) "I wish you would tell the story about how I observed you several times rooting round the garbage bins at conferences and such, re-sorting other people's recycling—an effect of Derek perhaps?" Probably an effect but, if not, certainly an affinity.

At the first session of a graduate seminar that Derek taught, Linton, on entering the room, got some water from the water cooler in a plastic cup, drank it, threw the cup in the bin,

> and then waited for the great man to arrive. He arrived, but the very first thing he did was to walk over to the bin, crouch down (it was a small bin), and fish out my plastic cup so he could use it himself. Not only was this immediately disarming, but it also brought home just how committed he was to ethics in even the smallest details of his life. He could have easily just taken a fresh cup like I did, but chose not to.

6 Precocity and Wit

Over the many years in which I knew him, I sometimes made notes about what Derek did or what he said to me. I also received most of the papers he had in his house at the time of his death. The materials in these notes and papers are heterogeneous and resist integration into the broad categories of the previous sections, so I am omitting most of them. A few, however, seem worth including and seem also to fit well under the headings of precocity and wit. I include them here in this final short section.

6.1 Precocity

Given his later brilliance, it is unsurprising that Derek was, to borrow a phrase from Dickens, an Infant Phenomenon. When he was a schoolboy at Eton, a new translation of the Bible appeared. It was, like the King James Version, the product of many hands. A newspaper at the time collected some comments on this new translation and published them under the headline "What they think of the New Bible." Among the entries, there is one credited to "Schoolboy: DP, Eton". It reads:

> Any new translation of the Bible brings out automatic riches. But is this new version better than its rivals? It avoids the occasional ridiculousness of Phillips, though also the chatty vitality. It is less stuffy than Knox, though not nearly so rhythmical. The general effect is simply polished and flawless. And that seems to me to be the trouble. Its virtues are all negative. The single translator may stumble, but lack of bruises is not a substitute for life.

> Moffatt's Sermon on the Mount, with its exciting verse form, at least vibrates. This New Testament reads like the product of a flawless calculating machine, giving us scientifically approved visions.

I do not know what Derek's exact age was when he wrote these words, but it is remarkable that anyone, particularly a "schoolboy" who was also an atheist, could be so familiar with so many translations, compare them with such insight, and describe the differences in such elegant prose.

6.2 Wit

In all the years in which I knew him, I am not sure whether I ever heard Derek really laugh. He would often chuckle—a soft "heh heh"—but that was largely phatic, a social gesture. I am certain I never saw him laugh uncontrollably, even for only a moment. Yet it is not that he was dour; on the contrary, he was almost always amiable and cheerful. And he had a very fine and discriminating sense of humor, though it was, by the time I came to know him, exercised far more often in the appreciation rather than the creation of humor. He delighted in the novels and short stories of P. G. Wodehouse, and reveled in the skits and films of Monty Python, as well as some of the offshoots, such as *Ripping Yarns*. Yet because, as I noted earlier, he very seldom saw people socially and, even when he did, sought to turn the conversation to matters of serious interest to him, he was not a witty conversationalist. I never heard him tell a joke.

When he was younger, however, both at Eton and as an undergraduate at Oxford, he often wrote in a manner that was exquisitely witty. Some of his writing for *Isis* reported on debates at the Oxford Union. In his account of a debate about atheism, at which Antony Flew was one of the speakers, Derek writes that one student spoke from the floor "with a logic so intensely formal you felt that you hadn't even been introduced." In another debate, April Carter, a lecturer in politics and a prominent pacifist and antinuclear activist, spoke in favor of British neutrality. Of one of her opponents, Derek writes:

> "I'm old-fashioned enough not to like doing the strong-arm stuff on women", said Brian Walden sanctimoniously. His weak arm is still pretty vicious.

Reporting on a further debate, Derek wrote of one speaker that he "looks so magnificent as he rises to speak that when he actually opens his mouth it is always something of an anti-climax." And of a titled speaker at the same debate whose concessions to the opposing view made it almost seem that he was speaking in favor of it: "At the risk of being pedantic, we might have referred him to the motion."

Finally, I have a note indicating that Derek once told me—explicitly as an example of his sense of humor—about a discussion he had had with his doctor many years earlier, long before he began to use a stationary bicycle in the evenings. The doctor told him that he was too sedentary and needed to get some vigorous exercise, perhaps participate in some games (a term sometimes used at British schools to mean "sports"). Derek's reply: "I suppose I shall have to buy some heavier chess pieces."

As I indicated, my notes for this memoir contain a great many more miscellaneous anecdotes, observations, and statements of the views he expressed to me about various matters—such as, for example, his view of who the greatest composers were (four best, listed chronologically: Bach, Mozart, Beethoven, Wagner; next four: Handel, Haydn, Schubert, Brahms—all, he noted, born within a period of 150 years in the German-speaking countries). But I have included what seems most important. I will therefore conclude by simply repeating the final lines I spoke in my tribute to Derek at his funeral: Derek was overall the most admirable and impressive person I have ever known, or ever hope to know. To have been his student, colleague, and friend has been the greatest privilege of my life.

6
"My Work Is My Life": How Derek's Identity Survived Across Time

Jonathan Glover

> There will later be some memories about my life. And there may later be thoughts that are influenced by mine.
>
> Derek Parfit, *Reasons and Persons* (1984)

We were undergraduates at the same time, though in different Oxford colleges. He didn't know me, but I knew him because in our student world he was famous. He was editor of *Isis*, and was also secretary of the Labour Club and so ran its termly programme. Previous speakers were often Labour MPs, unevenly interesting. Derek set up "Labour Club Lectures". They were far more intellectual, given by interesting academics whose work had a political dimension. Richard Titmuss spoke about the principles underlying the welfare state and about its looming dilemmas. The Marxist biologist J. D. Bernal spoke (unconvincingly but interestingly) about the relevance to biology of the Marxist dialectic. Isaiah Berlin talked about—I think—the role of imagination in politics. Stuart Hampshire spoke about psychoanalysis, freedom, and politics. It was unlike anything any other political club offered. For those of us who hoped politics could include broader ideas, it was exhilarating.

Several years later, as a young lecturer in philosophy, I was astonished and pleased to find Derek sitting at the back of a set of lectures I was giving about determinism, free will, and responsibility. He was going to John Mackie's lectures and to mine. He was pleased that both sets of lectures argued that determinism could be true and was worth discussing, not then the general view of Oxford philosophers. After each lecture he would come and make points, sometimes critical, always constructive. In Princeton, he had switched from history to philosophy. So, with genuine modesty, he saw himself as a

Jonathan Glover, *"My Work Is My Life": How Derek's Identity Survived Across Time* In: *Derek Parfit: His Life and Thought*. Edited by: Jeff McMahan, Oxford University Press. © Oxford University Press 2025.
DOI: 10.1093/9780191915307.003.0006

beginner, though the quality of his comments and questions brought out the absurdity of this.

1 Early Days

We saw a lot of each other. Around 1970 we collaborated on something we hoped would become practical politics. At that time, when some scientific development brought unexpected dangers, social mechanisms for responding were weak or non-existent. By the time the risks were noticed, the science could be unstoppable. A distinguished lawyer, together with Derek and me, set up a small group including scientists (one was my wife, Vivette) to consider what should be done. Derek came up with the idea we adopted. There should be an organization for concerned scientists to warn of risks. It should have access to scientific experts and, as needed, to lawyers, political insiders, philosophers, social scientists, and others. The task would be to think about social impact, to stimulate discussion, and to suggest policy responses. Not very radical now, but novel then.

It was agreed I would write a paper urging the social responsibilities of scientists, and making our proposal. Our lawyer successfully submitted it to *Nature*. After its publication the organization was set up. It produced a number of reports on potentially concerning developments.

When our paper appeared in *Nature*, I learnt something about the way of the world. I had assumed the paper would have three authors: Derek, whose idea it presented; our lawyer, who got it published; and me, who wrote it. The published version had the lawyer as sole author. He sent us a note saying *Nature* would accept only single-author papers. Perhaps he hadn't come across a famous *Nature* paper by Watson and Crick, or any of the thousands of other multiple-author *Nature* papers. Or perhaps he assumed that we had not. I was rather annoyed. Derek, more wisely, took it with Spinoza-like calm: people are sometimes like that; it is not rational to bother about it; what matters is that the article has appeared, etc.

It was the first time I had seen how Derek's approach to people didn't include reactive attitudes like blame or resentment. Ever since, when thinking of him, I have admired this. I too would like never to feel resentment, but haven't succeeded. (I also wonder how far such detachment may flatten relationships.) Then was also the first time I noticed an innocence in Derek's view of people. While he was explaining to me the irrationality of my annoyance, he clearly assumed that dispelling it was a purely intellectual matter.

Once I had understood his arguments, I would no longer be subject to the irrationality of my irritation. I too admire Spinoza's project of using reason to liberate ourselves from unwanted negative emotions. But I wonder if expecting liberation to follow explanation with quite such ease shows an innocence about people's psychology? An innocence that is not stupid, perhaps sublime. But innocence all the same.

1.1 Derek in Class Discussion

It is a myth that Oxford philosophy in the early 1960s had no concern with "real world" ethics. In lectures Herbert Hart coolly devastated Lord Devlin's case for keeping male homosexual acts illegal. Elizabeth Anscombe, citing the atomic bombing of Japan, had earlier opposed giving an honorary degree to Truman. Key to her arguments was what counts as intentionally killing innocent people. Richard Hare wrote on a range of military, medical, and other issues. Philippa Foot invented the trolley problem. Isaiah Berlin gave his inaugural lecture on "Two Concepts of Liberty". Iris Murdoch wrote on vision and choice in morality. Bernard Williams wrote on the idea of equality. Peter Strawson wrote about the reactive attitudes, and also defended ethical pluralism against "the single intense vision".

But, in the teaching and examining at Oxford, ethics was still almost entirely meta-ethics. The influence of ordinary language philosophy was strong. Saying we had a duty to help the world's poorest people could be met by the question: Would we ordinarily say giving to charity was a "duty"? And surely not an "obligation"? (I had been lucky in having Alasdair MacIntyre as a tutor in ethics. His tutorials fizzed with stimulus, discussing political and moral dilemmas from Homer to the Nazis. But few undergraduates had such luck.) Derek and I talked a lot about the importance of bringing real moral questions into the teaching. He, Jim Griffin, and I decided to give a class where they were central. I came up with the rather flat title "Life, Happiness, and Morality". Derek, with more flair, changed it to "Death, Misery, and Morality".

In the class we used ideas we were working on. Derek raised questions that would be central to *Reasons and Persons*. Jim's questions would appear in *Well-Being*, and mine in *Causing Death and Saving Lives*. Derek was the star. There he first presented some of his most brilliant and influential ideas, including the non-identity problem and the repugnant conclusion.

The class was repeated with variations for several years. It had large and lively participating audiences. Early students included people who would go on to be moral or political philosophers: Peter Singer, David Heyd, John Harris, Richard Keshen, and a number of others. In later years Oxford philosophers already distinguished came, including Stuart Hampshire, Herbert Hart, and Richard Hare. Derek was remarkable in the discussions. Tony Quinton made a tennis comparison, noting "his Laver-like ability, wherever the ball came from, to return it at speed".

Each week, one of us would read (or more usually talk round) a paper, to which one of the other two would prepare a reply. The respondent would be given the paper at the end of the previous week's session. One week, Derek was due to give me his paper for my reply next time. But, polite as ever, his apologies were profuse. His paper was very nearly ready, but there were a couple of points he had not quite settled. Could he let me have it either tomorrow or the next day? Of course, that was fine. He phoned up a day or two later, still struggling about solutions, would the next day be . . .? After several such calls, we finally agreed he would let me have it early in the morning on the day of our 2 p.m. class. When that morning came, it still wasn't ready. With absurd overconfidence, I said, "That's OK, Derek, I will listen and reply off the cuff." Little did I know.

When two o'clock came, he presented for the first time his paradoxes about population size. I was bowled over by the sheer originality of his talk. He covered the board in many block diagrams of different worlds with populations of different sizes and different average levels of happiness. He showed us that world A was better than B, which in turn was better than C, yet C was better than A. But, as he talked, underneath my delight about one of the best philosophy sessions I had known, was an anxiety. In replying, I would be walking unprepared into this minefield.

At the end of the talk I started to formulate my doubts for discussion. I was uneasy about representing these complex issues by block diagrams with only two dimensions: numbers of people and their average quality of life. I was struggling a bit to articulate this, when Derek interrupted. With characteristic kindness he said, "That is a very good point." Then he said, "I think your objection is . . ." and expressed it much better than I had. Then, "as you will have seen", he had three possible replies to the objection. "To my first reply, you of course will say . . . to which my reply will be . . . ." He thought his first response might work. But the second one (again, "as you will have seen") would allow me to say . . . .

It turned out that he had already thought out all three of "my" responses and his replies to at least four or five moves down the line. I felt like a novice chess player who had blundered into a game with a grand master. It was the first time I was fully aware of Derek's extraordinary capacity to work out and hold in his mind long chains of argument and counterargument. This was clearly part of what was behind the Laver-like speed and accuracy of return.

1.2 Acts of Kindness Behind the Scenes

Derek was not just honing his own philosophical skills. One aspect of his generosity has been acknowledged by many. He was an astonishingly willing reader of other people's drafts of books and articles. This continued throughout his life. And his acute comments made a real difference. I was an early beneficiary. My *Causing Death and Saving Lives* was improved both in argument and in style by his many suggestions.

Derek could also work behind the scenes as a peacemaker in the clashes that disfigure academic life. Richard Hare claimed that his account of universalizability gave a plausible version of Kant. In *A Theory of Justice,* John Rawls had a footnote sharply rejecting this. Hare wrote a hostile and dismissive review of the book, and Rawls felt hurt. Derek wanted to make peace in this sad conflict. So, when Rawls was lecturing in Oxford on Kant, Derek persuaded him to add a few sentences saying he had been wrong to reject Hare's claim.

After the lecture there was a drinks party. Frustratingly, it happened to be at the moment when Rawls was telling me why he wasn't convinced by Nozick's criticisms that Hare came up to him. Very polite/affable, clipped British: "There was really no need, but very kind of you to say what you did", etc. A mutually polite but also slightly awkward encounter. But Derek had some success in peacemaking. There were no further hostilities.

1.3 Renewal at All Souls

Soon after his first presentation of the population paradoxes, Derek's position at All Souls was to expire. He needed to apply for renewal. Some of the Fellows opposed him. He had been there several years, but only published a couple of short papers. (These were the papers that transformed the debate about personal identity. But clearly for some opponents what counted was *quantity.*) Derek was worried that they might win and so asked people to write references for him. As they included me, I was sent the list of his referees. Some opponents dismissed them, saying he had just got his friends to write in. They included John Rawls, John Mackie, Bernard Williams, and others in the same league. His opponents seemed not to have had the thought that someone with such "friends" just might not be negligible.

1.4 Derek and Dinners

The "tennis champion" side Derek displayed in argument was rightly central to his reputation. But that was only part of it. There was his originality in seeing new problems of fundamental importance, often questions that challenged deeply rooted intuitions. The non-identity problem is fundamental to choices between different kinds of future, but finding a solution that doesn't jar with some of our deepest responses is still elusive. The same goes for the issues about population size and the repugnant conclusion that I had imagined I could answer off the cuff.

But both sides, the tennis champion command of a complex network of arguments and the unearthing of new and deep questions, must have needed intense concentration for long periods. People hear that he always wore the same clothes, to avoid wasting time on such things. Or they hear that he used the time brushing his teeth for reading philosophy papers. Such things are often counted as mere eccentricity, whether absurd or charming. But I suspect that the scale of his thinking really would have been reduced if he had followed the conventions about such matters. This is especially true about socializing. How much time should he give to such things as going to dinners with people? If he did go, how should he use that time?

Once Derek sat next to Vivette at a college dinner. He didn't bother with small talk. The first thing he said to her was, "You probably think time is like a river we are in, that just flows, carrying us from one point to another. During this dinner I mean to change your mind about that." The perils of sitting next to a philosopher. But she found it fascinating. She greatly preferred that to another college dinner when she sat with two of the world's most eminent philosophers, by then very old—that is, about as old as we both are now. They made various complaints about their teeth and other misfortunes of age. As a dinner companion, Derek won by a mile.

Despite this, he *really* didn't want to go to college dinners. Once a year, New College had a special dinner, with the idea that Fellows would invite interesting people. Early in my friendship with Derek, I invited him. He was already reluctant to divert time from thinking to socializing. So, predictably, he refused. Considerate as ever, he gave a kind and polite excuse. But it was bizarre beyond belief. "There is nothing I would like more than an evening of conversation with you. But I know these college dinners. I would have to spend time talking to other people, and I don't want to have to do that." I have my share of vanity and self-deception. But it wasn't up to accepting this picture of the human race as divided into two. On the one hand me, worth Derek giving up an evening for. In contrast, all these appalling "other people" he couldn't face talking to. I fully respected the single-mindedness about his work. But his belief that his excuse was plausible reminded me again of his innocence about people.

2 Rationality

Rationality was central to Derek's approach to philosophy and to life. Its dominance had been clear in his optimism about how easily rational argument might dispel criticized reactive attitudes. It can be seen throughout *Reasons and Persons* and *On What Matters.* Of course, a large part of philosophy's contribution to the world is, and should be, challenges to irrationality. But in philosophy, as in life, there is room for disagreement over whether sometimes other values can trump even rationality.

2.1 A Conversation after a Gap of Years

For a long time I had quite little conversation with Derek. His own important and difficult questions increasingly absorbed him, and I wanted to think about philosophy in a very different way. His fame had greatly spread. There were huge numbers of graduate students and other young philosophers eager to discuss issues he raised. I didn't think I would be a particularly useful contributor to his own thinking and was fairly sure he would not be interested in my work. We remained on good terms, seeing each other at meetings of Ronnie Dworkin's philosophy group in Tony Honoré's room in All Souls, but with little deep talk. (I don't think either he or I thought we were no longer friends. For me he was still a friend, and it didn't surprise me when his wife, Janet Radcliffe Richards, recently told me he had thought the same.)

After this gap, Derek was to speak at University College London. Before the talk, I went into the large room where the drinks were. Derek was on his own at the far end of the room, looking at the pictures on the wall. Everyone else was clustered near the entrance door talking to each other. Were they shy about approaching the great man? This was absurd. I went to talk to him. Not wanting to waste his time with small talk, I asked, "Derek, all those years ago when we gave the class together, you must have had hopes about how your life would go. How close has your life come to those hopes?" He replied, "My life is my work. I believe I have found some good reasons showing that some things matter objectively, not just because we care about them. If I am wrong, my life has been wasted." That last sentence hit me hard, making it difficult to attend as he talked.

I am sceptical about claims about things mattering objectively, regardless of whether all or any people care about them. If something matters, mustn't it matter *to* someone? Perhaps the psychology of humans (or relevantly similar species) could have been a bit different, so that nobody at all in the past, present, or future cared even slightly about beautiful sunsets. What could it then mean to say that sunsets still mattered objectively? But Derek was quick and lucid as ever in outlining his view that some reasons for acting were based on objective values. And, with what his book later showed was tremendous compression, he indicated his great hopes. Appropriately adjusted, some of the main conflicting ethical theories might converge on the objectively true morality: one it would be rational for everyone to accept.

2.2 The Mountain Strategy

Nearly everyone reading this book will be familiar with the mountain strategy. Taking deontology (represented by Kant), consequentialism (represented by Sidgwick), and contractarianism (represented by Scanlon), he adjusted each until they began to converge. In early drafts he stressed the image of three people aiming at the same mountaintop, each climbing a different slope.

The theories and their exponents were well chosen. And the adjustments are not Procrustean: they are not chopping off bits simply to fit three theories into one bed. One case is Kant's principle about always treating people as ends in themselves and never merely as means. This obviously expresses something deep that resonates with many of us. But it is so hard to pin down precisely. Derek's discussion considers Kant's words and some interpretations by modern Kantians. At each stage the increasingly sophisticated versions are confronted with moral intuitions that signal possible inadequacies.

The resulting adjustments are plausible. And the discussion makes the issues sharper and clearer.

Despite these virtues, there are doubts about the project. One is: would its success be good? Ethics is about how we should live. Do we want some formula, even one based on an impressive theoretical consensus, to generate the values by which we should live?

Many are aware, in the context of religion, of the mixed results of trying to solve dilemmas by consulting a Holy Book. Some who do this are inspiring. But there are those who think they know that God forbids abortion or gay marriage. Others claim to know that God promised most of the Middle East to Abraham's Jewish descendants. Yet others claim to know that God supports the "sacrifice" of suicide bombings, or punishment by stoning people to death. Derek's principles, of course, are not backed by the "word" of any imagined Deity. And he disliked the moral views just mentioned. The principles he came up with are far more humane and flexible than those that others brought back from the mountaintop. Those who "look up the answers in Parfit" will be unlikely to commit the atrocities incited in some who look them up in their Holy Book.

This is partly because of the abstract level of his claims. A lot of hard thinking would be needed to work out how in practice to "follow the principles whose being universal laws would make things go best". But it is also because the intuitions Derek used to modify Kantian or utilitarian approaches are humane.

The sources of our intuitions are complex. Our values are shaped by parents and family, friends, and others we love. Our genetic or epigenetic history may be relevant. We are shaped by the society we live in and by the time when we live. Sometimes also by religion. And by events we are close to. (Someone whose sister died under a back-street abortionist may take one view of legalizing abortion. A different view may be taken by a nurse who spent the morning in the intensive care unit trying to save a premature baby, and in the afternoon had to assist an abortion at the same stage of pregnancy.) And we are influenced by motives and emotional responses perhaps coming from evolutionary pressures far back in human history.

Such causes shape people's values in different ways. Even when taking sides, we can accept that the world is enriched by the passionate disagreements. Variety of values is itself something we can value. Finding agreement at a very abstract level may not be much threat to human variety. But when questions are asked about what "things going best" means, the consensus seen from the mountaintop may start to fragment. If it doesn't, the threat of value uniformity may still lurk.

Human variety does not trump everything. I would be happy if it was reduced by the fading of values that allow genocide, climate destruction, racism, torture, abuse of children, and other cruelty. Some others would exclude values allowing blasphemy or gay marriage. The debate over different exclusions itself displays human variety. Perhaps tests of rationality may limit our options at the abstract level that mainly concerned Derek. But those of us who love many of the value disagreements at other levels may be wary of extending to them the veto power of the question "Would it be rational?"

2.3 Thoughts about Death

When young, Derek dreaded his own death: "My life seemed like a glass tunnel... at the end of which was darkness." But this faded in the light of his views about personal identity: "The walls of my glass tunnel disappeared... I became less concerned about my own life and more concerned about the lives of others." After his death no one living would be him. But he had a new account of what this would mean: "My death will break the more direct relations between my present experiences and future experiences, but it will not break various other relations. There will later be some memories about my life. And there may later be thoughts that are influenced by mine. This is all there is to the fact that there will be no-one living who will be me. Now that I have seen this, my death seems to me less bad."[1]

The comfort came from seeing death as less important than people suppose. But, if that is right, shouldn't it change how we think of the death of others too? I often wondered about this. The question pushed itself forward at Derek's funeral. All of us there had memories of him. Many of us will have had thoughts influenced by his. But none of that mattered. We had lost someone we cared about, someone special. A bright light had gone out.

One of my memories is of an often-repeated sequence. Having disagreed with something he said, I would hear his instant reply: "Ah yes. *But*..." That can't happen now and I miss it. Derek might have replied, "Ah yes. *But* that does not apply to your own death. When dead you can't miss anything." True. But when we *do* still have life we value, we may see its end as an evil to

[1] Derek Parfit, *Reasons and Persons* (Oxford: Clarendon Press, 1986), p. 281.

postpone. For me, life (what Derek when young thought to be a glass tunnel) is shared with others who make it rich. What if evidence makes me expect a virus to kill me? If it were possible, I would readily accept others having no posthumous memories of me in exchange for a few more years of life with them now. Derek might have said that his view of personal identity makes this response irrational. But the response is a deep human one, so deep that I don't care at all if it fails a test for some version of rationality.

2.4 Whims

My son David read Philosophy, Politics, and Economics at Oxford, although his approach to the whole thing was already more that of a television filmmaker than of a PPE student. But, going to Derek's classes, he became a fan. He borrowed my copy of *Reasons and Persons*. Later, I was at first a bit sorry to see he had written in it. But on a closer look I enjoyed his note. Derek was saying that acting on a whim need not be irrational, provided it has some good quality like aesthetic merit. He thought a whim mentioned by Thomas Nagel, that there should be parsley on the moon, was "an excellent whim", by contrast with "a poor whim" such as that there should be parsley in the sea. It was here that David gently mocked Derek, writing in the margin "Hello, Planet Parfit!"

The teasing may have been a bit hasty. Derek had a subtle sense of humour. But his disregard for what passes as common sense was so radical that sometimes it was hard to tell jokes from seriousness. He was probably joking about the parsley. But David's teasing was still apt. Derek probably wasn't joking in saying a whim need not be irrational if it has some good quality. But this makes rationality too dominant. If you feel like dancing naked in your garden under the moon, don't spend the first half of the night on an inner dialogue about the dance's rationality. Just do it. For the staider of us, the same goes for scattering parsley in the sea. One good thing in life is lots of space to act on whims without first getting them validated as rational. Is there room for this on Planet Parfit?

3 The Open Sea: Non-Religious Philosophy and its Potential

Derek's thought had two different modes. There were the long stretches of rigorous argument. And there were the quite impressionistic passages on some of the deepest questions there are. Famously, Derek said that ethics had started to escape the constraints of religion only since about 1960. (Does every generation feel bliss was it in *our* dawn to be alive?) He said that, if we can avoid the human race being wiped out, non-religious ethics will have at least a billion years in which to develop, as against the few thousand years of civilization so far. The epigraph to *Reasons and Persons* comes from Nietzsche: "At last the horizon appears free to us again . . . at last our ships may venture out again. . . the sea, *our sea*, lies open again; perhaps there has never yet been such an 'open sea.'"

Derek made two impressionistic ventures that were important.

One is not about values. (Though part of its motive may have been to remove an argument for theism, and so keep open the sea.) The question is why anything at all exists.

The other is about values. Has the history of the human species been on balance good or bad? And the follow-up: should we aim for our species' continuing survival?

3.1 The Deepest Question

Perhaps the deepest question is why anything at all exists. The alternative, of nothing ever existing, seems to have been a coherent possibility. So, can we explain why the "something" story came about instead of the (doubtless rather empty) "nothing" story? And, if we could explain why anything at all exists, there is perhaps the second-deepest question: why is the world like it is? The title of Derek's discussion is "Why Anything? Why This?"

If there were a God, His existence too would need explaining. He, as one Being, even if a rather grand one, would be part of the "something" story: part of the question, not its answer.

I am sceptical about Derek's approach, but there is something heroic about it. He is the chess grand master again, but this time playing against the universe. (In some way probably hard to defend, it reminds me of the knight playing chess against death in *The Seventh Seal*.)

Derek's own account of the main alternatives is agreeably minimalist. There are two. There is the Brute Fact view, which is no explanation: the universe just is the way it is; there *is* no explanation. And there is the alternative that there is what he calls a "selector": possibilities that become actual do so because they have some feature in virtue of which they are selected. (Selection need not be by some conscious being.)

He said the answer to "Why anything?" cannot be causal. Even if *all* events were caused by earlier events, an infinite series does not explain its own existence. He then appealed to intuitions about plausibility in the search for a non-causal explanation. He suggested that, if we have reason to believe in the Big Bang, we have even better reason to believe in many Big Bangs, leading to many worlds. It is hard to explain a single Big Bang that just happened to produce the conditions that made life possible. With many Big Bangs there is less to explain. He suggested that the hypothesis that all possible worlds exist is more plausible than that only some do, as again there is less to explain, with no residual question "Why *these* ones?" Or, in the case of only our world existing, "Why *this* one?"

Aldous Huxley's poem "Fifth Philosopher's Song" included these lines: "A million million spermatozoa. / All of them alive; / Out of their cataclysm but one poor Noah / Dare hope to survive. // And among that billion minus one / Might have chanced to be / Shakespeare, another Newton, a new Donne— / But the One was Me."

For any of us there is something to be explained: why, out of all the possibilities, was I the one born? The answer is said to include factors such as one sperm swimming faster and reaching the egg to be fertilized before others did. We live in a causal world and this leaves less to be explained about the stunning fact Huxley celebrates and/or mourns. Here "less to be explained" means roughly "fewer other causes are needed". And, in a causal world, the intuition to prefer accounts that leave less to be explained is a sound one.

If we move from "Why me?" to "Why anything?", Derek suggests the answer cannot be causal. But, if that is right, is the intuition to prefer accounts leaving less to be explained still sound? Our intuitions about plausibility are likely to have been programmed into our brains, either by our childhood experience of what works or through millennia by evolutionary pressures: what works helps survival. But "what works" in our world is so bound up with "what is causally effective". In these deep areas where physics and metaphysics overlap, if the answers are not causal, are our plausibility intuitions worth anything at all?

There are also problems about one of Derek's central intuitions here. What counts as "leaving less to be explained"? Some would say that belief in many Big Bangs, leading vast numbers of possible worlds to be actual, leaves, not less, but much more to be explained. We may be talking about how many unobservable entities or worlds we find plausible. Or the question may be about how many relevant kinds of explanation are plausible. (This is reminiscent of the debate in physics between Paul Dirac, who thought mathematical beauty was a sign of truth, and others who thought it was irrelevant.) Again, intuitions seem to flounder here.

Many think it very unlikely that humans will be able to answer the most fundamental question. Perhaps it has no answer: the Brute Fact view. Or perhaps there is an answer, but one so greatly transcending the human mind that even our future evolution will never produce the needed capacity.

Among those aware of the question this pessimism has much support. But making up the main exception are physicists who think about cosmology. Some of them say that the idea that a universe could come into existence from nothing does not mean that it has no causal explanation. Observations seem to support confidence in the view that laws of quantum physics will generate physical activity in empty space. The physicist Lawrence Kraus writes that "The structures we can see, like stars and galaxies, were all created by quantum fluctuations from nothing."[2]

One response is that a vacuum in which fluctuations take place in accordance with quantum physics is not "nothing" but something itself part of our universe and calling for further explanation. Different versions of "nothing" are in play. The intuitions of many physicists are in conflict with those who doubt the claimed "something from nothing". Physics has shown so many "impossibilities" not to be so that I am inclined towards the physicists' approach rather than to Derek's rather free-floating intuitions. But this is one of the cases where I wish Derek was here to say, "Ah, yes. *But* . . .".

3.2 With All the Suffering, Has Human History Been Worth It? The Importance of Human Survival

Derek, acutely aware of the vast suffering in human history, asked if the existence of humans had been a good thing. He said he was "weakly inclined" to think it had been, since "the sum of happiness has been greater than the sum of suffering". (On this, is it really possible to have a well-based view?) But he also thought this was not the only issue. He did think our future, if good, might outweigh even a past that on balance was bad: "We shall increasingly have the power to make life good. Since human history may be only just beginning, we can expect that future humans . . . may achieve some great goods

[2] Lawrence M. Kraus: *A Universe from Nothing* (London: Simon & Schuster, 2012), p. 105. I am impressed by the case Kraus makes, but I struggle even with expositions of quantum theory aimed, like his, at the general reader. So this endorsement counts for little or less.

that we cannot now even imagine . . . It may depend on us and our successors whether it will all be worth it. What matters now is that we avoid ending human history."

Suppose for a moment that Derek's weak inclination to think past human existence a good thing was wildly wrong. To cite two of Bernard Williams's witnesses for pessimism, suppose Sophocles and Thucydides got things roughly right. (We have to pretend—highly improbably—that we can work out these balances.) And suppose the human future will indeed have a favourable balance, though not so good as to outweigh the bad of the past. In those circumstances, should we hope for the human race to continue? One justification for saying "yes" would be that the bad past is over. Derek saw that, even though nothing in this scenario can make the *whole* history worth it, we can still go by our judgment that the future will be worth it. The case for human survival doesn't depend on a positive balance in some ledger that includes the past.

Making that case, Derek homes in on one important but often neglected aspect of it: "We are part of a universe that is starting to understand itself." Minds may have evolved in some other galaxy and may be working out answers to questions about the universe. But we may be the only ones. If so, the extinction of the human race could result in the universe never being understood. To some of us, this matters enormously. Even without accepting Derek's belief in objective values, we can agree that high on the list of "what matters" (to us) is that we avoid ending human history. Obviously, there are other hugely important reasons, linked to what we humans get out of our lives. But philosophers have said too little about this "understanding the universe" reason. It is terrible that our fragile defences against nuclear war or climate change may protect the only hope of the universe understanding itself. It is concerning that, even very recently, this huge possibility has been so much in the shaky hands of Mr Trump, Mr Putin, and the Central Committee of the Chinese Communist Party.

4 An Autobiographical Passage?

Writing in *Reasons and Persons,* Derek plausibly suggested that the world might be worse if we were all pure do-gooders, by which he means devoting all our energy to making the world a better place for people impartially. But, he thought, if most people are not pure do-gooders, the world may be better if a few people are.

> If most people remain as they are now, there will be much suffering, much inequality, and much of most of the other things that make outcomes bad. Much of this suffering I could fairly easily prevent, and I could in other ways do much to make the outcome better. It may therefore make the outcome better if I avoid close personal ties, and cause my other strong desires to become comparatively weaker, so that I can be a pure do-gooder.
>
> If I am lucky, it may not be bad for me to become like this. My life will be stripped of most of the sources of happiness. But one source of happiness is the belief that one is doing good. This belief may give me happiness, making my austere life, not only morally good, but also a good life for me.[3]

In philosophy the words "I" and "me" are generally used in an impersonal way, so that "I" stands for anyone. (Can I know that I am not a brain in a vat? Why should I be moral? etc.) In the paragraph just quoted the impersonal points are genuinely part of Derek's argument. But perhaps here, behind those points, is something autobiographical. For him philosophy, at its ethical end, was not a game but a search for how to live better. So, if done well, it is a way of being a do-gooder. And, with Derek's level of talent, it may be worth being a pure do-gooder, weakening other desires and turning down invitations to dinners. "One source of happiness is the belief that one is doing good." This interpretation fits with the strong impression that Derek was greatly fulfilled.

The pure do-gooder passage was written long ago. Married, he seemed to have an additional happiness. Despite the word "do-gooding" being laden with the hostile suggestion of smug interference, a life centring on it can be great, as his was. But letting human love draw you a bit away from the all-embracing "pure" version has something to be said for it too.

Though in Derek's old age there is also a sadness. As brought out in David Edmonds's very well researched intellectual biography, *Parfit: A Philosopher and His Mission to Save Morality* (2023), much of the engagingly wide non-philosophical range of his youth seems to have gone—replaced by such things as obsessive perfectionism over minute details of the publication of his book. But, looking at the video of the last lecture he gave, at Jeff McMahan's seminar in the November before he died, I was fascinated to see him include some of the problems he presented at our class when starting out. His

[3] Parfit, *Reasons and Persons*, p. 30.

thought, and he, seemed enriched and fulfilled by half a century of thought and discussion since then.

Yet that chilling sentence, "If I am mistaken, my life has been wasted", still reverberates. But he was completely wrong about that. Suppose, as is normal in philosophy, some of his arguments are challenged, and some of his conclusions don't gain acceptance? *Of course* his life wasn't wasted. He wrote some of the deepest and most brilliant philosophy of our time, likely to be thought about long after the rest of us are gone. In discussions that made us all think, he was a great stimulus to huge numbers of colleagues, students, and friends. If *his* life was wasted, what hope for the rest of us philosophy teachers?

5 A Final Note

In *A Mathematician's Apology* (1940) G. H. Hardy recounted how, when forced to listen to tiresome people, he could think, "Well, I have done one thing *you* could never have done, and that is to have collaborated with both Littlewood and Ramanujan on something like equal terms." I know no mathematics and can't assess how Derek compares with Littlewood or Ramanujan. But I have collaborated with Derek on classes, projects, and philosophical problems. As the account of my "reply" to Derek at our class shows, the phrase "on something like equal terms" would have to be greatly stretched. But knowing Derek was inspirational. Times of collaborating with him, however unequally, were high points in my life.

7
Derek, to My Mind

Ingmar Persson

Derek once—probably sometime in the summer of 2004 or 2005—said to me, "People never change." This remark came out of the blue, but I suppose that he had at least himself in mind. He may have thought that he did not change because, as he is quoted saying in Larissa MacFarquhar's article "How To Be Good" (2011): "I never get tired or sated with what I love most, so I don't want or need variety." For instance, he would take photographs of the same buildings in Venice and St Petersburg year after year, and he would watch his favourite films, Ingmar Bergman's *Wild Strawberries* and Ridley Scott's *The Duellists,* over and over again (but he changed the order of preference, from ranking *Wild Strawberries* first to putting *The Duellists* in this place). Nor did he change much in the superficial ways he regarded as not worth much consideration, such as the way he dressed or the food he ate. He frequently referred with approval to Ludwig Wittgenstein's statement that he did not care what food he was served as long as it was the same every day. I also have the impression that, perhaps out of fear that unclarity would slip in, he was unusually averse to stylistic variation if he thought he had found an accurate way of making a point. Therefore, you recognize at once that something is written by Derek even if it is the first time you read anything by him on a particular kind of topic, such as cosmogony.

It will, however, be seen that during his lifetime Derek underwent some quite significant changes. But he was nevertheless a man whose life was ruled or regulated by obsessions and habits. Some of his obsessions were long-lasting, like the already-mentioned aesthetic obsession that drove him to embark on numerous photographic expeditions to Venice and St Petersburg; others, to be exemplified, were short-lived. Firm habits regulated most of his day, to ensure that he could spend a maximum of time on his dominant obsessions. Some of his habits were designed to promote his health, like his hour on the exercise bike every evening. Others seemed evidently hazardous to his health in the longer run, like his ritual for drugging himself to sleep

Ingmar Persson, *Derek, to My Mind* In: *Derek Parfit: His Life and Thought*. Edited by: Jeff McMahan, Oxford University Press. © Oxford University Press 2025. DOI: 10.1093/9780191915307.003.0007

every night, which featured large doses of amitriptyline and vodka. Still others were quite innocent but downright curious, such as reading the endnotes of a book first.

It is true that during the third of a century in which I knew Derek, he changed in few respects, but he changed in at least one very important respect—indeed, the respect that he considered most important. Long before I got to know him, in his mid-twenties, he changed academic discipline from modern history to philosophy. And going by the testimony of people who knew him in his late teens and early twenties, he was then something of an outgoing man, with a wide range of interests, far from the monomaniacal recluse he became during the decade when he worked on the first two volumes of *On What Matters* (2011), when he even neglected his second great passion, that of architectural photography (for details of this period of single-mindedness, see Edmonds, 2023: ch. 19). It is tempting to compare this change of lifestyle to that of some people who underwent a religious conversion, such as St Francis of Assisi, who transformed from a youth who lived a leisurely life in luxury to a beggar immersed in religion. In Derek's case it was, of course, a conversion to philosophy, but there was something of a religious fervour in his attitude to *what matters* in the later part of his life; it was something without which his life would be "wasted".

It seems that his involvement with philosophy became increasingly all-consuming and single-minded as he grew older. When I got to know him at the time when he had just finished *Reasons and Persons* (1984), he was capable of effortlessly moving across an extensive array of philosophical problems. When he was working on the three volumes of *On What Matters*, roughly the last fifteen to sixteen years of his life, there was only a comparatively narrow slot in which what you wanted to discuss would have to fit in order for you to have a rewarding philosophical exchange with him. But the fact that in his last years he tended to concentrate on one philosophical problem after another may also have had to do with the increasing weakness of his memory.

Some remarks of his suggest that photography—a passion that he earlier described as only barely weaker than that for philosophy—dropped out of his life because, being increasingly aware of his mortality, he felt it necessary to focus more exclusively on philosophy to have time to carry out his projects. But I doubt that this forms a large part of the explanation since—being strongly inclined to look at things from the bright side—his feeling of having death breathing down his neck appears to me to have been rather less acute than what would be natural for someone with his health status. For instance, in his last year of life, he signed a contract with Rutgers University for five years of teaching, despite the fact that he had had a most serious health scare a couple of years beforehand (see Edmonds, 2023: ch. 22, for more details). So, evidently, he was reasonably confident that he would live for another five years and that the teaching would not prevent him from carrying out his philosophical projects.

It is especially noteworthy that the direction of his philosophy changed fundamentally midway between *Reasons and Persons* and *On What Matters*, as I have argued elsewhere (Persson, 2021). When Derek and I were walking along High Street in Oxford one summer a few years after the publication of *Reasons and Persons*, he suddenly said, "I don't want to become like Hare." He explained that what he had done in his book was to present various arguments rather than trying to defend any particular ethical position. What Richard Hare was known for having done for several decades was precisely to have passionately defended a certain ethical position, both in meta-ethics and normative ethics: a form of rule utilitarianism based on a meta-ethical position of universal prescriptivism.

In *On What Matters* (Vols 1 and 2, 2011, and Vol. 3, 2017), in contrast to *Reasons and Persons*, Derek, too, is largely preoccupied with basing normative ethics on meta-ethics. More specifically, he argues for a "Triple Theory" consisting of a combination of Kantian and Scanlonian contractualism and rule utilitarianism, on the basis of a non-naturalist theory of reasons which makes out normative reasons to be irreducible to natural or empirical matters. Like Hare, he takes what he calls the "High Road" in ethics (Parfit, 1984: 447), though his position both in meta-ethics and normative ethics is fundamentally different from Hare's. And Derek became doctrinaire about his meta-ethical position just as Hare was: when I arrived at Oxford as a graduate student in 1979, Hare told me that if I weren't a prescriptivist, he didn't care to talk to me; twenty years later, Derek told Julian Savulescu, and (according to Edmonds, 2023: 282–3) thirty years later Amia Srinivasan, that he did not have anything to say to them if they did not believe in his non-natural reasons.

Another point of similarity between Derek and Hare was that Kant eventually came to occupy a prominent place in their moral thinking. While Kant is barely mentioned in *Reasons and Persons*, he looms large in *On What Matters*. The last time Derek went to St Petersburg to do photography—it was probably in the spring or early summer of 2001—he had packed Kant's three books on ethics, *Groundwork of the Metaphysics of Morals*, *Critique of Practical Reason*, and *The Metaphysics of Morals*. Coming back, he excitedly told me that he had been astonished to discover how wrong Kant was about all ethical matters, and that he would spend the next couple of years showing this to be so. Unfortunately, I cannot remember the exact year, but it could not have been as late as 2002, since he gave his Tanner Lectures on Kant's ethics in November that year, and he was absorbed in Kant when the events of 11 September 2001 took place (Edmonds, 2023: 264). It is unlikely that this absorption started as early as 2000, since Kant appears not to have been mentioned in the preliminary lecture proposal that he presented to Samuel Scheffler in 2001. It is regrettable that I cannot remember the exact year; pinning it down is of interest because if there was a turning point in the development of Derek's philosophy, as I think can fairly be said, this is it. It was a turn from his concerns in *Reasons and Persons* to what would become *On What Matters*. He abandoned his project of writing three books which had developed out of his writing replies to critics of *Reasons and Persons* (their papers are collected in Dancy (1997)). Although I have not been able to have this confirmed, I also seem to remember that, on this last visit to St Petersburg, he broke his habit of going there in the winter because he had not got the snow he desired on his latest visits; instead, he went there early in the summer to find out whether the light of the "white nights" would do for his purposes.

So, Derek is not one of those philosophers, like Hume or Schopenhauer, who arrive at their basic philosophical position early on and then never deviate significantly from it. (In contrast, Hare told me that he had been unlucky in hitting on the truth straightaway and, thus, could do no other than repeat himself.) Derek was more like Wittgenstein in that you can discern an earlier and a later phase of his philosophy.

In his Preface to the first volume of *On What Matters*, Derek writes that (at the time of his last visit to St Petersburg) he "became unexpectedly obsessed with Kant's ethics", so that for "the next two or three years" he "thought about little else" (Parfit, 2011: xli). I think that we can divide Derek's philosophizing into three periods of roughly the same length: two obsession-fuelled periods, and a "fallow" period in between. The first obsessional period began in the late sixties when he was trying to "decide what really matters" (Parfit, 2011: Preface, xl) in order to spend his life pursuing it, and he found that Henry Sidgwick's *Methods of Ethics* offered assistance. This obsession culminated in Derek's first tome, *Reasons and Persons*, some fifteen to sixteen years later.

Then followed a fallow or interim period in which he largely busied himself with replying to critics of *Reasons and Persons* and published relatively little, especially relative to the time and energy he expended on philosophy.

Since he was no longer in the grip of any grander obsession, he was open to more short-lived obsessions, such as the obsession with buying a particular house in West Kennett. This obsession was nevertheless powerful enough to prod him to make a counter-offer which exceeded previous offers by a staggering £50,000 to guarantee his acquisition of the house.

The fallow period was succeeded in the beginning of the new millennium with a new obsessional period which resulted in an even more monumental tome in three volumes, *On What Matters*, at the end of his life. It seems that for a man who apparently needed to be ruled by an obsession in order to bring out the philosophically best in himself, he had now found an obsession with an ultimate or quintessential object, for is not *what really matters* to Derek what he could be lastingly obsessed with? If there was nothing that mattered in his sense, he felt that his life would be "wasted". So, although it was unexpected that he would become obsessed with Kant's ethics, it could be expected that he would be ignited by some new philosophical obsession and that it would have to do with "what matters".

The statement that Kant was all wrong about ethics is concordant with Derek's "confession" in the Preface that the "great energy" Kant injected in him "was, to start with, *almost* entirely negative" (Parfit, 2011: xli). He was "deeply opposed to some of Kant's main claims [e.g. about not using people merely as means], and to his way of doing philosophy" (2011: xli). By contrast, the "energy" he received from Sidgwick was largely positive: Sidgwick "gets very many things right" (2011: xl). Notwithstanding this difference, he dubs Kant his "master" alongside Sidgwick (2011: xxxiii). When I remarked that I understood well why he regarded Sidgwick as his master but could not see what he had learnt from Kant, he replied that he would switch around the order of their names from "Kant and Sidgwick" to "Sidgwick and Kant". This would make it clear to his readers, he conjectured, that Sidgwick was his more important master, since by both alphabetical and chronological order Kant would have to be placed first.

But he never replied to my request to specify some important insight that he had *learnt*—as opposed to wrenched by laborious revision—from Kant. The only positive claim that he succeeded in extracting from Kant is seemingly the formula that "everyone ought to follow the principles whose universal acceptance everyone could rationally will", which is a centrepiece of what he calls Kantian contractualism. It is, however, hard to understand why his arriving at this formula would necessitate such an intense, prolonged study of Kant. It is, after all, rather close to the familiar thought, "What if everyone did that?" I am inclined to hypothesize that the extensive attention he paid to Kant was, rather, motivated by Derek's association with the two philosophers to whom *On What Matters* 1 and 2 are dedicated, namely Thomas Nagel and T. M. Scanlon, and a wish to connect with the discussion at their universities where he taught intermittently for a couple of decades and where there were prominent moral philosophers inspired by Kant such as Frances Kamm and Christine Korsgaard.

Although Derek took over little of Kant's moral philosophy, there are some broad similarities between them as persons. Both of them were enormously erudite men who spent their entire lives securely ensconced in the academic establishment; they were scholars through and through. They both saw themselves as having to combat the threat of Humean scepticism; for Kant the threat was not only to "the moral law within" but also to scientific knowledge. Kant was obviously much more a man of science, with a number of scientific publications including some on cosmology. But, surprisingly, Derek wrote a couple of articles on cosmogony that may be seen as expressing that he, too, was filled with awe for the "starry heavens above". Furthermore, it has been said of Kant that when he was working on his critical philosophy in his sixties, it was only with the greatest difficulty that he could think himself into the system of someone else (Kuehn, 2001: 329). Likewise, when Derek was working out *On What Matters* 1 and 2, he became increasingly dogmatic with respect to his concept of normative reasons, and he regularly interrupted discussants, thinking that he knew what they were going to say (see Edmonds, 2023: ch. 19). In some other respects, though, they were opposites: Kant was pedantic or punctilious about practical matters, Derek was as disorderly as anyone could be; Kant was more social and enjoyed dinner conversations about matters other than his work, Derek abhorred them; Kant suffered from hypochondria, Derek was exceptionally sanguine about his life prospects.

As already indicated, in addition to the effort to reconcile the Kantian and consequentialist strands in his thinking, another respect in which the orientation of Derek's moral philosophy changed between *Reasons and Persons* and *On What Matters* is that the meta-ethical task of trying to establish the existence of irreducibly normative reasons is pushed to the forefront. In the first two volumes of *On What Matters*, his tactic is mainly to try to refute competing meta-ethical theories, whereas in the third volume his tactic is more conciliatory towards meta-ethics, as it is with respect to normative ethics. This preoccupation with meta-ethics was a later change in his philosophical orientation than his preoccupation with Kant, since as late as around 2005 he told me that he was relieved to have decided not to dive deeply into meta-ethics, into the different forms of naturalism, expressivism, and so on.

As a result of these changes in his philosophical orientation, Derek ended up, in *On What Matters*, with a way of doing moral philosophy more like Hare's than anyone would have anticipated in the 1980s. On the basis of their favoured meta-ethical theories, they were both hoping to show that there is a *"single true morality"* (Parfit, 2011: 2, 155), which involved rule-consequentialist as well as Kantian components. This is not to deny that there are great differences with respect to both their ways of proceeding and their conclusions; in particular, Hare's prescriptivism is diametrically opposed to Derek's non-reductionist view of practical reasons. They resembled each other, however, in that they both held their respective meta-ethical positions to be their most important philosophical positions. The fact that Derek was so firmly opposed to the view that reasons and values are subjective is probably linked to his extraversion, which I shall soon take up. It does not seem far-fetched to surmise that this trait could make him obsessed only with reasons and values that were external to him and that everybody could share and agree on, regardless of their individual personalities and interests.

A further noteworthy aspect of Derek's philosophical change is that some of his most controversial and widely discussed claims in *Reasons and Persons* are absent in *On What Matters*, even though they are highly relevant. For instance, the celebrated claim in Part III of *Reasons and Persons* that "personal identity is not what matters" is suppressed when, in section 19 of the first volume of *On What Matters*, Derek develops a version of Sidgwick's "dualism of practical reason", despite the claim's bearing on this dualism. Indeed, as I have tried to show in the paper earlier mentioned (Persson, 2021), in developing this dualism he even makes claims that are hard to square with his view of the insignificance of personal identity.

Another case in point is that no attempt is made to show how the Triple Theory could help us with respect to the leitmotif of Part IV of *Reasons and Persons*, the need to discover a "new theory of beneficence", "Theory X", which could deal with problems in population ethics like the non-identity problem and the repugnant conclusion. This lacuna is significant, for it was his belief earlier that to show that any moral "theory could be *objectively* the best theory", "we must find a theory which resolves our disagreements" about these matters (Parfit, 1984: 452). It is not that he had given up the hope of finding Theory X. Sometime after the publication of the first two volumes of *On What Matters*, he was very excited because he thought that he had discovered it. But this excitement was soon replaced by disappointment when he found it very tough to persuade people of the truth of his theory. Perhaps that is the reason why this theory did not find its way into the conciliatory project of *On What Matters* when it was continued in Volume 3.

Drawing on Peter Strawson's distinction between "two kinds of philosophy, descriptive and revisionary", Derek characterizes himself in the Introduction to *Reasons and Persons* as a revisionist "by temperament" (Parfit, 1984: x). Some years after the publication of this book, during the four years or so when he was working on replies to the papers collected in *Reading Parfit* (Dancy, 1997), he described his philosophical enterprise to me as an *exploration of the practical implications of metaphysics*, implications that he believed to be largely revisionary. He believed that not only personal identity harboured such implications but also, for instance, the nature of time, which is the topic of Part II of *Reasons and Persons*.

However, if Derek was a revisionist by temperament, he was also a "conciliationalist", and in *On What Matters* the conciliationalist streak in him apparently took the upper hand. As Samuel Scheffler remarks in his Introduction to this book, "The drive to eliminate disagreement . . . is a defining feature of Parfit's work" (Parfit, 2011: 1, xxxi). It is natural for someone as friendly and good-natured as Derek to find disagreement disturbing, at least disagreement with people with whom he was personally acquainted. On one occasion when he expressed regret because of the disagreement between him and me on practical reasons, I replied that it was to be expected that philosophers would disagree with each other, and that he did not mind disagreeing with Kant. His reply was: "But Kant is dead!" I suspect that the more embedded he became in the academic establishment, the stronger he felt a pressure to include more people in the agreement he aimed for. This agreement usually had to be accomplished by his convincing others of the truth of his views, or that their views really were not importantly different from his.

There is also a philosophical reason for his drive to eliminate disagreement. His fear is that "if we cannot resolve our disagreements . . . morality might be an illusion" (Parfit, 2011: 2, 155); we shall not have discovered what "could be *objectively* the best theory". The plausibility of the existence of his objective normative reasons would be jeopardized. Of course, revisionism is not incompatible with an elimination of disagreement and achieving reconciliation by these means, but it is immensely difficult to persuade people to revise their deeper convictions. An original thinker with a need for confirmation from others could hardly avoid a dilemma. It would then be tempting to let those of your ideas that you know by experience to have stirred up most disagreement recede into the background when your conciliatory aim takes precedence. But being an incurable optimist, Derek probably hoped someday to be able to incorporate even his most revisionary and controversial views into the conciliatory framework.

As already noted, Derek stopped going to St Petersburg to take photographs in 2001, or perhaps 2000, and to go to Venice a few years earlier, but there is no indication that his aesthetic taste changed, that he would not have gone on taking the same sort of photos had he continued his photographic expeditions. Against this background, the change in the orientation of his other main preoccupation, philosophy—which had the higher priority of the two—is all the more remarkable.

It is well known that Derek was a phenomenally fast reader. There are many anecdotes about how he was constantly reading: when he got dressed and put on his socks, cleaned his teeth, was on his exercise bike, and so on. As a result, he was incredibly erudite, not only as regards philosophy but also as regards visual art, architecture, music, film, literature, history, politics, and so on. The width of his erudition was revealed, for example, when on social occasions he was seated in the company of non-philosophers and had to entertain them about other matters of more interest to them. He was surprisingly good at this task, which he was so reluctant to undertake.

Being to an eminent degree a reader, Derek got his philosophical ideas first and foremost by reading and rereading texts—especially Sidgwick's *Methods of Ethics*—again and again rather than by sitting thinking with closed eyes. You cannot imagine him sitting thinking in a posture like Rodin's *Le Penseur*. If he was not reading, he would be at his computer, wearing out its keys at a speed that amazed computer people, or in a philosophical discussion with somebody: few, if any, have had as large a philosophical correspondence as he had. Locking Derek into a room without philosophical company and means of reading or writing even for just a couple of hours would be torture to him.

Earlier I suggested that Derek's philosophical development is similar to Wittgenstein's in that you can discriminate between two phases of it. But the procedure with which they developed their philosophical ideas could not have been more different. Derek's method was that of an extravert: as remarked, in his thinking he ruminated on a steady flow of inputs from fellow philosophers, alive and dead. Wittgenstein's procedure was decidedly introvert: after having been heavily influenced by Bertrand Russell's work on logic for a few years before World War I, his philosophy went on to unfold itself in splendid isolation from academic philosophy: in the solitude of his cabin in

Norway, as a soldier in the Austrian army in World War I, and as a schoolteacher in rural Austria. There were other differences of temperament and personality: Wittgenstein was pessimistic and suicidal; Derek was extremely optimistic and would not have dreamt of committing suicide as long as his mind was functioning. Wittgenstein was choleric and occasionally turned violent; Derek was invariably kind and benevolent, and almost never lost his temper with people (though he once yelled at a judge in a lawsuit about his deceased younger sister's son [Edmonds, 2023: 213]). Wittgenstein was a man of science, a wizard with technical devices, and was first drawn to philosophy by a love of logic; Derek was entirely a man of the arts who had no understanding of mechanics and hated logic. But they were both perfectionists, reluctant to publish and slow to finish anything of importance. They were both obsessives and in the grip of inflexible habits. Both have been placed along the autism spectrum, and they shared the early mark of autism of being remarkably late speakers in childhood, although they were evidently highly intelligent in general (I shall return to the issue of autism at the end of this piece).

If possible, Derek would always be hooked up to some medium: if he was not reading or writing, he would listen to music or watch a movie, or view works of art or photos. It seemed that he preferred to experience reality filtered through a medium. For instance, he liked watching wildlife on television, but did not care about experiencing it in nature. Characteristically, he says in "How To Be Good" that he has come to the conclusion that "most of the world looked better in reproduction than it did in life". He would touch up his photos and remove features in them that disturbed him. Accidentally, he might have had some philosophical idea while he was making his morning coffee, was out shopping, was taking a bath, or was engaged in something else practical that ruled out reading and writing, but it would have been inconceivable for him deliberately to adopt a practice like that of the Peripatetics and Nietzsche of strolling around as a means of stimulating philosophical thinking.

So, Derek lived *on* cultural products, but also, I think, he lived chiefly *for* them, in the sense that he lived in order to contribute to increasing their quantity and quality. His all-consuming passion and mission in life seems to have been to leave as good a record as possible for posterity. In a letter to MacFarquhar providing background information for "How To Be Good", he confesses, "I want people to admire what I produce." He desired admirable production to such an extent that it was almost unthinkable for him to put aside this ambition even for a few hours, let alone a whole day, to do something just because it was nice and pleasant; just "having a good time" probably meant nothing to him, unless it could serve as a means of recuperation. But although he did not *strive* for happiness, he *was* unusually happy, presumably mostly because he was so good and successful at that which he strove so hard to be good and successful at. One could hardly imagine anyone who was more perfectly cut out for the role of an academic, both in terms of talent and motivation. Because he had so little interest in social intercourse, it was easy for him to let it drop out of his life when the process of his philosophical "conversion" demanded it. He was not the least prone to join in anything like St Augustine's akratic prayer "Grant me chastity and continence, but not yet"; he would rather be impatient that he could not be granted it soon enough.

It is in line with this striving to produce first-rate cultural and intellectual products that it would not be enough for him just to enjoy a beautiful building; he had an urge to transform the experience into something of long-lasting value by taking a photo. He himself put his penchant for photography down to the fact that he had no mental images. He appears to have had some schematic ones, though, since he once told me that he imagined columns or boxes when he thought about such matters as population ethics and distributive theories like prioritarianism. We probably cannot recognize anything visual unless we have at least some vague images of it, and although Derek had the impression that he was bad at recognizing faces, he is reported to have been good at remembering the look of buildings.

By his own admission, he never introspected. Nor did he spend any time trying to figure out his own personality, as the ancient philosophical injunction "Know thyself!" commands philosophers to do. Although he could spend days in solitude, immersed in his work, and not missing company—unless it was needed to further his work—he was most definitely not introvert.

His ability to read and understand the emotions of others was below par. If people who were ill or miserable put on a happy face, he would often be fooled. If they turned to him with a problem that could not be solved by his standard methods of philosophical advice, favourable references, or generous cheques, he would in all likelihood be hopeless. He was easily embarrassed when he had to express in words his more personal emotions or deal with other people's emotions. His wife, Janet, has described how this trait manifested itself, for example, when he was courting her and later in their domestic life.

Something that mattered to the external or public world had to come out of his efforts, otherwise these efforts would be wasted, he apparently felt. It seems to have been a heavy burden on him that it took him so many years—twenty-seven to be precise—to publish a major work after *Reasons and Persons*. Therefore, it was of utmost importance to him that *On What Matters* should strike people as so marvellous that it compensated for all those years in which his efforts seemed to him to have been, in his own words, "disappointing". He was greatly upset if anyone who praised this book highly implied that it was still second to *Reasons and Persons*, even if they added that it was second to no other work in contemporary philosophy. The fact that he wrote in a draft of section 110 of the second volume of *On What Matters* that he was "now" 67 years old a couple of years before he turned that age made me suspect that, despite all delays, this volume would be published when he had to move out of All Souls at that age. He was certainly keen to show that all the research time that this college had generously granted him over decades had not been "wasted".

In the aforementioned letter to MacFarquhar he speculates that his being so hard-working "may be in part the result of my unusually competitive education, and to my frequent pleasure, as a child, in being ranked first" in the rankings that one of his schools arranged every fortnight in all subjects. If so, the fact that he was more hard-working than any other philosopher or academic I have known may not have been an outcome simply of his passion for discovering the truth. To cite just one instance of his diligence: in spite of the fact that he was 74 years old and was suffering from a severe cold, I have been told that he put in his usual full day's work from about noon to 10 p.m., with a short break for dinner—before he went to bed for the last time (see Edmonds, 2023: chs. 22 and 23, for more on Derek's health status towards the end of his life).

Since he was so humble and modest as a person, it is hard to believe that he had a craving for recognition. But signs of recognition, such as getting high-status awards, being hired by prestigious universities, and being highly paid by them *were* quite important to him. It was so important to him to teach at such universities that he was prepared to sacrifice time that he could have spent assiduously pursuing his own work thanks to his full-time research fellowship at All Souls. In addition, teaching came at the cost of having to write time-consuming references for the students whom he taught. He often told students who approached him unofficially that he was willing to read and comment on their work on condition that he did not have to write any references for them. He said to me that it counted in my favour that I had never asked him for a reference. I think what he detested with reference writing was the inflated vocabulary it forced on him, not that it involved reading a lot of what other people produced.

Time was so precious to him that he would occasionally not even sacrifice a tiny bit of it to boil water for his morning coffee, but rather took hot water from the tap, and late at night you could sometimes see him cycling through Oxford while brushing his teeth. Since he did not have any dependants, and his lifestyle was overall frugal—apart from a few extravagancies, such as paying through the nose to have his photos touched up before he could do it on his computer or buying new copies of CDs and DVDs that he could not find because he rarely put them back in their cases—he did not need any extra income. He would gladly give money away without thinking twice about it, so money meant very little to him, except as a means for acquiring what on rare occasions he coveted, like the house in West Kennett.

The only way I can make sense of all this is by hypothesizing that Derek's craving for agreement and his craving for recognition were flowing from the same source: a need to feel certainty about things that mattered to him. Due to his extraversion, he could not fully convince himself that he had found the truth when other people whose judgement he respected disagreed with him, and he could not fully convince himself that he was capable of finding the truth unless he was assured that these people regarded him has having this capacity. It may seem paradoxical to attribute a tendency to self-doubt and feelings of uncertainty to Derek, because in public discussion he generally exuded self-confidence. True, but he was from the start so successful in his studies—topping the rankings every second week in his schools, etc.—that he quickly amassed credentials to boost his self-confidence, and his arguments were usually so clever that they silenced all opposition, at least temporarily. His "original position" might have been a great deal more insecure.

In *On What Matters*, Derek quotes Hume's moving description of "that forlorn solitude, in which I am placed in my philosophy... utterly abandoned and disconsolate" (Parfit, 2011: 2, 452). It is remarkable that Derek should think that his "predicament" when he faced opposition to his meta-ethical convictions was even "partly similar" to Hume's. The young Hume had absolutely *no* standing whatsoever in the academic or learned world, and he was up against more or less *total* opposition: he could truly feel as though "All the world conspires to oppose and contradict me". Derek concedes that he is "not alone, since some other people have beliefs like mine". But this is quite an understatement: a *lot* of people have such beliefs, including some of the most influential moral philosophers, like Nagel and Scanlon. And, of course,

Derek was then—and still is—one of the most highly respected philosophers in the academic establishment. So, how could he believe that his situation was *in any way* comparable to Hume's? My tentative answer is, because the partial opposition he met was enough to stir up so much uncertainty and insecurity inside him that he felt his state to be comparable to Hume's. Imagine, then, what he would have felt had he *really* been in Hume's circumstances, with no external support or backing whatsoever.

In his letter to MacFarquhar he writes that he has "always enjoyed reading intellectual fights"—and in his youth he even participated successfully (of course!) in debating contests—though he is "worried by disagreements". It might be thought that there is an inconsistency here, because there cannot be intellectual fights without disagreements. But there is no inconsistency, because he did not enjoy intellectual fights when one corner was occupied by opposition to a position that mattered very much to him, such as his metaethical position. As I know from my own experience, disagreement with him about the issue of whether there are objective, non-natural reasons could quickly bring him to tears (which naturally made me reluctant to raise this issue with him). I remember one occasion in All Souls when Derek confidently told Jerry Cohen and me—as he was in the habit of telling people in this period of time—that he now believed Bernard Williams did not even have his concept of a practical reason as something irreducible to natural facts, so that there was no disagreement between him and Derek. When both Jerry and I objected that Williams rather thought there was no such coherent concept to be had, so that there *was* a disagreement, this visibly squashed Derek. (But perhaps he eventually came around to agreeing with us, for in *On What Matters* he writes that "Williams and others" believe that "there is no such intelligible concept of a purely normative practical reason" [Parfit, 2017: 255].)

Thus, the fact that he worked tirelessly to deliver arguments for his central philosophical doctrines was not due to his needing them to *directly* strengthen his conviction that they were true; it was to convince *others* of their truth and, *thereby*, boost his own confidence. His vast correspondence was designed to serve the purpose of assuring him that there was no objection that he had overlooked, that he could respond to all of them, so that nobody could reasonably disagree with him. Therefore, it is not paradoxical that someone whose life was in most respects that of a recluse conducted such an enormous professional correspondence. Here we also have a possible explanation of his perfectionism, his reluctance to let things go and be published: he wanted his publications to be perfectly irrefutable, so that they could not fail to win the assent of others and, thus, would quench his own residual doubts about his capacity to find the truth.

Although Derek sought prestigious positions and awards, and high salaries, it does not seem right to characterize him as competitive (as his father has been said to have been [Edmonds, 2023: 15]). In him there was very little, if any, pride because he had accomplished more than others, or boastfulness, or feelings of superiority. My hypothesis is, rather, that the fact that these distinctions would impress others was not an end in itself for him but a means that could serve to consolidate his belief in his own ability. He sought them chiefly as means of confirming that he had the capacity to find the truth, and he sought agreement chiefly as a means of confirming that he had found the truth.

Nasty aspects of competitiveness, such as being envious of the success of others or begrudging them progress, were entirely foreign to Derek. Quite the contrary, he was omnibenevolent, benevolent towards everyone, and generous with his assistance to promote their work. He was gentle even towards those who criticized him harshly and scornfully. He has been described as almost saintly, but I do not think that is quite accurate. If we strip saintliness of its religious connotations—which certainly do not apply to Derek—and take saints to be people whose overriding aim is to do what is morally good, Derek was not saintly. His overriding aims were to produce, first, as much high-quality philosophy as possible and, second, photographs that were as perfect as possible according to his aesthetic ideals, even if this meant spending exorbitant sums that could instead have been spent on charity. He was quite protective of his time to engage in these pursuits but was fortunate to be so well placed that he seldom had to make significant sacrifices in this respect. Examples will be given later to show that when such occasions arose, he was hard put to offer the requisite sacrifices. In addition, it was not beneath him to engage in some sucking up to the Warden of All Souls to secure a research fellowship there (Edmonds, 2023: 115).

I have characterized Derek as someone whose life was dominated by an ambition to produce works of long-lasting value and who desired recognition as a means of confirming his sense of having the ability to produce such works. Did he, then, perhaps desire to produce work of long-lasting value to gain posthumous fame? This does not follow: posthumous fame is different from the recognition of contemporaries. He thought it was a great tragedy that Mozart died so young because the world was thereby deprived of masterpieces that he would almost certainly have delivered, had he lived on for a longer period. It does not make much sense to consider it a tragedy that

Mozart died young because otherwise he would now have been more posthumously famous. This is an indication that it would be possible for Derek to think it important to enrich the world with such exquisite works, independently of the posthumous fame that it would bring the creator.

Derek wanted to teach because, as he says in "How To Be Good", he found it easier to persuade students than more mature and established philosophers to change their minds, but he taught more in the United States than in Oxford where he spent most of his time. Years after the death of my Oxford supervisor, John Mackie, in 1981, I learnt that Derek had complained of him that he "corrupted the youth" of Oxford by coaxing them to endorse his error-theory of moral judgments. But Derek would not consider putting up resistance against this alleged influence by taking up the White's Chair of Moral Philosophy, which would have restricted his opportunities of teaching in the United States. Derek's suspicions to the contrary, in my experience Mackie exhibited nothing remotely like the ardour Derek himself—or Hare for that matter—exhibited in order to win proselytes to his meta-ethical position. In fact, Mackie never even mentioned his error-theory in my tutorials with him, perhaps because he did not see himself primarily as a moral philosopher. Incidentally, when Mackie was going away to teach in the United States for a period, he proposed that Derek would replace him as my supervisor. I rejected this proposal because the only work by Derek I knew at the time was his 1971 paper on personal identity, and though I was greatly interested in that topic, it was irrelevant to my PhD thesis. As a result, I unfortunately did not get to know Derek until some years later, immediately after the publication of *Reasons and Persons*.

Derek was inordinately fixed on the sense modalities of sight and hearing, the transmitters of verbal communication, music and visual arts, almost to the exclusion of awareness of the whereabouts of his body and its sensations, whether tactile, olfactory, or gustatory. How fleeting his attention was to his body and its surroundings manifested itself, for instance, in how dangerously close he was to falling off the stage several times when he gave his lecture on the occasion of having been awarded the Schock Prize for Logic and Philosophy in Stockholm in October 2014. He was so engrossed in what he was talking about that a number of times he approached the edge of the stage, seemingly unaware of its existence. A low degree of bodily awareness could also make him adopt awkward facial expressions and bodily postures in public, completely oblivious to how he would look from the outside and to the public attention he might attract.

Another episode that illustrates this characteristic of scant consciousness of his physical position was when I called him from a phone booth in Exeter College to arrange a meeting with him sometime in the late 1980s. As happened so often with Derek, we immediately became entangled in a longish philosophical discussion. Eventually I had to tell him that we must stop because I was running out of coins. He replied that there was no problem because he could give me coins! That is, he responded simply to the statement he *heard*, oblivious to other circumstances that made this offer absurdly impracticable. If he wanted us to continue our discussion, the obvious thing would be to ask me to come over to his rooms at All Souls, which would mean only a five-minute walk from Exeter.

Derek gave an impression of being uncomfortable about being embodied, of not being entirely at home in his body. In MacFarquhar's words, there was "something not-there, . . . an unphysical . . . quality" about him. Perhaps this is reflected philosophically in the fact that he was inclined to accept a wide psychological criterion of personal identity, according to which the cause of the psychological continuity that he believed constituted our identity need not be the ordinary, neural one, but could be any cause. This criterion would, for instance, allow us to be teletransported and survive the destruction of our whole body. However, the claim about personal identity that was most important to him was not about what constituted it but that it "is not what matters". In his last publication on personal identity, he writes of the animalist or biological view of our identity—according to which we are identical to our human organisms—that, despite his arguments to the contrary, he has "a reason to *wish* that Animalism were true" (Parfit, 2012: 27), since this would make it easier for him to vindicate his claim that our identity does not matter.

Derek's ability to concentrate on work was extraordinary. Nonetheless, certain stimuli could break his concentration instantaneously. Then a pent-up tension could burst out in uncontrollable behaviour. For instance, if a house fly entered his room, its buzzing would immediately make him jump to his feet and start chasing it wildly, exclaiming, "Don't tell Janet that I'll kill it!" You could not find a better illustration of Blaise Pascal's aphorism in his *Pensées* about the power of flies to disturb our minds. Derek's intolerance of heat provides another example of a stimulus that could unleash his excitability. According to Janet, uncomfortable heat once made him take off not only his jacket but also his shirt and walk around with a bare torso in central Venice, with his luggage loudly rolling behind. This episode also illustrates how unaware he could be of how he would appear to others. Nevertheless, in some other respects he cared about his appearance—for instance, he would regularly use bronzer—as you might expect from someone with a keen interest in beauty.

A different type of example of how Derek's feelings could suddenly break out in uninhibited behaviour is provided by his lachrymosity. Some events or facts would make him cry profusely whenever he talked about them, even if this had happened many times. This was also demonstrated on the occasion of his receiving the Schock Prize, causing all those in the audience who were not familiar with this trait of his to gasp. The cause then was that he regarded it as tragic that J. S. Bach died before he completed his last work, *The Art of Fugue*. Another cause of crying was the fact that Nancy Cruzan was kept biologically alive in a persistent vegetative state for almost eight years, and her tombstone reading "Departed Jan 11 1983 At Peace Dec 26, 1990". A more philosophical cause of Derek's regularly breaking down in tears—and the one that seems most mysterious to me—was his regret that he did not get the opportunity to tell Bernard Williams that they had been talking past each other rather than disagreeing about reasons because Williams lacked his concept of irreducibly normative reasons. This "discovery" apparently brought him great relief as well, though as I have already hinted, I believe that Williams would have responded to this suggestion by nonchalantly shrugging it off.

That Derek took a more indulgent attitude to Williams than to other adversaries to his meta-ethical objectivism, like Hare and Mackie, seems to me to stem from factors external to philosophy, such as Williams having the air of being a "man of the world", of realizing what is sometimes said to be an ideal of their undergraduate college, Balliol—the ideal of "effortless superiority". MacFarquhar's article "How To Be Good" relates an episode of Derek showing Larry Temkin a photo of Williams, then Provost of King's College, Cambridge, and exclaiming, "Isn't he wonderful?" Derek's admiration of him, however, did not prevent Williams from treating Derek in ways that were downright humiliating. Consider, for instance, the following remarkable episode that Williams frequently repeated. At the time when he was living in Cambridge, Williams gave a talk on personal identity in Oxford. After the talk and the Q & A session, Derek "took the chance to buttonhole Williams and raise more objections. Williams needed to return to Cambridge and eventually fled to his car; Parfit pursued him, talking all the while. It was pouring with rain, and Parfit was still talking and pounding an arm on the bonnet, when Williams wound up the window and drove off, leaving his harasser standing there, drenched and bedraggled" (Edmonds, 2023: 258).

Although Derek's tenseness enabled him to work long hours with great energy and efficiency, it also had a negative effect on him in the shape of serious insomnia. This led him to drug himself to sleep each night for around forty years with a cocktail of amitriptyline and vodka. But when he was especially excited about something, not even this cocktail would send him to sleep. Amitriptyline is known to have a bad effect on memory, and this drugging of himself to sleep might well have prevented him from waking up on the night of his death if his reduced lung capacity and a severe cold made him stop breathing (see Edmonds, 2023: ch. 23, for the official cause of Derek's death).

How bad his memory was in his last year can be illustrated by the following anecdote. One afternoon Derek, Jeff McMahan, and I had decided to discuss some of his work when I was back from a brief errand. When I came back about fifteen minutes later, Derek told me that *Jeff* had gone out briefly, but that we would start the discussion as soon as he returned. I went to my room to wait for him. Around twenty minutes later, I heard Jeff asking Derek whether I had returned. Derek had misremembered my going out as Jeff's going out and, consequently, misled me into waiting for Jeff, while he was waiting for me.

Derek's tenseness or excitability also showed itself in his having no patience whatsoever with artefacts that would not function as they were supposed to. When his computer froze or malfunctioned in some other fashion, he would instantly start hitting the keys randomly and furiously. Just a few months before he died, when he found that he could not unlock the back door of his house in Beaumont Buildings, he immediately started to pull the handle violently and ineffectively. When I had unlocked it, he said emphatically, "We must never lock this door again".

On the extremely few occasions when he seemed annoyed with any person, or sentient creature like his cat Pushkin, his annoyance was only momentary. As already mentioned, he was a thoroughly benevolent and kind-hearted person who could not bring himself to respond harshly even to his most openly hostile critics. Ironies expressed by critics—including Williams—could easily pass by him unnoticed.

Unlike saints who generally do not have partners or spouses because they do not find their devotion to spiritual causes compatible with proper concern for them, Derek did have a partner, and subsequently a wife, Janet, for the last thirty-five years of his life. She could supply examples of how she suffered from various "sins of omission" on his part as the result of his overruling obsessions with philosophy and photography. Certainly, he would take pains to carry out such omissions as discreetly as possible because he would "find himself overcome by the mood of the person he is with, especially if that person is unhappy", as it is put in the MacFarquhar article. For instance, when they left the house in West Kennett and bought a house in Oxford, Janet assumed that they would live together in the Oxford house; Derek had not told her that he was intending to live mostly in college.

His great optimism about the future—his own as well as the future of others and humanity in general—may be linked to the fact that he found it hard to endure people being unhappy, even if it was their own fault. He was inclined to think that things would go well for people because he found it hard to bear that they would go badly. Already as a boy he began to doubt theories of desert because he could not believe that people could deserve to suffer, and he lost faith in the God of Christianity because He was conceived as sending deserving sinners to eternal torment in hell.

For a considerable time, Derek was curiously secretive about his relationship with Janet; for instance, if he happened to bump into her in public, he could refer to her as though she was a casual acquaintance, although there was no reason to be clandestine about their connection. For instance, before I got to know Janet, he said to me after a lecture where he saw her in the audience, "I should talk to that woman now", apparently without thinking of introducing us to each other. This may illustrate his disinclination to go into personal matters, but perhaps also that he felt it was somehow inappropriate for him, as a philosopher, not to live alone. In the letter to MacFarquhar already quoted, he makes an astonishing statement: "Though I have not been wholly solitary, I have never had children." This is an astonishing statement by someone who had a long-standing partner whom he had just married—and appeared to be delighted to have married. But it is a statement that many great philosophers of the past could have made with much more justification. It may be noteworthy that generally he did not call himself or his colleagues "philosophers"; he preferred terms like "writers". Perhaps this was because he viewed being a philosopher as an ideal which very few, if anyone, could live up to.

Psychiatrists would tick off some of the traits I have surveyed as belonging to Asperger's syndrome, such as Derek's tendency to monomania and his imperfect grasp of the codes of social intercourse. For a simple example that illustrates both traits, consider his standard answer, "On what matters", to the question of what he was working on—asked, for instance, by a nurse when he was hospitalized in 2014 (Edmonds, 2023: 316). This answer is likely to strike anyone but a few specialists as rudely uninformative, like "On something too important to tell you." Other traits of his, such as his undeniable great capacity for benevolence and sympathy, rather count against this diagnosis.

Earlier I hinted that Wittgenstein has been diagnosed as having Asperger's syndrome (see Fitzgerald, 2000). In 1946 Wittgenstein writes in his diary, in the words of his biographer Ray Monk, "as though it had struck him for the first time": "It is the mark of a *true* love that one thinks of what the *other* person suffers" (Monk, 1991: 492). If this is a discovery you make at the ripe age of 57, empathy and sympathy clearly do not come easily to you. This remark was occasioned by Wittgenstein's falling in love with Ben Richards. In 1938 he wrote chillingly about an earlier male companion, Francis Skinner: "Thought: it would be good and right if he had died, and thereby taken my 'folly' away"—the "folly" being his desire to have sex with Skinner (Monk, 1991: 387). So, Wittgenstein appears eventually to have made some progress in respect of his feelings for others. All the same, he fell far short of the sympathy found in such abundance in Derek. Instead, he was irascible and liable to aggression. I also noted that while Derek was extravert and optimistic, Wittgenstein was introvert and pessimistic. The bottom line is that if these philosophers can correctly be diagnosed as having Asperger's syndrome or being on the autism spectrum—and, not being a psychiatrist, I do not pretend to be able to decide this—this diagnosis is in any case far from being a complete characterization of their personalities. (In addition, it is vague and controversial, as psychiatric diagnoses in general are.)

Whenever I stayed in Derek's house, as I did on many occasions, and was about to leave, I always felt awkward about knocking on the door of his study and saying something like "I'm leaving. Thanks for letting me stay in your house", because I knew he would consider it completely superfluous. He had no time for small talk, even of this minimal sort. The last time we met, in November 2016, he had come to Oxford from Janet's house in London just to look at the latest proofs of the cover of the third volume of *On What Matters*, and to discuss them with Jeff and me. I was certain that he would leave without saying goodbye to me, just as he was in the habit of hanging up the phone without saying it. And sure enough, with simply a bang of the front door of 9 Beaumont Buildings, Derek in the flesh left my life forever.

I count myself lucky to have been born at the right time to enable me to experience first-hand not only the golden era of British rock music of the 1960s but also Derek at the height of his philosophical powers. I regard him as the greatest philosopher I have met, and he alone might have influenced me as much as all other living philosophers together.[1]

References

Dancy, Jonathan (1997), *Reading Parfit*. Oxford: Blackwell.
Edmonds, David (2023), *Parfit: A Philosopher and His Mission to Save Morality*. Princeton, NJ: Princeton University Press.
Fitzgerald, Michael (2000), "Did Ludwig Wittgenstein have Asperger's Syndrome?", *European Child & Adolescent Psychiatry*, 9: 61–5.
Kuehn, Manfred (2001), *Kant: A Biography*. Cambridge: Cambridge University Press.
MacFarquhar, Larissa (2011), "How To Be Good", *The New Yorker*, 5 September 2011.
Monk, Ray (1991), *The Duty of Genius*. London: Penguin.
Parfit, Derek (1984), *Reasons and Persons*. Oxford: Clarendon Press.
Parfit, Derek (2011), *On What Matters*, Vols 1 and 2. Oxford: Oxford University Press.
Parfit, Derek (2012), "We are not Human Beings", *Philosophy*, 87: 5–28.
Parfit, Derek (2017), *On What Matters*, Vol. 3. Oxford: Oxford University Press.
Persson, Ingmar (2021), "Parfit's Reorientation: From Revisionism to Conciliationalism", in Jeff McMahan et al. (eds), *Principles and Persons: The Legacy of Derek Parfit*. Oxford: Oxford University Press.

[1] In writing his, I have greatly benefited from discussions with David Edmonds, Jeff McMahan, and Janet Radcliffe Richards.

8
Not Quite a Person

Ruth Chang

I first met Derek Parfit when I was a graduate student in Oxford, sitting at the back of the 10 Merton Street Lecture Room, listening to him talk to a roomful of eager but intimidated philosophy graduate students. Derek posed a question to the class that occasioned silence and puzzlement in response. That silence emboldened me to raise my hand and to articulate, rather inchoately I'm sure, an idea I had when I was in law school.

If I may indulge in some autobiography to set the stage. The misery of law school drove me to spend as much time thinking about philosophical ideas as I could. It struck me as odd that, as far as I knew, all work in ethics assumed that value and reasons had the same structure as quantities, such as lengths, weights, and volumes. Why should we think that justice, beauty, and well-being were essentially like lengths, with one thing always being better than (longer than), worse than (less long than), or equal to (as long as) another? When I reflected on my own life, it seemed to me that all the important choices I faced were ones in which i) it wasn't true that one alternative was best, ii) it would be madness to think that they couldn't be compared at all, and iii) it would be a mistake to flip a coin to determine what to choose. It seemed to me that there was a fourth basic way things could be related evaluatively to one another and that it was a mistake to think that the world of value was like the world of nonvalue. I remember thinking that if I could wave a magic wand and make the world see normative reality as I saw it—full of comparable things that were neither better, worse, nor as good as one another but *just different*, we would have fewer wars. Instead of assuming, as leaders of nations do, that their way of life is best—and that there is a best way of life—every polity would accept that there could be various best ways of life, all comparable and none of which was at least as good as all the rest. Toleration would be "built into" the way we lived with one another.

Ruth Chang, *Not Quite a Person* In: *Derek Parfit: His Life and Thought*. Edited by: Jeff McMahan, Oxford University Press. © Oxford University Press 2025. DOI: 10.1093/9780191915307.003.0008

I remember being quite excited by this idea and thinking how, if I was right, then economic theory as a whole rested on mistaken foundations. That we would have a new grounding for affirmative action. That egalitarianism would need to be rejiggered. That we would have to reimagine reflective equilibrium as not geared towards a single point but towards multiple points. That Dworkin's "Right Answer Thesis" was wrong. And that I should no longer agonize about what path was best in the face of my hard choices. At some point I remember venturing to Littauer Hall to see Amartya Sen. I remember very little of the content of our talk, but I came away with two conclusions. First, Sen had sent me away with the assignment to read Debreu's *Theory of Value*, and I concluded that he—probably rightly—wanted me to learn to walk, that is, develop some formal chops, before I started to run with large, provocative ideas. Second, that, although he treated me with respect and politeness, he thought I was bonkers.

This is all by way of background to say how extraordinary and serendipitous it was that, on a different continent in a room far, far away, someone as distinguished as Derek Parfit asked a question that seemed to me to touch exactly on an idea I had filed away some time ago. That encounter in 10 Merton Street quite literally changed my life. Derek got very excited by what I was saying and told me to come see him so we could talk further. As it turned out, the idea that Derek was fishing for from the class was one about imprecision in ordering values. My idea was that there is a fourth, sui generis ordering relation and that the structure of normativity was not as ethicists thought. We were both interested in the implications of our views for thinking about normative reality. I was a mere graduate student, thrashing around in deep waters. Derek picked me up by the collar and got me to dry land.

I remember my first supervision in his room at All Souls. I was surprised by its decor—1960s mod, with two brown swirly upholstered chairs facing one another framing the fireplace. I remember thinking, "this guy is serious and he's going to listen to me". (I've now set up my own rooms at University College in this way—with two chairs facing one another for some serious, focused talk). Talking philosophy with him was utter joy. I had no trouble writing reams and reams of material for him, and it was wonderful to write them down for someone who was actually interested. I can't recall whether our first supervision was long, but thereafter, our supervisions were regularly five-to-eight-hour events. We were both in flow—talking about all things philosophical and not always about my thesis—so the time flew quickly. The usual way things would go is that he would invite me to come talk with him over lunch at All Souls, which I later learned was roughly when he woke up, and then we'd continue talking all afternoon until dinner time at All Souls, where he had some trick for hanging at the edge of the Common Room so we could go in last and sit together at the end of the table and continue talking philosophy without having to chit-chat with others. I infer that he had had his knuckles wrapped over this procedure, since sometimes the Warden would come up and introduce himself in a way that seemed to be a gentle rebuke for not following All Souls rules, which encourage guests to be seated next to the Warden at dinner. But they must have given up on him because eventually we went back to the usual drill. After postprandial discussion, eventually I'd declare I was tired and had to go back to my rooms. He was, I guessed, nearly thirty years my senior, but I always started flagging before he did.

What was especially lovely about talking philosophy with Derek in those early days was that he made me feel fearless—he made it clear that it was okay to be confused now and again. It wasn't that he was full of Pollyannish encouragement; it was, rather, that he treated me like a peer and took what I said seriously and engaged in vigorous argument with me. I remember also talking with Bernard Williams on occasion, who was also lovely and not scary but much less argumentative and more centred in his own way of seeing things (I can still see him pacing from behind his desk to a large window overlooking a gorgeous garden and back again while we talked about predicative and attributive value attributes). I remember thinking way back then that some other distinguished philosophers I talked with on occasion were scary because I didn't always understand what they were saying, and I felt that I should. Because I was embarrassed by my own lack of understanding, I couldn't engage with them deeply about the issue at hand. I now regret that I lacked the courage to say "I don't understand, please explain" to them. I wish every graduate student would feel comfortable saying that. People have very different intellectual styles, and I was inordinately lucky to have Derek, who allowed the artifice and noise of being a graduate student to fall away so that I could just focus on the philosophy. One of the most striking things about Derek was that his ego was absent in philosophical discussion, which encouraged his interlocutor to shed theirs as well. I've never encountered another philosopher—nay, academic!—for whom that seems true.

Back then, we were both very fast thinkers, but he was much faster than I and, of course, knew orders of magnitude more. I would sometimes use the fact that I needed to powder my nose as an excuse to think in the loo about something especially challenging that he said, and that always worked—I could come up with something that was at least a relevant consideration in the argument. One thing I never understood about him was that he almost never had to powder *his* nose during our meetings, even though sometimes he would sip about .01 oz of water at a pretty steady clip while we were talking. I remember, when I returned from the loo Derek always seemed a tad impatient—how inconvenient to have bodies that needed tending to during philosophical discussion! Another fact about Derek as an interlocutor: he would *never* take sides in an argument for the sake of argument but would only push for what he thought was true. I, on the other hand, would flip-flop and think of arguments on both sides because I often wasn't sure what I thought. One of the strange things about our intellectual rapport is that we rarely agreed. He once said to me that we were a great intellectual fit because we agreed with each other just enough to have profitable disagreements that pushed things further.

Without Derek, I most certainly would not have become a philosopher. He was many things to me, and over time our relationship changed. He started off as a godlike figure to me, then became a kind of wonderful crazy uncle, and then, during the last twenty or so years of his life, a dear friend and someone towards whom I felt deeply protective and even maternal. As I grew older, I began to realize how innocent and unworldly Derek was. Larissa MacFarquhar, who wrote a stunning profile of Derek for *The New Yorker,* told me that I was like a mother bear when she interviewed me for the piece. I insisted that the things I told her be used only as background and that I didn't want to be quoted.

After I left Oxford, Derek and I didn't talk as much, and he became more and more obsessed with his own views and would relate everything to what he was thinking. I remember spending *hours and hours* arguing with him about whether Bernard Williams, who had then died, had the concept of a normative reason. I *knew* Bernard, and it seemed to me very clear that he had Derek's concept of a normative reason. I went through passages of "Internal and External Reasons" and other work of Bernard's showing how the way Derek was interpreting Bernard was not the only way to interpret him. He was clearly alarmed at my confidence that Bernard had the concept, and whenever I would see him—when he was at Rutgers, for instance—he would renew our argument. In the end, however, I failed to convince him. I had the sense that I could not convince him of anything—he had to come to a view by himself. Derek was through and through an autodidact.

Derek stayed with me and my husband, Kit Fine, at Harvard one term when he was teaching there and stayed with us in New York on and off over many years, giving me a photographer's advice about the horrific lighting in the guest room. I greatly enjoyed feeding him, since he tended not to eat hot meals. I remember one evening in New York when I made him a ginormous bowl of hot, steaming seafood noodles, which he slurped up and then asked for more. Did he have a hollow leg? He ate copious quantities, even by Chinese standards, and I remember being happy that I could give him warm nourishment—we had a running argument about the importance of warm food for the body. When I visited him at his and Janet's beautiful house in London, he would feed me with a carton of Covent Garden soup—I couldn't help but think heated up for my benefit—and cold berries doused with fizzy water. I knew that he regarded eating as an inconvenient waste of time, necessary only to fuel his thinking. He was famously averse to socializing and chit-chat. He would sometimes tell me that so-and-so invited him to dinner, and could I let the person know that he didn't really socialize? He found it stressful that people wanted to socialize with him when he would rather be doing philosophy.

One day, in New York, when he was living uptown, he called me to say that he thought he was having a heart attack. After grilling him about immediate symptoms and ascertaining that he was not going to drop dead right there and then, I instructed him to get a cab and meet me at the hospital. When I arrived at the hospital, he was in a gown surrounded by doctors in the emergency room, and I pushed through them to see how he was. He was obviously very glad to see me, and the first thing he said was "What are you working on?" They ran tests and decided that he had indigestion of some sort, and Derek's reaction was one of utter embarrassment. Very English. He seemed to feel better when I reminded him that it was extremely difficult to distinguish heartburn from a heart attack.

The second major medical episode happened when he was at Rutgers. He was living in Jeff McMahan's house at the time, and Jeff can tell the story with more detail than I. But I remember several of us visiting him in turn every day and our being utterly exhausted dealing with medical records and whatnot, while Derek was trying to talk philosophy with us. He even insisted on conducting a PhD viva of Johann Frick from his bed! (Johann passed with flying colours.) One day in hospital Derek excitedly reported to me that one of the doctors had pronounced that his X-ray films were "incompatible with life". He was thrilled. (Jeff later told me that the doctor had actually said "*almost* incompatible with life".) His glee reminded me of a similar glee I saw in Isaiah Berlin, with whom I was fortunate to have had regular lunches; Isaiah would regularly pause on our way to the lunch room to regale me with a story about each of the great and the good whose portraits hung on the walls outside the Senior Common Room, *always* ending his tale with a perfunctory "Now dead", along with a slight twinkle in his eye signalling appreciation that he himself was still alive and kicking.

As Derek was readying Volume 3 of *On What Matters,* we talked about his future intellectual plans. He was planning a reboot of *Reasons and Persons,* as he was dissatisfied with various aspects of it. He would then turn to metaphysics. He was fascinated by time and time's arrow. And he wanted to think more about why there was something rather than nothing. I remember arguing with him about whether he should devote his energy solely to *Reasons and Persons 2.0* as his next project and encouraging him to turn to his projects in metaphysics immediately. About two weeks before he died, we were in communication about a pair of articles he had agreed to write for a volume co-edited by Kurt Sylvan and me. The point of the volume was in part to name a subfield in philosophy, "the philosophy of practical reason", which then consisted of work scattered throughout metaethics, moral psychology, the philosophy of action, and mind and epistemology, and to create a teaching volume centred around the set of issues about practical reason that cut across the usual subdisciplines of philosophy. Derek agreed to write a piece on objectivism about reasons and another on nonnaturalism in normativity, both of which would update, while drawing upon, his published work in *On What Matters.* Sadly, Derek died before he could write those pieces.

Towards the end of his life, Derek became more openly emotional. He would weep readily, sometimes in public over meals, usually occasioned by his talking about his family. He felt the suffering of others acutely. He was hurt by unkind and disrespectful feedback he had received on *On What Matters.* He was nervous before the Schock Prize ceremony in Sweden, but he was typically brilliant and gracious at what was a glorious event. In his later years, he would talk to me about various emotional things in his life, and I was always grateful that he felt safe and loved in my company. I remember one occasion on which he was clearly feeling conflicted about something in his personal life, and he wanted to talk with me about how he *should* feel instead of just letting himself feel the conflicting emotions. He seemed to feel negative emotions very rarely and was unsure how to handle them. Sometimes I would tell him how strange he was; more than once—and only half in jest—I wondered aloud whether he might be a changeling. Months before his sad and untimely death, I said to him, "You're not quite a person, you know?" Unfazed, he replied that Janet Radcliffe Richards, his dear wife, would often say the same thing. I think only his closest friends will know that this was our way of saying that we saw him, understood him, and loved him.[1]

[1] Thanks to Jeff McMahan for helpful editorial comments.

9

“Some Philosophical Questions Are Sublime”: Memories of Derek Parfit

Thomas Kelly

Along with my children, Derek Parfit is one of the only human beings for whom I retain a fairly vivid memory of the first time I was ever in his presence.

It was twenty years ago, in a lecture hall at Harvard University. The first meeting of a class that he was giving that term, “Topics in Metaphysics.” There were a bunch of students in the room, both undergraduates and graduates. I was a second-year graduate student, who had signed up to be the teaching assistant for the course. Not only had I never met Derek before, but we had never communicated in any way. (This was before he was on e-mail.) Derek was scheduled to fly in from Oxford a few hours earlier. So my plan was just to show up at the first lecture and then go up afterwards and introduce myself.

Derek walked in and proceeded directly to the podium at the front of the room.

And for those of us who had never seen him before, this was *already* kind of interesting, even before he had said anything. Because, as you can see, Derek was an interesting-looking person. His physical appearance, the way he carried himself—in these respects as well as in other, more important, respects, he was unique. Just as, once you had read some of his philosophical prose, there would never again be any question—was this passage written by Parfit, or by someone else? He wasn’t the kind of person who, if you saw him on the street, you’d be in any danger of mistaking him for someone else.

In any case, he started right in: “I’m Derek Parfit. This is Topics in Metaphysics. Here are my topics in metaphysics.” He then began enumerating the topics that he planned to lecture on that term.

And although Derek himself was oblivious to this, a number of us in the room found what happened next rather remarkable.

Thomas Kelly, *“Some Philosophical Questions Are Sublime”: Memories of Derek Parfit* In: *Derek Parfit: His Life and Thought*. Edited by: Jeff McMahan, Oxford University Press. © Oxford University Press 2025.
DOI: 10.1093/9780191915307.003.0009

Because back then, a certain kind of freewheeling, speculative metaphysics was definitely *not* in vogue in the Harvard philosophy department.[1] (The attitude was more like: that's the kind of thing that they're doing at Princeton.) But it wasn't just metaphysics. It was also mainstream philosophy of mind and mainstream epistemology. In fact, if you weren't doing a certain kind of ethics or historical scholarship, it was at least a little bit unclear what you were supposed to be doing. Because on the metaphysics and epistemology side of things, there wasn't much of a certain kind of traditional approach which just says: "Here's a philosophical question; now, let's take it more or less at face value, and get to work trying to answer it, by coming up with a positive view and then offering arguments for that view (and considering objections, etc.)." Where the goal is to make progress by trying to answer the original question.

In the wing of the department in which I found myself, the most important philosopher was the later Wittgenstein. But it wasn't Saul Kripke's later Wittgenstein, or Crispin Wright's later Wittgenstein, where you read the *Investigations* and it seems as though there are some interesting philosophical problems here! Rather, it was much more Burton Dreben's later Wittgenstein—where, if you really understood the *Investigations*, you'd see that, really, the whole thing (that is, philosophy, in anything like the way it had traditionally been practiced) was some kind of mistake. And if you were young and idealistic about philosophy, this could be discouraging at times.

So that's the local environment that Derek stepped into that day, when he began by simply listing the topics that he planned to address. And it's fair to say, I think, that even by the standards of a metaphysics class, Derek's list consisted of just about the most "out-there" topics anyone could have come up.

> First topic: Why the Universe Exists, or: Why is There Something Rather Than Nothing?

(So, a nice easy question to start off the semester: Why *is* There Something Rather than Nothing?)

> Second topic: the metaphysics of personal identity, with a special emphasis on thought experiments involving people teletransporting from one end

[1] I should emphasize that everything that I'm about to say was (at most) true of the Harvard department twenty years ago, as opposed to the Harvard department of today. Indeed, many of these things had already changed significantly during my time as a student.

of the galaxy to the other, as well as thought experiments involving transplanting people's brains into other people's bodies.

The metaphysics of time's passage. The metaphysics of free will...

By this point, we graduate students were shooting each other looks, as if to say: "This is going to be a little bit different!"[2]

Then he just started right in, lecturing. Topic #1: Why the Universe Exists. Just passed out the syllabus. Get your notebooks out, get ready to take notes, I have a lot of ideas about this, we're going to figure it out. And then, he delivered this great lecture.

Fifteen years later, he finally brought himself to publish that material. It appears as Appendix D in Volume 2 of *On What Matters*. So this is 623 pages deep into Volume 2, and over 1,100 pages deep into the two volumes. (You might think—Appendix D of Volume 2!?! Couldn't be that significant! But, of course, that wouldn't be a safe inference in Derek's case. Famously, some of the appendices of *Reasons and Persons*—material that, for one reason or another, didn't make the cut for main text—gave rise to entire literatures of interesting philosophy.)

In any case, I was pleased to see that the opening of the lecture that Derek gave at Harvard on that day twenty years ago was preserved more or less verbatim in the published version. I'm going to read you a few lines from that opening, where he offers a brief *apologia* of his addressing these questions. So here's Derek. (Again, the questions he's referring to are—Why is there a universe? Why is there something rather than nothing?):

> Many people have assumed that ... these questions ... cannot have any answers. Some therefore dismiss these questions, taking them to be not worth considering. Others conclude that they do not make sense, assuming that, as Wittgenstein wrote, "doubt can exist only where there is a question; and a question only where there is an answer."
>
> These assumptions are, I believe, mistaken. Even if these questions could not have answers, they would still make sense, and they would still be worth considering. Such thoughts take us into the aesthetic category

[2] It wasn't just the graduate students, either. You have to picture all of these nerdy Harvard undergraduates, who grew up reading all of this science fiction and playing these sci-fi games, and so on. Now, here they are at Harvard College, taking a class from the world's Greatest Living Ethicist. He's telling them that they're going to spend roughly a third of the class arguing about thought experiments that involve people teletransporting from one end of the universe to the other. And they were going to get college credit for this!

of the *sublime*, which applies to the highest mountains, raging oceans, the night sky, the interiors of some cathedrals, and other things that are superhuman, awesome, limitless. No question is more sublime than why there is a Universe: why there is something rather than nothing.

And, even if reality cannot be fully explained, we may still make progress, since what is inexplicable may become less baffling than it now seems.

Now, of course, that's just me reading these words to you. But, for people who knew Derek: you have to hear him, and picture him, delivering those words in his distinctive way. For me, as a young graduate student, it was kind of electric. (Or at least, as close to electric as it gets, in a philosophy class, where the professor has just finished passing out the syllabus.)

And I admit—for me, even now, twenty years later, looking at Derek's picture, thinking about him saying these things—*some* philosophical questions are *sublime*, just like the interiors of some cathedrals are sublime—it ***still*** feels electric.

* * *

Years later, when we had gotten to know each other, I told Derek that story and said that it had made a big impression on me. He was clearly very interested but waited for me to finish. He then said: "It's just like the very first time I ever discussed those questions at Oxford!"

As a relatively young philosopher Derek had given a public lecture on these topics. And he was quite anxious about how it would be received, because in the audience were three of the great Oxford philosophy luminaries of the previous generation, including P. F. Strawson and Michael Dummett. (I forget who the third luminary was in Parfit's telling of the story—it might have been Grice.)

After the public lecture, there was a question and answer session. At some point, Strawson got the floor. And Strawson said: "Well, Derek, it's all very ingenious. But really, the question 'Why is there something rather than nothing?'—it just isn't a very good question." (Strawson thought that the question didn't make any sense, for some reason.)

The young Parfit was somewhat deflated by this.

And then at some point, Oxford Luminary #2 (maybe it was Grice) got the floor. And Grice said: "Well, I agree with Strawson: it's all very ingenious, but it's not really a good question, it ultimately doesn't make any sense."

Parfit, a bit more deflated.

Finally, Dummett gets the floor. And Dummett says: "Look, I strongly disagree with my colleagues Strawson and Grice. The question 'Why does the Universe exist?' is a perfectly good question!"

So Derek, in his recounting of the story, is heartened by this.

But then Dummett continues: 'Why does the Universe exist? Perfectly good question! In fact, not only is it a perfectly good question, but it's got a perfectly good, straightforward answer: The universe exists, because God created the universe. Now, if you accept that answer, you might think that there's this *other* question to ask: namely, Why Did God Exist? But *that's* the question that's not a good question, the question that doesn't make any sense!"

So the young Parfit was deflated by these reactions. And I noticed that, while he's telling me the story years later, he's getting visibly deflated all over again, as he relived his failure to convince these philosophers, whom he respected, that these were profound questions, and that trying to answer them was worthwhile. And that's a natural reaction, of course. But in Derek's case, I think it was even more pronounced. Because Derek cared deeply—too much, I would say!—that we're converging in philosophy. And it bothered him when he couldn't bring people around to what he thought was the true view—*even in cases where he was certain that he was right.* It bothered him that he could never persuade Bernard Williams that there really are external reasons for action, and that the man who is mistreating his wife really does have a reason to stop, even if the man doesn't care about her well-being. So it really bothered him, all of these years later, that he had failed to bring some of the people he most respected around, and to appreciate that these are profound questions, and it's worth philosophizing about them.

But then, all of a sudden, he kind of perked up. And he looked at me with a twinkle in his eye and said: "But you can't get discouraged!"

* * *

As I said, I first came to know Derek by being his teaching assistant. I suppose it's possible that someone, somewhere, once got more out of being someone's teaching assistant than I did that semester. But I tend to doubt it. It wasn't just that I was getting paid to sit there and listen to Derek deliver a set of fascinating lectures. At some point, Derek said to me: "Tell me about *your* work in philosophy." (I would never have brought it up.) So we started to have regular conversations about philosophy—his work, my work, and other questions we were interested in. And as you won't be surprised to hear, Derek had *lots* of penetrating ideas about what I was doing—things that I had never thought of before, and probably would never have thought of. At some point, he asked me: Would I consider adding him to my dissertation committee, as an outside member, when I had one? Answer: Absolutely!

At this point, I was already thinking: Boy, signing up to be this guy's teaching assistant is working out pretty well, so far . . .

But it got better. Right before the students were about to turn in their first papers of the semester, Derek called me into his office in order to propose a radical change in plan. Officially, our division of labor was supposed to be this. He would give a couple of lectures each week; and then he would lead a discussion section for graduate students who were taking the course for credit, and he would grade and comment on their papers. Meanwhile, I would lead a discussion section for the undergraduates and be responsible for grading and commenting on their papers.

Parfit's radical plan was that when the undergraduates submitted their papers to me, I should just forward all of their papers to him. He would then do *all* of the grading and commenting for the class, both for the undergraduates—of whom there were many—and for all of the graduate students.

When he first explained this new plan to me, I literally didn't understand what was being proposed. (Because, after all, it's not often in life that you find yourself in this situation. There's already a clear institutional understanding in place: this is my job; this is your job; we're splitting it up. But then the other person comes to you and says: "Look, let's keep this just between you and me, but let's try this instead: 'I'll do all the work, you'll do nothing!' ")

Once I understood what he was suggesting, I resisted. After all, grading the undergraduate papers was my job, and a big part of what I was getting paid to do that semester. (Although, to be honest, I don't think that Harvard was in danger of putting any kind of dent in its endowment with what they were paying teaching assistants in those days.)

But Derek insisted. He said: "You've got your own research to think about." And, moreover—and somehow he managed to say this without any touch of arrogance, and without any touch of putting me down—". . . it's just so much *easier* for me to grade and comment on the papers than it would be for you; it's just *better* if I do all of the grading and commenting than if we divide it up."

Finally, I agreed. And for the rest of the semester, whenever the undergraduates would send me their papers, I'd immediately forward them on to

Derek, and he would return them with grades and comments. And boy, did he give comments. Since Derek's death, you see a lot of people commenting online about just how incredibly generous he was when it came to giving them feedback on their work. All of that's true. But really, it understates the case by at least an order of magnitude. After all, the people commenting online are all professional philosophers— professors of philosophy and philosophy graduate students. In order to really appreciate just how generous Derek was when it came to giving people feedback on their work, you'd have to take into account all of the initially indifferent undergraduates who turned in some half-assed five-page double-spaced paper that they probably fired off the night before it was due—only to receive back two days later (often to their astonishment!) three single-spaced pages of incredibly incisive comments from one of the greatest living philosophers.

Derek took a lot of people more seriously than they expected to be taken, and more seriously than they took themselves. And often enough, people noticed that and started to take themselves more seriously as a result.

During the years I was officially his student, he spent most of his time in Oxford, and his time in the United States was divided between his two regular visiting appointments, at Harvard and at NYU. In many cases, this might have been an issue—having a crucial member of your committee, one of the main people you're working with, only be around for six weeks or two months out of every year. But because it was Derek, it never so much as crossed my mind to worry about it. It didn't matter if we hadn't seen each other in ten months, or if we were thousands of miles away: the penetrating comments and good advice always kept coming, just as fast as I could get him my latest draft. He was a fantastic teacher and mentor.

Many people benefit from the generosity of their teachers, in ways that they will never be able to come close to repaying. And there's a question about the morally appropriate response to that. After all, typically, you're not in a position to help your teachers professionally. So there's this idea: if your teachers treated you well, then "pay it forward" by treating your students well.

Treat your students the way your teachers treated you. I like the sentiment, and I agree with it in theory. But, for those of us who were fortunate enough to be Derek's students, there's something more than a little bit absurd about trying to apply it in practice. You might be conscientious and go out of your way to help your students, and do supererogatory things for them. But if you think that you're treating your students like Derek treated his students, you're fooling yourself.

(So, for the Princeton graduate students: if you ever end up as one of my teaching assistants, you definitely should *not* expect me to insist on doing all of your grading for you . . .)

* * *

Another thing that still makes me smile when I think about Derek saying to me, all those years ago, "It's just so much easier for me to do the grading and commenting than it would be for you, so it's just *better* if I do everything," is this. Even compared to other philosophers, Derek was a person of deep philosophical convictions. But I'm not sure that any conviction was deeper—Larry Temkin can correct me if I'm wrong here—than his conviction that some states of affairs really are better than other states of affairs, objectively speaking. It's not just what would be better-for-Tom-Kelly, or better from Tom Kelly's point of view, or what would be better-for-Derek-Parfit, or better from Derek Parfit's point of view. There's also what would be *impersonally better*. As his hero Henry Sidgwick would have put it: what would be better or worse from The Point of View of the Universe. And I think that he just concluded: from The Point of View of the Universe, it really would be better if I, Derek Parfit, grade all of the papers, because it's just so much easier for me to do it.[3]

* * *

One last story. I mentioned earlier how disappointed Derek was by the reaction of some of the great Oxford philosophers of the previous generation to his first public lecture on "Why There Is Something Rather than Nothing?" If I left it there, I worry that people who never met him might get the wrong idea. Because the way I told the story almost makes it sound as though Derek was concerned to *impress* Strawson or Dummett. But that was definitely not the kind of thing that motivated him in philosophy. Probably more than anyone I've ever known, Derek's relationship to philosophy—his commitment to the questions he was working on, his love of the subject—was so pure that things like reputation or status seemed not to matter at all. Now, it's not

[3] Incidentally, I thought then, and still think now, that this was a non sequitur on his part. I'm sure he was right that it was much easier for him than for me, given how good he was at doing it. But I don't think he was right to infer that, therefore, it would better from the point of view of the universe if he took time out from his own research to do it, as opposed to me taking time out from mine. (Ricardo's Law of Comparative Advantage, and all that.)

that he was completely oblivious to to whom he was talking. For example, when he was talking ethics with Tim Scanlon or Tom Nagel or Jeff McMahan or motivated him in philosophy, he knew who he was talking to, and he had tremendous respect for these people. But then you'd see him engage in much the same way with a beginning undergraduate or some random person who had just asked him a question. It was deeply admirable, even inspiring, in my opinion. I could go on about this, but instead let me just share one last quick anecdote that sticks in my head and which, I think, really illustrates what I'm talking about.

This story also takes place at Harvard, although a few years later. And back then, as I said, Derek wasn't on e-mail. (He typically wasn't at the cutting edge of technology.) In fact, back then, whenever he was in the United States, his main way of communicating with people back in England and elsewhere was via fax. So he was constantly receiving these extremely long faxes. And this, understandably, drove the secretaries in the philosophy department a little bit crazy.

Just imagine, trying to do your job, and then, all day long: here comes the latest, seemingly never-ending, incoming fax for Parfit. They knew he was this famous and important person, so they tolerated it and didn't say anything, but they confided in me: this was not something that they enjoyed.

So one day, I happened to be in the office for something, and sure enough, here comes the latest extremely long fax for Parfit.

Derek was in the office too, waiting for his fax to finish coming in.

And the two secretaries were there. One of the two secretaries, Betty, had worked in the department for decades, or for about as long as anyone could remember. Betty was a wonderful person. She also was the kind of person who had an opinion about everything, and who always shared her opinions. The other secretary, Ghanda, would spend much of her time nodding at whatever Betty happened to be talking about. No one was ever really sure to what extent Ghanda actually agreed with what Betty was saying, or whether Ghanda just wanted to keep the peace and avoid any office drama. But, in any case, pretty much any time you were in the office, that's what was going on.

I want to emphasize: it's not as though Betty was ever mistreated, or disrespected, or anything like that. But it's also not as though it ever would have occurred to Hilary Putnam, or Bob Nozick, or Stanley Cavell to actually *talk philosophy* with Betty. And why would it?

So there we are one day in the office. Derek waiting for his long fax to finish coming in.

Betty talking to Ghanda. Ghanda nodding her head. Who knows what I was doing there.

And on this day, Betty happened to be talking to Ghanda about *death*, and airing her opinions about what exactly happens when people die.

Of course, Derek was very interested in, and thought a lot about, death—death in general, his own death, and so on. But it didn't seem like Derek was paying any attention at all to what Betty was saying. He was just waiting for his fax, in one corner of the large office, with Betty and Ghanda on the other side of the room.

Finally, the fax finishes. Derek gathers it up under his arm and starts rushing off someplace. (He was often in a hurry.)

He's on his way out the door. And then, in the middle of the office doorway, he just STOPS, dead in his tracks. And for a moment it's as though he's frozen or paralyzed, in the middle of the doorway, just standing there. And then, he pivots, doing a 180-degree spin in the doorway, and rushes back into the office. And he walks over to Betty's desk, and looks her right in the eye and says very excitedly: *"I have a view about what you just said!"*

With that, he literally pulls up a chair, puts it right in front of her desk, and proceeds to explain his view, how it relates to what she was just saying, and to ask her questions about what she thought. And, more generally, to engage with her about what he took to be their shared object of philosophical concern.

But, for once, Betty was speechless.

10
Philosophy and Art with Parfit

F. M. Kamm

My interactions with Derek centered on philosophy and art.

At the suggestion of Gerald Dworkin, I first contacted Derek by phone when I was a graduate student at MIT and he was a visiting professor at Harvard. Jerry thought our interests in possible future people overlapped. Unfortunately, he was leaving Cambridge that very day. We did not actually meet until he came to be a visiting professor at NYU. many years later and, at the suggestion of Thomas Nagel, he read some work in progress of mine when I was not yet tenured. It was from that point onward to the end of his life that I had the greatest good fortune to have him read and offer voluminous comments in short order on whatever work I offered up for examination. Having someone as brilliant as Derek do this for one is an extraordinary gift, for which I am immensely grateful. He went on to approve for publication in his Oxford Ethics Series five of my books. Sometimes more of Derek's detailed comments might come even past the copyediting stage, which could be frightening, but he expected such a reaction and would kindly preface the comments with "don't worry." Derek was always kind; one need never be afraid of a cutting remark or a put-down. I am sure that having his ear and interest in my work helped encourage me to keep on working, and even today the thought of what he might say has the same effect.

Did I return the favor by as faithfully reading and commenting on the work he gave me? The short answer is "no." Being a slow reader and producer of publishable work, I tried to preserve as much time for my own work as I could. There was one exception. Derek asked me to comment on three chapters on deontology that he planned for Volume Three of *On What Matters*, and originally there was some rush in doing this. In August 2015 I wrote, "I am almost finished reading the last chapter (you must think I read a word a day)." He thanked me for my comments but said there was a change of plans. The deontology chapters were to be included in Volume Four, which wouldn't come out before the second half of 2016, and so he would put aside

F. M. Kamm, *Philosophy and Art with Parfit* In: *Derek Parfit: His Life and Thought*. Edited by: Jeff McMahan, Oxford University Press. © Oxford University Press 2025. DOI: 10.1093/9780191915307.003.0010

considering my comments further. However, it turned out that the chapters were actually included in Volume 3 after all, and several years later Derek wrote to say that when he was cleaning out his quarters, he had found a print out of my comments and was sorry that he hadn't reread them before publishing Volume Three. So I hadn't helped him much by written comments even when I tried.[1]

Derek and I would mostly discuss his work over dinner in restaurants when we were in the same city in the US or the UK. He would present his thesis or case to me for comments. Since Derek and I had very different views in moral philosophy, I was often very critical, and since we both took these issues seriously, this could often lead to increasingly loud disagreements and, given our topics, reactions from other diners. I remember one such dinner meeting at Legal Sea Foods in Cambridge, Massachusetts, that went something like this: "How many people would you kill to save five? Would you topple them from the bridge? What if you had to crush someone under the trolley to stop it turning?" And so on. I thought we might get thrown out or have the police called to investigate.

We both loved art, so Derek and I would often go to museums and there we only talked art. Derek's favorite colors were black and white, and having focused on drawing when I was a high-school art student, I could appreciate that. I remember that we went to see an exhibit of Matisse's black-and-white drawings at MoMA, but I took that opportunity to take him up to the floor with abstract expressionist and color field painters. I am happy to say that he appreciated the colors in Sam Francis and showed real insights into Philip Guston's abstract work. Despite the fact that his own wonderful photographs of buildings were in color, he once said that he thought the best depiction of buildings were only black-and-white. I pulled out a book of American Precisionists whose paintings of buildings in colors were new to Derek, and he was happy to revise his view. The very next day, we went to the Fogg (with me going through the galleries calling out "masterpiece alert") and saw some of those very paintings. Derek really appreciated good architecture of any period, and for me one memorable dinner to which I took him was outdoors in New York City where we could see both the Seagram Building and the

[1] Some of those comments are to be found in my article "Parfit on the Irrelevance of Deontological Distinctions," published in *Oxford Studies in Normative Ethics*, ed. M. Timmons (Oxford: Oxford University Press, 2020), and in "Duties that Become Supererogatory or Forbidden?" in *Principles and Persons*, ed. J. McMahan et al. (Oxford: Oxford University Press, 2021). These articles are reprinted in revised form in my *Rights and Their Limits: In Theory, Cases, and Pandemics* (New York: Oxford University Press, 2022).

Citicorp behind it and witness the “floor show” as the evening light changed what they reflected. Then we continued what I call an architectural walk down Park and Lexington Avenues with their memorable art deco buildings. I hope this shows that, as passionate as Derek was about philosophy, his interests were not limited to it.

I am so grateful to have known him and for having shared some philosophical and artistic adventures with him. I am also glad that remembrances of him are being collected because I remember how much he appreciated those who had benefited from his attention celebrating him at a conference at Rutgers for his sixtieth birthday. He and I returned to New York by train after that event, and in Penn Station he was crying tears of joy because he had found out how much he meant to so many people. (The only other time I saw Derek cry involved tears of sorrow when he talked about how badly African Americans had been treated for so long.)

Index

For the benefit of digital users, indexed terms that span two pages (e.g., 52–53) may, on occasion, appear on only one of those pages.